Poet's Choice

Poet's Choice

———

EDWARD HIRSCH

HARCOURT, INC.

Orlando   Austin   New York   San Diego   Toronto   London

www.HarcourtBooks.com

Library of Congress Cataloging-in-Publication Data
Hirsch, Edward.
Poet's choice/Edward Hirsch.—1st ed.
p.   cm.
1. Poetry—History and criticism.   I. Title.
PN1111.H57   2006
808.81—dc22   2005026890
ISBN-13: 978-0-15-101356-2   ISBN-10: 0-15-101356-x

Text set in Adobe Garamond
Designed by Cathy Riggs

Printed in the United States of America

First edition
A   C   E   G   I   K   J   H   F   D   B

Permissions acknowledgments appear on pages 409–419,
which constitute a continuation of the copyright page.

For André Bernard

CONTENTS

PART 2

INTRODUCTION

Sun-struck mornings, rainy afternoons, starry nights of poetry, come back to me now, remember me. Do not desert me, lifetime of encounters, lifelines, sentencings. I stumbled upon poetry as a teenager in Chicago—I was at sea and it offered me a raft—and it has sustained me for the past forty years. I have carried poetry with me like a flashlight—how many small books have I crammed into my pockets?—and used it to illuminate other lives, other worlds. I discovered myself in discovering others, and I have lived with these poems until they have become part of the air that I breathe. I hope they will become part of the reader's world too.

Many of us remember with an eerie precision where we were when we first read certain crucial things:

I remember the spidery light in the second-floor warehouse of Wertheimer Box and Paper Company where I pored over Pablo Neruda's "The Heights of Macchu Picchu," which I then shared with a couple of Puerto Rican workers whose job it was to feed corrugated cartons through enormous iron machines. *Sube a nacer conmigo, hermano,* one of them quoted ("Rise to be born with me, brother").

I remember the circle of lamplight that ringed the page in my college dorm room where I was first stung by Gerard Manley Hopkins's so-called terrible sonnets ("I wake and feel the fell of dark, not day"). These lonely poems made me feel less lonely—I recognized their inner desolation—and I read through the night until I washed up on the crisp Iowa morning ("There lives the dearest freshness deep down things").

I recall the cramped bookstores and branch libraries, the cafés and fast-food joints, the book-lined studies. I can still feel the drizzly homesickness of a café in London where I was pierced by Ezra Pound's adaptations of Li Po. I think of the bugged hotel room in Leningrad—it was more like a closet—where I was mesmerized by Osip Mandelstam's

"Tristia" ("I have studied the science of goodbyes"). And I do not forget the dusky blues of an empty Warsaw café in midwinter where I was changed by Zbigniew Herbert's "Mr. Cogito" poems ("you were saved not in order to live / you have little time you must give testimony").

These poems have had a kind of talismanic power for me, and I keep them close at hand. I have kept my early loves in poetry nearby; I have held them as a touchstone and a reminder during the years I have been writing this book. They have dreamt with me through the night; they have been companions of the day. I have tried to remember throughout that poetry is made by flesh-and-blood human beings. It is a bloody art. It lives on a human scale and thrives when it is passed from hand to hand.

Poetry is as ancient as the drawing of a horse at Lascaux, or an Egyptian hieroglyphic, and yet it also feels especially relevant to a post–9/11 world, a world characterized by disaffection and materialism, a world alienated from art. The horrors we face daily around the globe—terrorist bombings, ethnic cleansing, the ravages of the HIV epidemic, children becoming soldiers—challenge us to find meaning in the midst of suffering. Poetry answers this challenge. It puts us in touch with ourselves. It sends us messages from the interior and also connects us to others. It is intimate and secretive; it is generously collective.

We live at a time when the pervasive influence of media and consumer culture blurs national boundaries and identities. The poems featured in *Poet's Choice* consistently grapple with death, suffering, and loss. They defend the importance of individual lives, and rebel at the way individuals are dwarfed by mass culture. They are unaccommodating. They portray, and communicate on behalf of, people at the margins of society: exiles, transplants, refugees, nomads, people with no country, people split between two different countries, split between the past and the present. They search for meaning—in language and forms particular only to poetry—in the realm of emptiness, for company in the face of isolation. Poems are always in dialogue with other poems and in conversation with history, and they invite readers into that conversation, which offers a particular form of communication, communion, and fusion.

This book seeks to befriend the reader on behalf of poetry, which trembles with sensuous music, human presence. Each of these short pieces contains at least one entire poem that is worth our full attention. These individual poems—urgent, formal, insistent—need individual readers to experience them. It is an honor to introduce and present them to you. My idea throughout is to help unveil them, to explain their sometimes challenging formal devices and to provide a context for reading them, whether biographical, literary, or historical. I hope to accompany the reader in the experience of reading and internalizing a poem, which ultimately bypasses rational mind and lodges inside of us. It enters the dream life, and the dream works. It circulates in the bloodstream.

Poetry is a means of exchange, a form of reciprocity, a magic to be shared, a gift. There has never been a civilization without it. That's why I consider poetry—which is, after all, created out of a mouthful of air—a human fundamental, like music. It saves something precious in the world from vanishing. It sacramentalizes experience. It is an imaginative act that starts with the breath itself. It arises from breathing. It is a living thing that comes from the body, from the heart and lungs, and thus seems hardwired into us. It enters our bodies through the material stream of language. It moves and dances between speech and song. These words rhythmically strung together, these electrically charged sounds, are one of the ways by which we come to know ourselves. A poem beats out time.

Poetry speaks with the greatest intensity against the effacement of individuals, the obliteration of communities, the destruction of nature. It tries to keep the world from ending by positing itself against oblivion. The words are marks against erasure. I believe that something in our natures is realized when we use language as an art to confront and redeem our mortality. We need poems now as much as ever. We need these voices to restore us to ourselves in an alienating world. We need the sounds of the words to delineate the states of our being. Poetry is a necessary part of our planet.

PART I

IT SEEMS NATURAL to me to converse with writers from other countries. I come from a family of Eastern European immigrants and grew up with the sounds of other people's languages, echoes of their stories, which became my own. My grandfather used to scrawl poetry in the backs of his books, and I remember leaning over his shoulder and peering down at the magical letters of the Hebrew alphabet blooming from right to left under his hand. Later, I traveled to Europe and heard poetry in Gaelic, Romani, Polish, German, and all the Romance languages. I heard Florentine schoolchildren reciting Dante's *Inferno*. I heard two Yiddish poets dueling in a café in Vienna. I recognized my world in the strange and compelling foreign sounds that were chanted and sung. I heard my ground notes in other people's songs. The melody resonated with my own.

The canonical poetry I read in school, the poetry of high modernism, seemed undeniably great to me, but also a little distant. I found the alternative I was looking for—a poetry of radical directness, intense intellect, and deep emotional clarity—when I discovered César Vallejo's *The Black Heralds,* and Nazim Hikmet's *Things I Didn't Know I Loved,* and Yehuda Amichai's *Amen.*

And in this frigid hour, when the earth
smells of human dust and is so sad,
I want to knock on every door
and beg forgiveness of I don't know whom,
and bake bits of fresh bread for him
here, in the oven of my heart . . . !

—CÉSAR VALLEJO, "OUR BREAD"

Let's say we're in prison
and close to fifty,
and we have eighteen more years, say,
          before the iron doors will open.
We'll still live with the outside,
with its people and animals, struggle and wind—
          I mean with the outside beyond the walls.
I mean, however and wherever we are,
     we must live as if we will never die.

                    —NAZIM HIKMET, "ON LIVING"

     I have nothing to say about the war,
     nothing to add. I'm ashamed.

     All the knowledge I have absorbed in my life
     I give up, like a desert
     which has given up water.
     Names I never thought I would forget
     I'm forgetting.

     And because of the war I say again,
     for the sake of a last and simple sweetness:
     The sun is circling round the earth. Yes.
     The earth is flat, like a lost, floating board. Yes.
     God is in heaven. Yes.

          —YEHUDA AMICHAI, "PATRIOTIC SONGS"

These Peruvian, Turkish, and Israeli poets are both intimate and political, ancient and modern, ruthless, tender, and heartbreakingly human.
    The translation of poetry is of the utmost importance, even
though it is an impossibility. How impoverished we would be if we
couldn't experience something of the T'ang Dynasty poets, or the Sufi
mystics, or the Provençals, who invented romantic love. I am one of

many readers who have been deepened and changed by the tragic fragmentation and despairing beauty of Paul Celan and Nelly Sachs, the transfigured suffering and nobility of Osip Mandelstam and Anna Akhmatova, the anguished grandeur of Czeslaw Milosz and Joseph Brodsky. These figures are models of integrity and seriousness. They are necessary to American poetry. I have also included in the following section the British lyric poets who have especially called out to me—from Caedmon to Denise Levertov, from John Clare to Thomas Hardy, Charlotte Mew, and Edward Thomas. I have always been surprised and moved by the holy eccentrics of English poetry.

The poems in this international section of the book, which move roughly from the ancient to the contemporary, come to us bursting with news. Many of their speakers have been initiated into the apocalyptic fires of history in ways that Americans have only recently come to understand. They speak to us directly. We recognize their sorrows, their losses, their joys. Suffering is one of the central elements of these poems, but part of the majesty of poetry is that it works against the suffering it describes. It restores us to what is deepest in ourselves. It consoles us.

I

NIGHTINGALES

spring's messenger, the lovelyvoiced nightingale
—Sappho

I WISH I'D BEEN on the street in Madrid on that night in 1934 when Pablo Neruda, who was then Chile's consul to Spain, told Miguel Hernández that he had never heard a nightingale. It is too cold for nightingales to survive in Chile. Hernández grew up in a goatherding family in the province of Alicante, and he immediately scampered up a high tree and imitated a nightingale's liquid song. Then he climbed up another tree and created the sound of a second nightingale answering. He could have been joyously illustrating Boris Pasternak's notion of poetry as "two nightingales dueling."

I once told this story to the writer William Maxwell, and he said that learning how to sing like nightingales in treetops ought to be a requirement for poets. It should be taught, like prosody, in writing programs. The Romantic poets might have agreed: Wordsworth called the nightingale a creature of "fiery heart"; Keats inscribed its music forever in his famous ode ("Thou wast not born for death, immortal bird!"); John Clare observed one assiduously as a boy ("she is a plain bird something like the hedge sparrow in shape and the female Firetail or Redstart in color but more slender then the former and of a redder brown or scorched color then the latter"); and Shelley declared:

A poet is a nightingale, who sits in darkness and sings to cheer its own solitude with sweet sounds; his auditors are as men entranced by the melody of an unseen musician, who feel that they are moved and softened, yet know not whence or why.

The singing of a nightingale becomes a metaphor for writing poetry here, and listening to that bird—that natural music—becomes a metaphor for reading it.

One could write a good book about nightingales in poetry. It would begin with one of the oldest legends in the world, the poignant tale of Philomela, that poor ravished girl who had her tongue cut out and was changed into the nightingale, which laments in darkness but nonetheless expresses its story. The tale reverberates through all of Greco-Roman literature. Ovid gave it a poignant rendering in *Metamorphoses,* and it echoed down the centuries from Shakespeare (*Titus Andronicus*) to Matthew Arnold ("Philomela") and T. S. Eliot ("The Waste Land").

One of my favorite poems about "spring's messenger" is by Jorge Luis Borges, the Argentine fabulist, who may never have heard a nightingale, and yet, through poetry, had a lifelong relationship with the unseen bird.

TO THE NIGHTINGALE

Out of what secret English summer evening
or night on the incalculable Rhine,
lost among all the nights of my long night,
could it have come to my unknowing ear,
your song, encrusted with mythology,
nightingale of Virgil and the Persians?
Perhaps I never heard you, but my life
is bound up with your life, inseparably.
The symbol for you was a wandering spirit
in a book of enigmas. The poet, El Marino,
nicknamed you the "siren of the forest";
you sing throughout the night of Juliet
and through the intricate pages of the Latin
and from his pinewoods, Heine, that other
nightingale of Germany and Judea,
called you mockingbird, firebird, bird of mourning.
Keats heard your song for everyone, forever.

There is not one among the shimmering names
people have given you across the earth
that does not seek to match your own music,
nightingale of the dark. The Muslim dreamed you
in the delirium of ecstasy,
his breast pierced by the thorn of the sung rose
you redden with your blood. Assiduously
in the black evening I contrive this poem,
nightingale of the sands and all the seas,
that in exultation, memory, and fable,
you burn with love and die in liquid song.

(TRANSLATED BY ALASTAIR REID)

2

GERARD MANLEY HOPKINS

There lives the dearest freshness deep down things.

GERARD MANLEY HOPKINS's sonnet "God's Grandeur" is one of the poems that many readers, including poets, have been reciting with special intensity since the events of September 11, 2001. Hopkins wrote the poem in 1877, the year of his ordination to the priesthood, and it is filled with his sacramental impulse to praise the natural world, to affirm its intrinsic pattern and beauty. Mankind may have defaced and blackened the human realm, Hopkins argues, but an eternal freshness, an electric majesty, animates nature itself.

GOD'S GRANDEUR

The world is charged with the grandeur of God.
   It will flame out, like shining from shook foil;
   It gathers to a greatness, like the ooze of oil
Crushed. Why do men then now not reck his rod?
Generations have trod, have trod, have trod;
   And all is seared with trade; bleared, smeared with toil;
   And wears man's smudge and shares man's smell: the soil
Is bare now, nor can foot feel, being shod.

And for all this, nature is never spent;
   There lives the dearest freshness deep down things;
And though the last lights off the black West went
   Oh, morning, at the brown brink eastward, springs—
Because the Holy Ghost over the bent
   World broods with warm breast and with ah! bright wings.

Hopkins's poem is an argument of praise. Praise restores us to the world again, to our luckiness of being. It is one of the permanent impulses in poetry. Praise is clearly inscribed in the Egyptian Pyramid Texts, the oldest lyrical fragments in existence. It is a defining motive in *The Iliad* (the praise poem of Achilles) and in *Genesis* (the praise poem of Yahweh). *"Rühmen, das ists!"* Rainer Maria Rilke exclaims in the seventh sonnet to Orpheus: "To praise, that's it!"

In a splendid essay entitled "Making, Knowing, and Judging," W. H. Auden declared:

> Whatever its actual content and overt interest, every poem is rooted in imaginative awe. Poetry can do a hundred and one things, delight, sadden, disturb, amuse, instruct—it may express every possible shade of emotion, and describe every conceivable kind of event, but there is only one thing that all poetry must do; it must praise all it can for being and for happening.

Praise lays claim to as much of the extant world as possible by uttering the names of things. It catalogs our blessings. It speaks to our need to overcome circumstances and reclaim the world as our own. It represents a dream of transcending history. It is an impulse to more life, a form of blessing, a way of cherishing a world that shines out with radiant particularity.

One of my favorite praise poems is Hopkins's quirky lyric "Pied Beauty," which he named a "curtal sonnet"—literally, a sonnet curtailed or cut short from its usual fourteen lines to ten and a half lines. "Pied Beauty" rejoices not in perfection but in "dappled things," in patchy or flawed beauty, in everything mottled, splotched, variegated in appearance. Hopkins's highly concentrated verbal music, which has its own idiosyncratic and piebald beauty, delights in imperfection, in the splendid oddity that marks individual beings, that lets each thing emerge and stand out as its own most exact and distinctive self, a process he termed "selving." He celebrates variety and flux even as he revels in unexpected unities.

PIED BEAUTY

Glory be to God for dappled things—
    For skies of couple-colour as a brinded cow;
      For rose-moles in all stipple upon trout that swim;
Fresh-firecoal chestnut-falls; finches' wings;
    Landscape plotted and pieced—fold, fallow, and plough;
      And all trades, their gear and tackle and trim.
All things counter, original, spare, strange;
    Whatever is fickle, freckled (who knows how?)
      With swift, slow; sweet, sour; adazzle, dim;
He fathers-forth whose beauty is past change:
           Praise him.

3.

CAEDMON

Now we must praise

ENGLISH POETRY began with a vision. It started with the holy trance of a seventh-century figure called Caedmon, an illiterate herdsman, who now stands at the top of the English literary tradition as the initial Anglo-Saxon or Old English poet of record, the first to compose Christian poetry in his own language.

The story goes that Caedmon invariably fled when it was his turn to sing during a merry social feast. He was ashamed he never had any songs to contribute. But one night a voice came to Caedmon in a dream and commanded him to sing about the beginning of created things. "Thereupon," as Bede tells it in his *Ecclesiastical History,* "Caedmon began to sing verses which he had never heard before in praise of God the Creator."

Here is a West Saxon rendition of the inspired poem called "Caedmon's Hymn":

Now we must praise   the Protector of the heavenly kingdom
the might of the Measurer   and His mind's purpose,
the work of the Father of Glory,   as He for each of the wonders,
the eternal Lord,   established a beginning.
He shaped first   for the sons of the Earth
heaven as a roof,   the Holy Maker;
then the Middle-World,   mankind's Guardian,
the eternal Lord,   made afterwards,
solid ground for men,   the almighty Lord.

Caedmon's dream was a sign he had become a poet. It was a signal of poetic vocation. His hymn is a praise poem to the Lord, like the Latin canticle *Benedicte, omnia opera domini,* which embraces all of creation ("O all ye Works of the Lord, bless ye the Lord: praise Him, and magnify Him for ever"). Caedmon's poetry of praise inaugurates a tradition that would look forward to Traherne, Vaughan, and Christopher Smart, who sings of the transcendent virtue of praise itself. Here is stanza fifty of Smart's eighteenth-century poem of benediction, "A Song To David":

> PRAISE above all—for praise prevails;
> Heap up the measure, load the scales,
>   And good to goodness add:
> The gen'rous soul her Savior aids,
> But peevish obloquy degrades;
>   The Lord is great and glad.

Smart's catalog of praise looks forward to Blake and Hopkins, and to Whitman, who embraces (and challenges us to embrace) all the works of creation: "Divine I am inside and out, and I make holy whatever I touch or am touch'd from." I think, too, of W. H. Auden's radiant and intricate sonnet of instruction, "Anthem" ("Let us praise our Maker, with true passion extol Him").

Denise Levertov's poem "Caedmon" retells Caedmon's story in his own words. It captures the sheer unlikelihood of Caedmon's experience. Levertov dramatizes the radical shock of a clumsy unschooled peasant who is suddenly gifted with the power of song. She also pays homage to the alliterative power of Anglo-Saxon poetry. Like other Christian poets, Levertov connects the energy of language with the power of divine spirit.

CAEDMON

> All others talked as if
> talk were a dance.
> Clodhopper I, with clumsy feet

would break the gliding ring.
Early I learned to
hunch myself
close by the door:
then when the talk began
I'd wipe my
mouth and wend
unnoticed back to the barn
to be with the warm beasts,
dumb among body sounds
of the simple ones.
I'd see by a twist
of lit rush the motes
of gold moving
from shadow to shadow
slow in the wake
of deep untroubled sighs.
The cows
munched or stirred or were still. I
was at home and lonely,
both in good measure. Until
the sudden angel affrighted me—light effacing
my feeble beam,
a forest of torches, feathers of flame, sparks upflying:
but the cows as before
were calm, and nothing was burning,
        nothing but I, as that hand of fire
touched my lips and scorched my tongue
and pulled my voice
                into the ring of the dance.

4.

OLYMPIAN ODES

Mother of games, gold-wreathed, Olympia . . .
—Pindar

There's a long and even jubilant tradition in poetry of celebrating athletic achievement. It begins with the Greek poet Pindar, who wrote a series of choral odes to commemorate athletic victories. Pindar's triumphal odes from the fifth century B.C. are the first truly written narrative texts of any length. Greeks simultaneously sang the poems and danced to them at shrines or theaters, though now the words are all that remains of the complete Pindaric experience. The movement of the verse, which mirrors a musical dance pattern, tends to be emotionally intense and highly exalted.

The Olympian Games, which were held at Pisa in Elis, a spot sacred to Zeus, were the oldest and most honorable of the competitions that took place at regular intervals throughout the ancient world. Pindar's "Olympian Ode 1" commences:

> Water is preeminent and gold, like a fire
> burning in the night, outshines
> all possessions that magnify men's pride.
> But if, my soul, you yearn
> to celebrate great games,
> look no further
> for another star
> shining through the deserted ether
> brighter than the sun, or for a contest
> mightier than Olympia—

The epinician odes were commissioned victory poems (named for epi-Niké-an, the goddess of victory) about sports, and they had stories of gods and heroes woven into them. Each ode focuses on a triumphant athlete who has a symbolic connection to a god, and thus it incorporates a mythology. The poems have their roots in religious rites, and each one called for an ecstatic performance that communally reenacted the ritual of participation in the divine.

The Latin poet Horace compared Pindar to a great swan who conquered the air by long rapturous flights. He claimed that athletes were given more glory by Pindar's voice "than by a hundred statues standing mute / Around the applauding city." I am also an admirer of the Greek poet's fifth-century contemporary Bacchylides, who has often been considered a "lesser Pindar," but who flew with appealing modesty and grace.

One thinks of Bacchylides as something of an underdog because he was known after antiquity by a mere 107 nonsequential lines (in 69 fragments) until 1896, when a papyrus in Egypt was discovered containing his work. The papyrus was bought, cut up into sections, smuggled from Egypt, and delivered to the British Museum. There an eminent papyrologist, Frederic Kenyon, reassembled 1,382 lines: fifteen epinician odes and five dithyrambs. Here is the sixth ode in David Slavitt's agile colloquial translation:

> Lachon has brought home the bacon
> or, say, the glory from Almighty Zeus:
> the first prize in the sprint. By Alpheus'
> mouth, chalk up yet another Olympic
> win for vine-rich Ceos, home of the greatest
> boxers and runners,
> who stand there as the anthem plays,
> and feel the weight of those luxuriant
> victory garlands they wear
> on their high-held heads.
> Now by the goddess Niké's will,
> we sing, at the gate of your house,

Urania's hymn to honor
the son of Aristomenes,
fast as the wind.
Your triumph in this race
brings glory to Ceos.

5

THE GREEK ANTHOLOGY

Take what you have while you have it: you'll lose it soon enough.
A single summer turns a kid into a shaggy goat.
—ANONYMOUS GREEK EPIGRAM

PURE PAGAN, selected and translated by Burton Raffel, is a small, superb gathering of seven centuries of Greek poems and fragments. Raffel adds titles to otherwise untitled pieces and translates with great transparency and panache a marvelous array of lesser-known poems and poets from ancient Greece. He concentrates on figures who have rarely been translated into English, such as Anyte (early third century B.C.), Phocylides (mid-sixth century B.C.), and Terpander (mid-seventh century B.C.), and culls gems from the four thousand poems that constitute *The Greek Anthology.* These brief and entrancing lyric intensities ("drink, and get drunk with me," Alkaios insists) are perennially fresh and inviting, surprised by time, and quick with life.

The Greek poets, many of them anonymous, had a special gift for poignant inscriptions, such as this two-line epigram by an unknown author:

EARTHQUAKE

Once corpses left the city behind them, dead,
But now the living carry the city to her grave.

The Greek term *epigramma* means "inscription," and, indeed, the epigram began as a poem compressed enough to be carved onto the limited space of a monument, a tombstone, or the base of a statue. Precision of language has always been the hallmark of the form. Some of the anonymous Greek epigrams have the elements of proverbial or commonplace wisdom:

MESSAGE TO THE LIVING

I'm dead, but waiting for you, and you'll wait for someone:
The darkness waits for everyone, it makes no distinctions.

Plato delivered a similar message to the living in this well-balanced, closely reasoned epitaph, which has the same shine as his prose:

AN EPITAPH

I am a drowned man's tomb. There is a farmer's.
Death waits for us all, whether at sea or on land.

Simonides took this sort of deeply measured inscriptional epigram to its peak in such short poems as the one Raffel entitles "Sailors":

These men lying here were carrying honors to Apollo.
One sea, one night, one ship carried them to their graves.

The epitaph ("writing on a tomb"), an abbreviated or foreshortened elegy, is one of the types of lyric that the Greek poets perfected. These poems were suitable for placing on gravestones, though it's evident this was often never really intended. The idea of a commemorative poem on a tombstone addressed to a passerby served as an enabling fiction, and it fostered a type of a lyric that was short, pithy, and summative. Theodoridas wrote:

AN EPITAPH

This is a drowned man's tomb. Sail on, stranger,
For when we went down the other ships sailed on.

And here is how Antipater of Sidon eulogized a dead soldier. This poem is no doubt as relevant today as when it was written sometime around 120 B.C.

AMYNTOR

Amyntor, Philip's son, lies in this Lydian soil.
His hands were full of iron war.
No sickness led him into the darkness:
He died holding his shield over a wounded friend.

6.

SAPPHO

Eros the Limb-loosener shakes me again—
that sweet, bitter, impossible creature.

THE POET SAPPHO, who lived some twenty-seven centuries ago on the Greek island of Lesbos, invented the lyric meltdown. She was an initiate of Eros, which she characterized as an irrational force; a dread, sacred, and overwhelming power; an insatiable desire; a delicious, bittersweet illness that shakes one to the very core. Thus she testified in one fragment:

> Then love shook my heart like the wind that falls on
> oaks in the mountains.

Sappho wrote in a spare, limpid, wonderfully direct style. Her poems, which survive in fragments, have a startling personal immediacy. They have never lost their dramatic impact. One of her most intense lyrics, fragment 31 (*Phainetai moi*), has made readers shiver over the centuries. The physical symptoms of love (the heart trembling inside the breast, the fire spreading beneath the skin, and so forth) are still recognizable. The diagnosis holds.

The poem sets up the geometry of a love triangle: Sappho stares at and ardently desires a woman who is unavailable because she favors a man who sits with her. So enviable is his position that he seems, to the speaker, like a peer to the gods. It is from intimately watching the woman, and listening to her voice, and hearing her laugh, that Sappho begins her fiery meltdown, though one can't help but note the cool precision with which the poet describes the epic helplessness of the lover.

I admire here the way the translator, the poet Jim Powell, re-creates Sappho's idiom in contemporary American English, preserves her rhythm as much as possible, and re-creates the expanding and contracting movement—the pulse—of the Sapphic stanza.

> In my eyes he matches the gods, that man who
> sits there facing you—any man whatever—
> listening from closeby to the sweetness of your
>   voice as you talk, the
>
> sweetness of your laughter: yes, that—I swear it—
> sets the heart to shaking inside my breast, since
> once I look at you for a moment, I can't
>   speak any longer,
>
> but my tongue breaks down, and then all at once a
> subtle fire races inside my skin, my
> eyes can't see a thing and a whirring whistle
>   thrums at my hearing,
>
> cold sweat covers me and a trembling takes
> ahold of me all over: I'm greener than the
> grass is and appear to myself to be little
>   short of dying.
>
> But all must be endured, since even a poor [

Sappho's meter was brilliantly adapted by the Latin poet Catullus, who turned it into a lyric (#51: *"Ille mi par..."*) addressed to the woman he called "Lesbia." But the fragment only survives because it was cited by Longinus in his treatise *On the Sublime* in the first century A.D. He considered it a prime example of "love's madness." I leave you with his haunting perception—Sappho's catalog and complex of symptoms—that echoes down the centuries and continues to influence and characterize the language of erotic love:

. . . are you not amazed how at one and the same moment she seeks out soul, body, hearing, tongue, sight, complexion as though they had all left her and were external, and how in contradiction she both freezes and burns, is irrational and sane, is afraid and nearly dead, so that we observe in her not one single emotion but a concourse of emotions? All this of course happens to people in love . . .

7

THE POET AS MAKER

Making is the mirror in which we see ourselves.
—FRANK BIDART

"THERE IS SOMETHING missing in our definition, vision, of a human being: the need to make," Frank Bidart writes in "Advice to the Players": "We are creatures who need to make."

Poiēsis means "making," and, as the ancient Greeks recognized, the poet is first and foremost a maker. The Greeks saw no contradiction between the truth that poetry is inspired and, simultaneously, an art (*technē*), a craft requiring a blend of talent, training, and practice. In the Renaissance, the word *makers*, as in "courtly makers," was an equivalent for poets. (Hence William Dunbar's glorious "Lament for the Makers.") The word *poem* came into English in the sixteenth century and has been with us ever since to denote a form of fabrication, a verbal composition, a made thing.

This idea of the poet as maker is essentially a Horatian notion of poetry, and it stands behind Horace's conclusive Ode (iii.30), which rings with confidence and pride:

> Today I have finished a work outlasting bronze
> And the pyramids of ancient royal kings.
> The North Wind raging cannot scatter it
> Nor can the rain obliterate this work,
> Nor can the years, nor can the ages passing.
> Some part of me will live and not be given
> Over into the hands of the death goddess.
> I will go on and on, kept ever young
> By the praise in times to come for what I have done.

So long as the Pontiff in solemn procession climbs
The Capitol steps, beside him the reverent Vestal,
So long will it be that men will say that I,
Born in a land where Aufidus' torrent roared,
Once ruled by Danaus, king of a peasant people,
Was the first to bring Aeolian measures to Latin.
Melpomene, look kindly on the honor
The muse has won for me, and graciously
Place on my head the garland of Delphic laurel.

(TRANSLATED BY DAVID FERRY)

Ben Jonson referred to the art of poetry as "the craft of making." The old Irish word *cerd*, meaning "people of the craft," was a designation for artisans, including poets. It is cognate with the Greek *kerdos*, meaning "craft, craftiness." Two basic metaphors for the art of poetry in the classical world were carpentry and weaving. "Whatsover else it may be," W. H. Auden pointed out, "a poem is a verbal artifact which must be as skillfully and solidly constructed as a table or a motorcycle."

In his entertaining mock-interview poem "Not a *Paris Review* Interview," F. T. Prince takes up the question "So the poet is a 'maker,' / Not seeker, seer or world-forsaker?"

    A. Surely he undertakes,
       Whatever as a man
       He may do, like the bees and birds
       To make something, but in words;
       And surely then he can
       Do or not do, or half do it.

       In a painting once said to be
       By Giorgione, one could see
       A small boy with a kit
       Of tools, watching a bearded man,
       His tutor, bent, intent

On testing a new instrument,
An astrolabe. Below them ran
A motto on a sill
In Latin, with the moral
Of which I would not quarrel:

INGENIUM 'Our skill'
Or 'mother wit' (of which we see
The boy with file and mallet is
Symbolical) NON VALET 'is
Not worth a damn' NISI
FACTA VALEBUNT 'unless
What we have made will
Work.'

"The thing gets made, gets built, and you're the slave / who rolls
the log beneath the block," Thomas Lux asserts in his tellingly funny
poem "An Horation Notion." "It's how a thing gets made—not /
because you're sensitive, or you get genetic-lucky," he declares:

Grow up! Give me, please, a break!
You make the thing because you love the thing
and you love the thing because someone else loved it
enough to make you love it.

8

THE ARS POETICA

Poetry is the subject of the poem.
—WALLACE STEVENS

THE ARS POETICA is a poem that takes the art of poetry as its explicit subject. It proposes an aesthetic. Self-referential, uniquely conscious of itself as both a treatise and a performance, the great ars poetica embodies what it is about.

Horace's *Ars Poetica* is our first known poem on poetics and the fountainhead of the tradition. Horace introduces himself as both poet and critic in what was probably his final work (10 B.C.), a combination of the formal epistle and the technical treatise. It is an eloquent defense of liberty at a time when freedom was imperiled in Rome. Horace speaks of art and ingenuity, of the poet's need to fuse unity and variety, to delight as well as to be useful. He wittily defends the usefulness of artistic constraints and the necessity for creative freedom. He writes on behalf of both writer and reader, the poet and the audience. Here are some key lines from J. D. McClatchy's translation:

> It's not enough that poems be exquisite.
> Let empathy prevail and lead the listener's
> Heart. A face will smile to see a smile,
> Or weep at tears. If you would have me grieve,
> Then first feel grief yourself.

Horace also speaks of the sacred role of poets in earlier times.

Byron alludes to the *Ars Poetica* in his 1811 "Hints from Horace," which he ranked as one of his own best poems, and expands on these lines with an easy galloping cleverness:

'T'is not enough, ye bards, with all your art,
To polish poems; they must touch the heart:
Where'ver the scene be laid, whate'er the song,
Still let it bear the hearer's soul along;
Command your audience or to smile or weep,
Whiche'er may please you—anything but sleep.
The poet claims our tears; but, by his leave,
Before I shed them, let me see *him* grieve.

An anthology of the ars poetica would include Pope's "Essay on Criticism," the exemplary treatise of the Enlightenment; passages from Wordsworth's *Prelude,* which traces the growth of the poet's mind, and from Whitman's "Song of Myself" ("I speak the pass-word primeval . . . I give the sign of democracy"); Emily Dickinson's poem #1129 ("Tell all the Truth but tell it slant"); Wallace Stevens's "Of Modern Poetry"; and Hugh MacDiarmid's "The Kind of Poetry I Want" ("A poetry that takes its polish from a conflict / Between discipline at its most strenuous / And feeling at its highest"). It would include Marianne Moore's adversarial ars poetica "Poetry" ("I, too, dislike it"), Czeslaw Milosz's conditional "Ars Poetica?" ("The purpose of poetry is to remind us / How difficult it is to remain just one person"), and James Wright's harrowing "Ars Poetica: Some Recent Criticism" ("Reader, / We had a lovely language, / We would not listen"). The ars poetica, like the defense of poetry, becomes a necessary form when poetry is called into question and freedom is endangered.

Here is the lead poem in *Scars,* a lively translation of poems by the Bulgarian poet Blaga Dimitrova. I admire the way the translator, Ludmilla G. Popova-Wightman, captures Dimitrova's intense urgency and force, the way she writes every poem as if it were a final statement. Her work has the sting of long experience.

ARS POETICA

Write each of your poems
as if it were your last.
In this century, saturated with strontium,

charged with terrorism,
flying with supersonic speed,
death comes with terrifying suddenness.
Send each of your words
like a last letter before execution,
a call carved on a prison wall.
You have no right to lie,
no right to play pretty little games.
You simply won't have time
to correct your mistakes.
Write each of your poems,
tersely, mercilessly,
with blood—as if it were your last.

9.

THE BARDIC ORDER

Great is the art,
Great be the manners, of the bard.
—RALPH WALDO EMERSON

THE PROFESSIONAL LITERARY caste of the bardic order in Ireland lasted from the thirteenth to the seventeenth century. It was serious business to become a bard and serve the prince, and the training period could extend for as long as twelve years. In *The Book of Irish Verse,* John Montague says that one way to describe the training is as "seven winters in a dark room." He quotes an early-eighteenth-century memoir:

> Concerning the poetical Seminary or School . . . it was open only to such as were descended of Poets and reputed within their Tribes . . . The Structure was a snug, low Hut, and beds in it at convenient Distances, each within a small Apartment. . . . No windows to let in the Day, nor any Light at all us'd but that of Candles, and these brought in at a proper Season only. . . . The reason of laying the Study aforesaid in the Dark was doubtless to avoid the Distraction which Light and the variety of Objects represented thereby occasions.

The poets who came through this strict regimen created poems that sometimes let deep emotion break through their virtuoso technique. Some of their most poignant poems mourn the passing of their order. In his essay "The Poet," Emerson wrote, "The ancient British bards had for the title of their order, 'Those who are free throughout the world.' They are free, and they make free."

In the eighteenth century, with the decline of traditional schools of learning, poets no longer needed to belong to special families to practice their profession. But after the Battle of the Boyne in 1690, as the Irish poet and novelist Seamus Deane has said, "the old Gaelic culture had lost all coherence. Its leaders were gone, the bardic schools dispersed, its land reduced, its political power extinguished." This led to what the poet Dáibhi Ó Bruadair (c. 1625–1698) referred to as "the break-up of the old custom," and it sounded the death knell for one major kind of poetry. "Tonight Ireland is lonely," Aindrias Mac Marcais declared in his seventeenth-century Gaelic poem "The Deserted Land," which deals with the plight of the people after the Irish chieftains fled to continental Europe: "No praise poem is recited, no bedtime story told, no desire to see a book, no giving ear to the family pedigrees . . ."

Here is the contemporary Irish poet Eavan Boland's poignant lamentation for the bardic order itself, for the last nameless bard wandering the lost land. The poem, called "My Country in Darkness," dramatizes the passing of a kind of oral poet, as well as a kind of Gaelic poetry, a way of life. It takes the loss personally and becomes an elegy "for a dead art in a dying land," for an entire communal world that has faded away before the onslaught of English colonization. The poem stands as the first section of her twelve-part sequence "Colony" in her ninth book, *The Lost Land,* and it has a powerful mythic resonance:

1. MY COUNTRY IN DARKNESS

After the wolves and before the elms
the bardic order ended in Ireland.

Only a few remained to continue
a dead art in a dying land:

This is a man
on the road from Youghal to Cahirmoyle.
He has no comfort, no food and no future.
He has no fire to recite his friendless measures by.
His riddles and flatteries will have no reward.
His patrons sheath their swords in Flanders and Madrid.

Reader of poems, lover of poetry—
in case you thought this was a gentle art
follow this man on a moonless night
to the wretched bed he will have to make:

The Gaelic world stretches out under a hawthorn tree
and burns in the rain. This is its home,
its last frail shelter. All of it—
Limerick, the Wild Geese and what went before—
falters into cadence before he sleeps:
He shuts his eyes. Darkness falls on it.

10

AZTEC POETS

Now I have come
I am standing,
I will compose songs,
make the songs burst forth,
for you, my friends.
—"Poem of Temilotzin"

I FIND TREMENDOUS power in the native chants of ancient Mexico. In Nahuatl, the language of the Aztec world, one key word for poet was *tlamatine,* meaning "the one who knows," or "he who knows something." Poets were considered "sages of the word," who meditated on human enigmas and explored the beyond, the realm of the gods.

The pre-Hispanic Aztec poets of the fourteenth and fifteenth centuries are perhaps the first known poets of the Americas, but their work comes down to us at some remove. Their indigenous texts were painted in what are now lost pictoglyphic codices. These were later recited to ethnographer-friars, who in turn transcribed them in Roman letters. The "ancient word" of the Nahuatl texts was preserved in a few sixteenth-century manuscripts.

The Aztec poets had a keen sense of transience. They sang often of *cahuitl,* "that which leaves us." Here is a poem by the song-composer Nezahualcóyotl (1402–1472), a well-known figure who was not only a poet but also the supreme ruler of Tezcoco. I discovered it thirty years ago in a free adaptation by Peter Everwine in his first book, *Collecting the Animals:*

I Nezahualcóyotl ask it—
You live on this earth?
No, not forever
Only a short time.
Be jade. Jade breaks.
Be gold. Gold tears away.

The broad plumes of the quetzal unravel.
No, not forever.
Only a short time.

"I comprehend the secret, the hidden / O my lords!" Nezahual-cóyotl declares in another poem: "Thus we are, / we are mortal, / humans through and through, / we will all have to go away, / we will all have to die on earth . . ."

In his immensely helpful *Fifteen Poets of the Aztec World,* Miguel León-Portilla summarizes the biographies of fifteen masters of Nahuatl verse and reproduces their work in both the Nahuatl and English languages. León-Portilla points out that these composers had all been instructed in the *calmecac,* or priestly schools, where "they had mastered the science of the calendar, the divine wisdom, the books of the annals, the ancient songs, and the discourses."

One of my favorite poets in this group is Ayocuan Cuetzpaltzin, who lived in the second half of the fifteenth century in what is now Puebla. He seems to have been a *teohua,* or priest, a "White Eagle." He was a seeker after heights who believed that "[f]riendship is a shower of precious flowers" and that "Earth is the region of the fleeting moment." From a lapidary statement in a poem sometimes entitled "Let the Earth Remain Forever," I have an image of him walking and chanting his songs on ancient roads. Here is Everwine's adaptation:

> Let the earth last
> And the forests stand a long time
>
> Ayocuan Cuetzpaltzin said this, traveling
> The road to Tlaxcala
> The road to Huexotzinco
>
> Let field after field
> Unfold with brown corn
> Flowers of cacao
>
> Let the earth last

RIDDLES

Men are fond of me. I am found everywhere . . .

THERE IS A CUNNING riddle in Daniel Hoffman's ninth book of poems, *Darkening Water*:

A RIDDLE

If all but one deny me, I am not.
The Greeks had gods for everything but me.

                                                        Since then
How could I live on earth, in heaven? Yet see
If you can find me in the hearts of men.

The answer is ancient, simple, and timely: *Peace.*

There are many riddles of war, such as this anonymous eighth-century Anglo-Saxon one, which is translated by John Hollander in his encompassing anthology, *War Poems*. I like the way that Hollander imitates the alliterative-stress meter of the original. In Anglo-Saxon poetry, each line is broken into distichs by a strong cut or break in the line.

A RIDDLE

Injured by iron   I am a loner
Scarred by the strokes   of the sword's edge
Wearied of battle.   War I behold
The fiercest foes   yet I hope for no help

No comfort for me   to come out of battle
Before among people   I perish completely
But the keen swords   skillfully forged,
The handiwork hard-edged   of hammering smiths,
Bite into my stronghold.   I must ever abide
An encounter more dire;   never a doctor
Will I ever find   on the field of fighting
To heal with herbs   the grievous hurts,
But my sword-wounds   are ever widened
By death-blows dealt me   day and night.

The answer was key to the Anglo-Saxon warrior: *A shield.*

The riddles of war and peace are inexhaustible. Think of *After the First Rain: Israeli Poems on War and Peace,* a deeply moving and crucial anthology of Hebrew poems that are filled with a revulsion against war and a powerful hunger for peace. Some of the poems I've known for a long time, such as T. Carmi's "Military Funeral at High Noon" ("Everything is ground down, razed, forgotten") and Yehuda Amichai's heartbreaking "Seven Laments for the War-Dead" ("And everything / in three languages: Hebrew, Arabic, and Death"). Others I'm discovering for the first time, such as Ella Bat-Tzion's haiku-like poem "Peace," translated by Barbara Goldberg and Moshe Dor, and Eytan Eytan's splendid "The Wind Grinds," translated by Merrill Leffler and Moshe Dor, which has a driving sincerity and urgency, an incantatory power.

PEACE

Peace is a sea
whose waves
will carry us far.

THE WIND GRINDS

The wind grinds bones to dust
In the courtyard of death
Grinds clouds, vehicles

In a low continuous burning
Grinds soldiers, grinds cannon and guns
Grinds buildings, grinds animals, grinds you and me

Listen, leave your explosives, your vehicles, your soldiers
Leave your animals, your wars, your people
They all left you long ago

You have the wind with you
You have the burning light, the land and the dew with you
You have the whole pulverized earth with you

Set your face toward begetting
Set your face once more towards rising

12.

CHARMS

Whose wreathed friezes intertwine
The viol, the violet, and the vine.
—Edgar Allan Poe

A CHARM IS A SPELL or incantation spoken to invoke and control supernatural powers. Charms, which are universally known, are among the earliest form of recorded literature. They carry the resonance of magic rites in archaic cultures and, indeed, the Old English charms (against wens, against the theft of cattle, for taking a swarm of bees, for a land remedy) are some of the first written works in our literature.

Charms can be used for positive or negative ends, to ward off the spirit of evil or to invoke it, to destroy an enemy or attract a beloved, to enchant objects, to ensure good luck with supranormal power. I've always loved this charmed and charming love poem by Thomas Campion, which obsessively repeats the magic number three. It appeared in his *Third and Fourth Book of Ayres* (1617):

> Thrice tosse these Oaken ashes in the ayre,
> Thrice sit thou mute in this inchanted chayre;
> Then thrice three times tye up this true loves knot,
> And murmur soft, shee will, or shee will not.
>
> Goe burne these poys'nous weedes in yon blew fire,
> These Screech-owles fethers, and this prickling bryer,
> This Cypresse gathered at a dead mans grave:
> That all thy feares and cares an end may have.
>
> Then come, you Fayries, dance with me a round,
> Melt her hard hart with your melodious sound.

In vaine are all the charmes I can devise:
She hath an Arte to breake them with her eyes.

In her collection *The Charm,* Kathy Fagan uses the charm as an
ironic contemporary form. I find something both very old and very
new in her wisecracking charms to assuage grief and despair, to ward
off misfortune and heartbreak. Often she writes here under the spell of
childhood. Fagan creates linguistic charms from an English grammar
as well as quasi-surrealist ones for the artists Joseph Cornell and Max
Ernst. She includes a group of short satirical poems she calls "Charm
Bracelet." She exorcises the novelist in herself by writing "Charm for
an Unwritten Character" ("She'd be a woman with a lot of brothers, /
a woman who wore charm bracelets") and imagines a "Late Night
Charm" for watching old movies while her lover sleeps beside her
("Life, you say, is like TV"). She even comes up with a charm from the
Egyptian Book of the Dead to avoid dying a second time.

One of my favorites among these poems is "Little Bad Dream
Charm." The speaker has just been startled awake from an afternoon
nap and thus fractures English in her sleepy, semiconscious state. Her
recitation of the dream has the funny, off-key precision of a nightmare:

LITTLE BAD DREAM CHARM

We haven't found enough dreams.
We haven't dreamed enough.
—GEORGIA O'KEEFFE

I just woke up from a start afternoon nap. I
dreamed of whole time. I dreamed I woke up
lists of times. I wanted to make up, because
all my drears were nightmares. The only reason
I thank I'm awake now is that I'm steel sleepy.
I dreamed about goldfish except they were boys,
and there were hundreds of ether boys, some
so tinny they were trapped in the weave of a green

carpet that shone like water or glass—sea, that's
why it was a bad dream. They were all dying
because they were leafing out of their tanks. I
had scooped them up and threw them back into any
whaler I could find—I had stuffed, even, two
plastic cups full. And then, in order to save
as many lines as I could, I scooped a whole
bunch into an aquarium, awe at once—and that's
what they became soddenly, enormous carrots
sinking to the bittern of the dark.

13

JOHN CLARE

a language that is ever green

JOHN CLARE (1793–1864), who was born in the village of Helpston, Northamptonshire, in the eastern flatlands of England, found his poetry in the woods and fields, in the intricate nests of birds and the avid renewal of wildflowers, in a green language. He was enabled by what he read—James Thompson's poem "The Seasons" inspired him to become a poet—and often wandered through the fields with a book jammed in his pocket. "The fields were our church," he later recalled, "and we seemed to feel a religious feeling in our haunts on the sabbath." A secular religious sensibility—"the quiet love of nature's presence"—animates his work, early and late.

Jonathan Bate's capacious and detailed book *John Clare: A Biography* tells the story of England's greatest lower-class poet with deep sympathy and understanding. Bate's edition of Clare's selected poems also demonstrates the complete range of Clare's achievement, which is no mean feat since he wrote more than thirty-five hundred poems over three and a half decades. The punctuation is a bit too regularized for my taste—Clare was a madcap and eccentric punctuator at best—but the trade-off in literal accuracy does give the poems fuller accessibility to a wider audience. He breathes in these pages.

Clare was "addicted" to poetry, helpless before his rural muse. He was an agricultural laborer who published four poetry books during his lifetime, less than one-quarter of his total output. He was taken up as a "peasant poet" in London, supported by rival patrons, cultivated, condescended to, neglected. He was dogged by poverty most of his life. Clare had a keen ear for the vernacular and championed local customs, yet was considered peculiar by his neighbors. He stuck out everywhere—an alien at home, a lonely visionary. He empathized with outsiders, such as gypsies, whom he characterized as "a quiet, pilfering, unprotected race." It is no wonder, then, that shy, vulnerable creatures especially called to him: the snipe, the marten, the badger, the field mouse.

Clare was a prodigious walker, a solitary who sought out the secret recesses of nature, a hidden, underappreciated, overlooked country, which he detailed with a sharp eye and a naturalist's sensibility. Accuracy was a scrupulous habit and a moral imperative. He had a powerful capacity to identify with what he observed. Bate points out that more than fifty of Clare's poems begin "I love." "Poets love nature and themselves are love," he wrote in a late sonnet. "For everything I felt a love, / The weeds below, the birds above," he declared in "The Progress of Rhyme." Bate also notes that the most common noun in Clare's mature poetry is *joy*. One distinguishing feature of Clare's work is the ethic of reciprocity that he brought to his encounters with the natural world.

Clare's poetry intimately chronicles a world that was rapidly disappearing, that was systematically divided up into rectangular plots of land, fenced off and restricted, enclosed. This gives particular social and political relevance to his highly personal first subject, the lost Eden of childhood, a world that he never forgot but that seemed to have abandoned him. It also gives additional poignancy to his love poems, which are typically invitations: "Let us go in the fields, love, and see the green tree; / Let's go in the meadows and hear the wild bee; / There's plenty of pleasure for you, love, and me / In the mirth and the music of nature."

> We'll down the green meadow and up the lone glen
> And down the woodside far away from all men,
> And there we'll talk over our love-tales again
>   Where last year the nightingale sung.

Clare loved to roam so freely through open fields, through wilds and waste places, through uncultivated regions, that it comes as something of a shock to find him suddenly looking back over his shoulder for magistrates and gamekeepers:

> I dreaded walking where there was no path
> And pressed with cautious tread the meadow swath
> And always turned to look with wary eye
> And always feared the owner coming by;
> Yet everything about where I had gone
> Appeared so beautiful I ventured on
> And when I gained the road where all are free
> I fancied every stranger frowned at me
> And every kinder look appeared to say
> "You've been on trespass in your walk today."
> I've often thought, the day appeared so fine,
> How beautiful if such a place were mine,
> But, having naught, I never feel alone
> And cannot use another's as my own.

Clare was alert to both social and economic alienation. E. P. Thompson recognized that "Clare may be described, without hindsight, as a poet of ecological protest: he was not writing about man here and nature there, but lamenting a threatened equilibrium in which both were involved."

Clare suffered from a disconcerting number of physical and mental troubles. Bate scrupulously chronicles the tormented years from 1837 to 1864 that the poet spent in the High Beach Asylum and the Northampton General Lunatic Asylum. He suggests that Clare "conforms to the classic pattern . . . of manic depression or 'bipoloar affective disorder,'" though in the end concludes that Clare was most likely schizophrenic. He had periods of lucidity mixed with bouts of depression and episodes of mania. He was emotionally volatile. He suffered from delusions and obsessively identified himself with Lord Byron. One of his strangest literary performances is "Don Juan: A Poem," which begins, "'Poets are born'—and so are whores—the trade is / Grown universal."

Clare was also gripped by the notion that he had two wives. One was his actual wife, the other his youthful crush and early muse, Mary Joyce. "To Mary" begins:

> I sleep with thee and wake with thee
> And yet thou are not there;
> I fill my arms with thoughts of thee
> And press the common air.
> Thy eyes are gazing upon mine
> When thou art out of sight;
> My lips are always touching thine
> At morning, noon and night.

Clare continued writing all through his asylum years: "I wrote because it pleased me in sorrow," he said, "and when I am happy it makes me more happy and so I go on."

Some of Clare's finest works were asylum poems: "A Vision," "An Invite to Eternity," a poem addressed to his namesake, and two disconsolate self-revelations that begin "I am," one a sonnet ("I feel I am—I only know I am"), the other a lyric that stands as his most haunting memorial, a poem with a simple eloquence, a shocking lucidity:

LINES: "I AM"

> I am—yet what I am, none cares or knows;
> My friends forsake me like a memory lost:
> I am the self-consumer of my woes—
> They rise and vanish in oblivion's host
> Like shadows in love-frenzied stifled throes—
> And yet I am and live—like vapours tossed
>
> Into the nothingness of scorn and noise,
> Into the living sea of waking dreams
> Where there is neither sense of life or joys
> But the vast shipwreck of my life's esteems;

Even the dearest that I love the best
Are strange—nay, rather, stranger than the rest.

I long for scenes where man hath never trod,
A place where woman never smiled or wept,
There to abide with my Creator, God,
And sleep as I in childhood sweetly slept,
Untroubling and untroubled where I lie,
The grass below—above, the vaulted sky.

14

CHRISTMAS POEMS

His beams shall cheer my breast, and both so twine,
Till ev'n his beams sing, and my musick shine.
—GEORGE HERBERT

THOMAS HARDY published "The Oxen" in the London *Times* on December 24, 1915. He based the poem on the traditional legend of oxen kneeling in their stables at midnight on Christmas Eve, which he first heard from his mother. He may also have recalled the carving of "a kneeling bovine" that he saw as a youth when he was working as an architect's apprentice on the restoration of Rampisham Church.

Hardy always associated the supernatural with the celebration of Christmas. I feel that in this poem he envied the people who sat comfortably in a Christian "flock" and never doubted the veracity of the tale of the kneeling animals. He had been one of them once. But, in the midst of World War I, which cast, as he said, "a shade over everything," that faith was forever denied him.

"The Oxen" is written, appropriately enough, in the common meter of the ballad stanza. It has a rustic English vocabulary (a "barton" is a farmyard, a "coomb" a valley) that reverberates with Christian overtones. There is a keen element of childish wonder in the poem, which he included in his book *Moments of Vision* (1917). Many years later, when Hardy was asked to choose twelve of his own poems for the library of Queen Mary's quirky doll's house, "The Oxen" was his first choice. His eyesight was too weak to manage it, but otherwise he would have transcribed the poem in miniature in his own handwriting.

Here, then, is my favorite Christmas Eve poem:

THE OXEN

Christmas Eve, and the twelve of the clock.
  "Now they are all on their knees,"
An elder said as we sat in a flock
  By the embers in hearthside ease.

We pictured the meek mild creatures where
  They dwelt in their strawy pen,
Nor did it occur to one of us there
  To doubt they were kneeling then.

So fair a fancy few would weave
  In these years! Yet, I feel,
If someone said on Christmas Eve,
  "Come; see the oxen kneel

"In the lonely barton by yonder coomb
  Our childhood used to know,"
I should go with him in the gloom,
  Hoping it might be so.

Hardy's poem is also collected in *Christmas Poems,* an erudite little anthology selected and edited by John Hollander and J. D. McClatchy. The editors point out that Christmas is both a holiday and a holy day, which has always been associated with poetry. Their garland traces a dramatic arc from the Annunciation to the Epiphany, and reaches a pinnacle in a sublime group of poems that centers on the Nativity, including pieces by John Milton, John Donne, Henry Vaughan, Christopher Smart, and T. S. Eliot. It contains requisite poems, songs, and carols everyone recognizes, such as "A Visit from St. Nicholas" and "The Twelve Days of Christmas," as well as lesser-known but equally enchanting lyrics, such as this elegant little "Epiphany" by Robert Fitzgerald, which consists of one sentence strung across two rhyming quatrains:

Unearthly lightning of presage
In any dark day's iron age
May come to lift the hair and bless
Even our tired earthliness,

And sundown bring an age of gold,
Forgèd in faëry, far and old,
An elsewhere and an elfin light,
And kings rise eastward in the night.

15

CHARLOTTE MEW

Over my head the curlews call,
And now there is the night wind in my hair;
My heart is against the grass and the sweet earth . . .

IT IS HARD to understand why the English poet Charlotte Mew (1869–1928) isn't better known. She deserves more readers. Virginia Woolf recognized that she was "very good and interesting and unlike anyone else," and Thomas Hardy, whom she revered as the "King of Wessex," considered her "far and away the best living woman poet, who will be read when others are forgotten."

Mew's poetry has a strange, agitated beauty. She published two books of poems: *The Farmer's Bride* (1916) and *The Rambling Sailor* (1929), which appeared posthumously. She was part Victorian, part modernist, and her work is "God bothered." Her irregular rhythms and rhyming free-verse experiments make her something of a formal anomaly among the Georgian poets with whom she is usually associated, and her romantic focus on women gives her work a feminist perspective and intensity. In her life, Mew was secretive, thwarted, and guilt-ridden—she believed in maintaining proprieties and keeping up a front of gentility—but in her work, reticence gives way under the extreme pressure of emotion, as in the heartbroken poem "Rooms":

> I remember rooms that have had their part
>   In the steady slowing down of the heart.
> The room in Paris, the room at Geneva,
> The little damp room with the seaweed smell,
> And that ceaseless maddening sound of the tide—
>   Rooms where for good or ill—things died.
> But there is the room where we two lie dead,

Though every morning we seem to wake and might just as well seem
   to sleep again
  As we shall somewhere in the other quieter, dustier bed
  Out there in the sun—in the rain.

Mew was a master both of the interior and the dramatic monologue. She liked to tell stories at an odd angle, a fictionalized distance,
and thus she often displaced herself into other speakers. The men in
her work tend to be nondescript, whereas the women are distinctive
and need passion, which is usually negated. This gives her poetry the
undercurrent of a heartfelt cry. What Mew said about Emily Brontë re-
veals something true about herself as well: "Never perhaps has passion
been portrayed as she portrayed it—wayward and wild as a storm . . .
And nature is presented to us by the same unerring hand." Like Brontë,
Mew could describe uncanny experiences with an eerie fatalism:

THE CALL

  From our low seat beside the fire
     Where we have dozed and dreamed and watched the glow
   Or raked the ashes, stopping so
We scarcely saw the sun or rain
   Above, or looked much higher
Than this same quiet red or burned-out fire.
      To-night we heard a call
     A rattle on the window-pane,
     A voice in the sharp air,
And felt a breath stirring our hair,
   A flame within us: Something swift and tall
  Swept in and out and that was all.
Was it a bright or a dark angel? Who can know?
   It left no mark upon the snow,
     But suddenly it snapped the chain
    Unbarred, flung wide the door
    Which will not shut again;
  And so we cannot sit here any more.

We must arise and go:
The world is cold without
And dark and hedged about
With mystery and enmity and doubt,
But we must go
Though yet we do not know
Who called, or what marks we shall leave upon the snow.

16

W. B. YEATS

There floats out there
The shape that I shall take when I am dead,
My soul's first shape, a soft feathery shape,
And is not that a strange shape for the soul
Of a great fighting-man?

W. B. YEATS completed his penultimate poem, "Cuchulain Comforted," just two weeks before his death. Here the heroic warrior inexplicably finds himself welcomed into the otherworld by singing cowards, his exact opposites in life, whom he joins in death. "The hero, absorbed into a purgatorial otherworld, has to await resurrection and reincarnation," as R. F. Foster puts it in the conclusive second volume of his biography of Yeats, in which he observes, "WBY's last poetic vision of the afterlife is not a refuge 'where the blessed dance,' nor the transforming dolphin-journey to Byzantium, nor even the reunion rehearsed in numerous séance rooms, but a banishment to the company of outcasts."

Yeats first tackled the death of the Irish hero in an 1892 poem that he later rewrote as "Cuchulain's Fight with the Sea" (1925). Between 1904 and 1939, he wrote five plays about the ancient saga figure. "Cuchulain Comforted" was intended as a kind of sequel to his final play, *The Death of Cuchulain.* As his life drew to a close, Yeats struggled to link the circumstances of his own death to that of his chosen Irish hero.

Shortly before 3 A.M. on the morning of January 7, 1939, Yeats awoke from a vivid dream and dictated the prose draft of the poem to his wife. This outline, included in Foster's biography ("A shade recently arrived went through a valley in the Country of the Dead"), was transposed into the poem, which Yeats first entitled "Cuchulain Dead."

Yeats borrowed the image of the sewing shades directly from Dante's *Purgatorio.* Even more tellingly, he wrote "Cuchulain Comforted" in terza rima, a verse form that Dante invented for the *Commedia.* Terza rima consists of interlocking three-line stanzas rhyming *aba, bcb, cdc,* and so forth. Rhyming the first and third lines gives each tercet a sense of temporary closure; rhyming the second line with the first and last lines of the next stanza generates a strong feeling of propulsion. The effect is both open-ended and conclusive, like moving through a set of interpenetrating rooms or going down a set of winding stairs; you are always traveling forward while looking back. The ingenious form is perfectly suited to Yeats's mysterious and purgatorial poem, which he dated 13 January 1939:

Cuchulain Comforted

A man that had six mortal wounds, a man
Violent and famous, strode among the dead;
Eyes stared out of the branches and were gone.

Then certain Shrouds that muttered head to head
Came and were gone. He leant upon a tree
As though to meditate on wounds and blood.

A Shroud that seemed to have authority
Among those bird-like things came, and let fall
A bundle of linen. Shrouds by two and three

Came creeping up because the man was still.
And thereupon that linen-carrier said
'Your life can grow much sweeter if you will

'Obey our ancient rule and make a shroud;
Mainly because of what we only know
The rattle of those arms makes us afraid.

'We thread the needles' eyes and all we do
All must together do.' That done, the man
Took up the nearest and began to sew.

'Now we shall sing and sing the best we can
But first you must be told our character:
Convicted cowards all by kindred slain

'Or driven from home and left to die in fear.'
They sang, but had nor human notes nor words,
Though all was done in common as before,

They had changed their throats and had the throats of birds.

17

RABINDRANATH TAGORE

Such splendor illuminates a deathlessness
hidden in the everyday by our senses' limits.

DURING THE last year of his life, while he was suffering from an ex-
cruciating illness, Rabindranath Tagore (1861–1941), one of the great
cultural figures of modern India, wrote and dictated four volumes of
poems. In this quartet of books—*Sickbed, Recovery, On My Birthday,*
and *Last Poems*—the writer unblinkingly faces his own death. It is
thus a long-awaited and abiding pleasure to have Tagore's *Final Poems,*
selected and translated from the Bengali by the poet Wendy Barker
and the philosopher Saranindranath Tagore, a descendant of Rabindranath himself. This collection gives English-speaking readers an opportunity to take the measure of Tagore's last act.

The translators treat the four books as a single cohesive body of
work. Their version is so evocative that one can't help wishing they
had translated all four volumes in their entirety. Yet what they have
provided is sufficient for us to experience the rich complex of feelings—terror, grief, awe, uncertainty, exhilaration, acceptance, wonder, courage—with which the most multifaceted of Indian writers
confronted his own mortality.

Tagore is known for his highly musical verse (he also composed
more than two thousand songs), but here he writes in a free-verse style
that is stark and austere, utterly simple, poignantly direct. He writes
in the clarifying light of last things. The art of such finality is an art
pared away to what is absolutely essential, an art of making language
at the edge of a void where everything is undone, unmade. Language
is put to a grave test as it faces a poet's permanent silence.

Here, for example, is a lyric of departure. It has the radiance of a deep farewell poem, a final acceptance:

LAST POEMS 10

> I'm lost in the middle of my birthday.
> I want my friends,
> their touch,
> with the earth's last love.
> I will take life's final offering,
> I will take the last human blessing.
> Today my sack is empty.
> I have given completely
> whatever I had to give.
> In return if I receive anything—
> some love, some forgiveness—
> then I will take it with me
> when I step on the boat that crosses
> to the festival of the wordless end.

Tagore's *Final Poems* were written from the vanishing point of life. "They are replete," as S. Tagore puts it, "with images of *bhāshāhī-natā*—the state of 'languagelessness,' of Silence." They enter a sacred space as they deliver us back to a primal unity. These poems take us to the very edge of human consciousness, to a place beyond words. Here is one of the last three poems Tagore dictated to his secretary less than two weeks before his death. Even as this poem approaches a final threshold, it echoes the "Creation Hymn" of the *Rig Veda*, which stands at the dawn of ancient Indian literature:

LAST POEMS 13

> The first day's sun
> questioned
> the new appearance of being—

Who are you?
There was no answer.

Years went by.
Day's last sun
asked the last question from the shores of the west
in the soundless evening—
Who are you?
There was no answer.

18.

GIUSEPPE BELLI

Christ made great houses and palaces
for prince and earl, marquis, queen and duchess.
He made the earth for us, the dog-faces.

THE NINETEENTH-CENTURY Italian poet Giuseppe Belli (1791–1863)
created sonnets that are small, explosive, highly compressed dramas.
He was a lifelong resident of Rome and wrote in the Romanesco di-
alect of Trastevere, which Miller Williams, who has brilliantly translated Belli into an earthy American idiom, calls a sister language of
Italian. When I lived in Trastevere for a year in the late 1980s, I discovered that the Romani or Trasteverians still tend to call themselves
Noiantri: "we others." It was for these proud, irrepressible "others"
that Belli wrote more than two thousand sonnets over a thirty-year
period.

Belli had a strong theatrical streak and liked to tell stories. He
had a tough, streetwise wit, a terrific ear for slang, and a deep sympathy for working people. His poems are cunning, ironic, and robust.
They are unexpected and shocking, as when one gravedigger says to
another:

So what are we gonna do? Nobody dies.
That smell of malaria wasn't worth a damn.
People are holding onto their crazy lives.
You'll love gravedigging, they said. So here I am.

Williams notes that Belli all but turned the sonnet into a ballad
form. He gave it raw, narrative energy. A good example is "La nottata
de spavento," a chilling poem that he wrote on January 22, 1835:

Night of Terror

You're not going back out, as mad as you are?
Look, I don't like the way you're acting tonight.
Jesus! What is it? What have you got under there?
Holy Virgin, you're looking for a fight!

Pippo, my darling, you're not in any shape
To be out there carousing around town.
Pippo, listen to me, for pity's sake.
Okay, give me the knife. Just put it down.

You're not going out. I'm not yours anymore
The minute you leave. Cut me, go ahead.
There's no way you're going through that door.

Look at our sleeping angel. What a surprise
Not to find his father beside his bed
Smiling at him when he opens his eyes.

Belli despised cant. He worked as a petit bureaucrat, and completely identified with the poor people of Trastevere. He was darkly funny and approached the world with the eye of a disabused lover. He knew how things worked. Belli developed a healthy contempt for crass wealth, dirty politicians, and corrupt ecclesiastical authorities. His political poems are forthright, knowing, and scornful. The people he writes about are instantly recognizable. Have things changed? Here is *"Li padroni de Roma,"* which he wrote in April 1835:

The Bosses of Rome

These are the bosses of Rome; take a good look.
They know how to deal with scum like us. They learn
To cook us on both sides as no other cook
Could cook us, turned out perfectly, done to a turn.

First comes the pope, for all the afflicted. Now
The cardinals, like endless rows of roses,
And then the bishops, holier-than-thou,
Making up laws and looking down their noses.

Each one in his place, and number four,
The heads of the orders of monks to kill the bull,
To finish us off. Coming behind them, the corps

Of foreign diplomats with open knives
To claim the bull's ears. And last of all
The gentlemen of Rome with their beautiful wives.

19

GIUSEPPE UNGARETTI

I have never held
so hard
to life

I'VE BEEN HAUNTED for years by the Italian poet Giuseppe Ungaretti's memorial poem to his friend Mohammed Sceab. The two young foreigners, each trying to discover himself and seal his vocation, each wildly excited and disturbed by the adventure of modernism, lived in the same obscure Parisian hotel in 1912 and 1913.

I think of them roaming around the City of Light together, both in their early twenties, both displaced—one an Italian from Alexandria, the other a descendent of Arab nomads. They declared their principles to each other, like young poets everywhere, and talked endlessly about Baudelaire and Nietzsche, whom Sceab especially loved, and Leopardi and Mallarmé, whom Ungaretti felt were sublime. They were two literary kids from the provinces dreaming of greatness in the modern capital.

Sceab was "a boy with clear ideas," as Ungaretti later said, but he was also lost and tormented, filled with self-hatred, and he committed suicide in 1913 "because he had been unable to feel at home in any country." We see every day now the dire consequences of absolute cultural dislocation, and we recognize what can happen when people feel unable to liberate the song of their own homeless desolation.

Here is the poem *"In memoria"* that Ungaretti wrote in 1916 from a trench in the midst of World War I. By then, Ungaretti feared, no one remembered his friend anymore, no one knew who he was or what he might have become. And it's true that Sceab's name is known to posterity only because of the tender, dedicatory elegy that opened Ungaretti's first volume of poetry. The poem appears in Andrew

Frisardi's splendidly fresh and definitive translation of Ungaretti's *Se-lected Poems*, which I am eager to recommend.

IN MEMORY OF
Locvizza, September 30, 1916

His name was
Mohammed Sceab.

Descendent
of emirs of nomads
a suicide
because he had no homeland
left

He loved France
and changed his name

He was Marcel
but wasn't French
and no longer knew
how to live
in his people's tent
where you hear the Koran
being chanted
while you savor your coffee

And he didn't know how
to set free
the song
of his desolation

I went with him
and the proprietess of the hotel
where we lived in Paris
from number 5 Rue des Carmes
an old faded alley sloping downhill

He rests
in the graveyard at Ivry
a suburb that always
seems
like the day
a fair breaks down

And perhaps only I
still know
he lived

20

EUGENIO MONTALE

I always begin with the real . . .

THE ITALIAN POET Eugenio Montale (1896–1981) was an aficionado of the void, of thresholds and enclosures, of stony enclaves and seacoasts. He wrote often of his first landscape, a walled-in garden near the Tuscan coast, the sea churning against the cliffs, the unforgiving sun in an endless blue sky. This is the world stripped to the bone, the "rocky and austere" Ligurian shore, where he spent summers until he was thirty. It served as the mirror held up to his turbulent inner realm, the place where he was always "waiting for the miracle."

Here, then, is the earliest piece from Montale's first book, *Cuttlefish Bones,* in which he evokes the landscape of his childhood. The untitled lyric, which he wrote in 1916 and revised again in 1922, belongs to a group of poems he called "my rondels."

> Sit the noon out, pale and lost in thought
> beside a blistering garden wall,
> hear, among the thorns and brambles,
> snakes rustle, blackbirds catcall.
>
> In the cracked earth or on the vetch,
> watch the red ants' files
> now breaking up, now meeting
> on top of little piles.
>
> Observe between branches the far-off
> throb of sea scales,

while cicadas' wavering screaks
rise from the bald peaks.

And walking in the dazzling sun,
feel with sad amazement
that all life and its torment
consists in following along a wall
with broken bottle shards imbedded in the top.

(TRANSLATED BY JONATHAN GALASSI)

Almost all of Montale's poetry is addressed to an imaginary inter-
locutor, a *"tu,"* who is sometimes the reader, sometimes an unnamed
companion, sometimes an absent beloved, most frequently the fierce
and angelic figure of Clizia and her later counterpart, the earthly vixen
Volpe. For Montale, the beloved is a spur and an inspiration, a spiritual twin, an alter ego. She becomes a "goddess who won't become
flesh," a celestial light, a cosmic force that he has absorbed into himself, a power that counters the evil in history.

"The Eel" (*"L'anguilla"*), one of Montale's most widely admired
poems, consists of a single sentence that runs for thirty lines. It describes an eel coming down from the north with lightning-like speed
and becoming a "torch, whiplash, / arrow of Love on earth":

The eel, siren
of cold seas, who leaves
the Baltic for our seas,
our estuaries, rivers, rising
deep beneath the downstream flood
from branch to branch, from twig to smaller twig,
ever more inward,
bent on the heart of rock,
infiltrating muddy
rills until one day
light glancing off the chestnuts
fires her flash

in stagnant pools,
in the ravines cascading down
the Apennine escarpments to Romagna;
eel, torch, whiplash,
arrow of Love on earth,
whom only our gullies
or desiccated Pyrenean brooks lead back
to Edens of generation;
green spirit seeking life
where only drought and desolation sting;
spark that says that everything begins
when everything seems charcoal,
buried stump;
brief rainbow, iris,
twin to the one your lashes frame
and you set shining virginal among
the sons of men, sunk in your mire—
can you fail to see her as a sister?

(TRANSLATED BY JONATHAN GALASSI)

21

RAINER MARIA RILKE

. . . what I needed was not so much an instrument of emotion, but, rather: clay.

RAINER MARIA RILKE'S early work is intensely subjective, but beginning in 1902, when he first came to Paris and put himself under the wing of the sculptor Rodin, he started to conceive a poetry that belonged more to the world of things than to the realm of feelings. The twenty-seven-year-old focused on the artist's labor, the actual process of making something material, and objectified his practice to match something of what he referred to as Rodin's "art of living surfaces." He called his new work *Dinggedicthe,* or "thing-poems."

Rilke put himself to school by wandering around Paris, gazing intently at things. Like Marianne Moore, who called her second book *Observations,* Rilke often practiced the art of observation by spending whole days at the zoo studying animals. The poems that resulted have their own character—I find them outwardly impersonal, inwardly nervous. (In his fine book *Slow Air,* Robin Robertson puts together three of these poems under the rubric "From the Jardin des Plantes.")

In *"Der Panther,"* Rilke seems to combine his description of a real animal with his memory of a small Greek statue of a panther (or a tiger) in Rodin's studio:

THE PANTHER

Exhausted, he sees nothing now but the bars
that flicker past him in a blur;
it seems there are a thousand bars
and behind the thousand bars an empty world.

The drill of wheel and return: turning on his heel till
he seems to pass through his own body—like whiskey
swilled to the neck of the bottle then back on itself.
He swings on the pivot of his numb and baffled will.

Sometimes, though, the sprung shutter of the eyes
will slide open and let an image enter—a face, perhaps—
shooting through the tensed muscles, lightening
the limbs, streaming into his heart to die.

"Yesterday I spent the whole morning in the Jardin des Plantes,
looking at the gazelles," Rilke wrote to his wife, Clara, on June 13,
1907. He found himself particularly drawn to a single female gazelle,
lying a few feet apart from the others:

> And when a horse whinnied, the single one listened, and I saw
> the radiance from ears and horns around her slender head . . . I
> saw the single one stand up, for a moment; she lay right down
> again; but while she was stretching and testing herself, I could
> see the magnificent workmanship of those legs (they are like rifles
> from which leaps are fired). I just couldn't tear myself away, they
> were so beautiful.

Rilke's experience resulted in his sonnet "The Gazelle," subtitled
Gazella Dorcas (a gazelle from lower Egypt) and dated July 17, 1907.
Unlike the male panther, whose world has become a cage, the gazelle
doesn't seem weighed down by captivity. The poet works to find a language for his enchantment and has a keen sense of the precarious relationship that obtains between the perceiver and the thing perceived.
The key turning point in the poem comes when the speaker closes his
eyes and lets his imagination take over.

The Gazelle

Tranced creature: no rhyme or ringing words
can match the pulse that rolls

through you like a charm. Horns spring
from your head, adorning you with leaf and lyre,

and you are your own metaphor,
just as the words of a love-song
are like a drift of rose-petals, closing
the eyes of a tired reader, so as to see you—

there—hair-triggered,
four legs pointed, ready
to recoil and ricochet away

but waiting, listening: just as
the bathing huntress heard the forest stir,
and turned, the quivering pool reflected in her face.

22

SELF-PORTRAITS

I paint myself.
—Pablo Picasso

Rainer Maria Rilke was thirty-one years old and living in Paris when he wrote his searching, off-balance sonnet "Self-Portrait in the Year 1906." My favorite translation, if that is the right word, is Robert Lowell's version in *Imitations,* a book that can be reread in Frank Bidart and David Gewanter's definitive edition of Lowell's *Collected Poems.*

Lowell took his idea of "imitation" from Dryden, who in turn borrowed the term from Crowley. "I take imitation of an author . . . to be an endeavour of a later poet to write like one who has written before him, on the same subject," Dryden declared in *Ovid and the Art of Translation* (1680); "that is, not to translate his words, or be confined to his sense, but only to set him as a pattern, and to write as he supposes the author would have done, had he lived in our age, and in our country."

Lowell could be so free with his texts that they become virtually unrecognizable—"I have been reckless with literal meaning," he confessed—but I find his rhyming version of Rilke's self-portrait utterly convincing. Here, Rilke's seriousness finds a formal American idiom that also feels natural:

Self-Portrait

The bone-build of the eyebrows has a mule's
or Pole's noble and narrow steadfastness.
A scared blue child is peering through the eyes,
and there's a kind of weakness, not a fool's,

yet womanish—the gaze of one who serves.
The mouth is just a mouth . . . untidy curves,
quite unpersuasive, yet it says its *yes,*
when forced to act. The forehead cannot frown
and likes the shade of dumbly looking down.

A still life, *nature morte*—hardly a whole!
It has done nothing worked through or alive,
in spite of pain, in spite of comforting . . .
Out of this distant and disordered thing
something in earnest labors to unroll.

Lowell captures Rilke's playful and anguished tone, the ruthless self-critical gaze of a young artist who feels unfinished, incomplete, haunted by his own weakness. Rilke used the occasion not only to recognize but also to declare his own inner conviction, his deep sense of artistic mission. He had already apprenticed himself to Rodin when he wrote this poem, and he had taken from the master an unshakable sense of "the great work."

Lowell's version of Rilke's sonnet stands behind Frank Bidart's poem "Self-Portrait, 1969," which appeared in his breakthrough first book, *Golden State* (1973). Bidart adds something more open and hesitant, something more radically self-questioning to the form. His complex, original mode of punctuation gives the sense of a man brooding, of consciousness at work. It nails down the way the poet hears phrases coming to him. He stares at himself in the mirror; he responds intensely to what he has just written. Bidart brings to the self-portrait a Yeatsian sense of lyric as a form of arguing with oneself.

SELF-PORTRAIT, 1969

He's *still* young—; thirty, but looks younger—
or does he? . . . In the eyes and cheeks, tonight,
turning in the mirror, he saw his mother,—
puffy; angry; bewildered . . . Many nights
now, when he stares there, he gets angry:—

something *unfulfilled* there, something dead
to what he once thought he surely could be—
Now, just the glamour of habits . . .

                                 Once, instead,
he thought insight would remake him, he'd reach
—what? The thrill, the exhilaration
unraveling disaster, that seemed to teach
necessary knowledge . . . became just jargon.

Sick of being decent, he craves another
crash. What *reaches* him except disaster?

23.

ERNST STADLER

Mensch, werde wesentlich!

WE ARE FOREIGN to ourselves. There are times when we seem to be sleepwalking through our daily lives, superficially skating along the surface, strangers to our motives and desires, to our own actions, which we do not recognize or comprehend. We coast along until an old saying, or a phrase from a long-forgotten song, or a poem itself suddenly wells up and shocks us awake. We are startled back into authenticity, into a deeper and truer relationship to our inner lives, into a greater feeling for the genuine mysteries of the different realms we inhabit. I believe we should treasure these words like a talisman, since they deliver and restore us to ourselves.

A certain kind of inner alienation seems to come with modern urban life. This spiritual state, which has been brilliantly anatomized by Baudelaire, Hofmannsthal, and Kafka, is characterized in a startling poem by Ernst Stadler (1883–1914). Stadler was a vital German Expressionist poet (often associated with Georg Heym and Georg Trakl) who was killed by a British shell on the Western Front. What is compelling is the intensity of his poems, his Whitmanian cadences, his fierce determination to pierce the shimmering surfaces of the modern world and somehow penetrate the core of reality itself.

I first read Stadler's poem "The Saying" as a literal translation in an anthology of twentieth-century German verse. I rediscovered it updated and refashioned into a strong contemporary American idiom by Stephen Berg in his book of versions and free translations, *The Steel Cricket: Versions 1958–1997* (1997), which is the most compelling book of its kind since Robert Lowell's controversial *Imitations* (1961).

An imitation is different from a literal rendition of a poem. It takes greater license. A looser adaptation, a wider departure, it moves in more ambiguous literary space. Thus Lowell confessed that he had been reckless with the literal meaning of poems, but labored hard to get the right tone. The same may be said of Berg's versions. When an imitation succeeds, it accomplishes something closer to a fusion of two poetic selves. Look, for instance, at how Stadler's final command, *"Mensch, werde wesentlich!"* ("Man, become substantial!"), is strikingly refigured in the last line of Berg's version.

THE SAYING

In an old book
I stumbled across a saying.
It was like a stranger
punching me in the face,

it won't stop
gnawing at me.
When I walk around at night,
looking for a beautiful girl,

when a lie or a description
of life or somebody's fake
way of being with people
occurs instead of reality,

when I betray myself with
an easy explanation
as if what's dark is clear,
as if life doesn't have thousands

of locked, burning gates,
when I use words without really
having known their strict openness
and put my hands around things

that don't excite me,
when a dream hides my face with soft hands
and the day avoids me,
cut off from the world,

cut off from who I am deeply,
I freeze where I am
and see hanging in the air in front of me
STOP BEING A GHOST!

24

NELLY SACHS

Peoples of the earth,
do not destroy the universe of words . . .

NELLY SACHS (1891–1970) is one of the great poets of lamentation in the German language. She has deep affinities with her friend Paul Celan (their sixteen-year correspondence is a remarkable twentieth-century document), whose work is now more widely read and frequently discussed. They are true peers. One could say that each of them formulated a brave and unnerving lyric response to the unbearable catastrophe of the Holocaust, which is unimaginable but nonetheless needs to be remembered and imagined. Celan spoke of passing through "the thousand darknesses of deathbringing speech." Sachs declared: "The frightful experiences that brought me to the edge of death and darkness are my tutors. If I couldn't have written, I wouldn't have survived . . . my metaphors are my wounds."

Sachs grew up in a prosperous upper-middle-class Jewish family in Berlin. She was an only child and later referred to her privileged early life as a "hell of loneliness." She began by writing a kind of high, neo-Romantic poetry, but in the 1930s increasingly turned to biblical themes and Hasidic mystical subjects. She was deeply bonded to her mother—her father died in 1930—and, with the aid of the Swedish writer Selma Lagerlöf, the two of them escaped to Stockholm in May 1940. Sachs lived the rest of her life in Sweden. After her mother's death in 1950, she had the first of many psychiatric breakdowns. She earned a modest living as a translator of Swedish poetry into German, and created a full and heartbreaking body of her own work. She won the Nobel prize in literature in 1966. The citation praised her for "lyrical laments of painful beauty and . . . dramatic legends."

Sachs bore the burden of writing in German during the dumb-founding horrors of the death camps. She carried the lifelong weight of continuing to write in the language of Goethe and Schiller in the wake of the Final Solution. She entered her true poetry under the shadow of the Holocaust, which is why *In the Habitations of Death* (1947) was her first wholly characteristic work. It begins by evoking the crematoriums:

> O the chimneys
> On the ingeniously devised habitations of death
> When Israel's body drifted as smoke
> Through the air—

Hans Magnus Enzensberger has pointed out that metamorphosis is at the heart of Sachs's work. Transformation was her enduring theme. "I hold instead of a homeland / the metamorphoses of the world," she wrote in *Flight and Metamorphosis* (1959). The sense of renewal is key to Sachs's enigmatic and grief-stricken poetry that takes, to use one of her titles, a *Journey into a Dustless Realm* (1961). That's why the butterfly is one of her signature figures, an airy fundamental.

BUTTERFLY

> What lovely aftermath
> is painted in your dust.
> You were led through the flaming
> core of earth,
> through its stony shell,
> webs of farewell in the transient measure.

> Butterfly
> blessed night of all beings!
> The weights of life and death
> sink down with your wings
> on the rose
> which withers with the light ripening homewards.

What lovely aftermath
is painted in your dust.
What royal sign
in the secret of the air.

(TRANSLATED BY RUTH AND MATTHEW MEAD)

25

WOMEN AND WAR

My Blue Piano

At home I have a blue piano.
But I can't play a note.

It's been in the shadow of the cellar door
Ever since the world went rotten.

Four starry hands play harmonies.
The Woman in the Moon sang in her boat.
Now only rats dance to the clanks.

The keyboard is in bits.
I weep for what is blue. Is dead.

Sweet angels, I have eaten
Such bitter bread. Push open
The door of heaven. For me, for now—

Although I am still alive—
Although it is not allowed.

—Else Lasker-Schüler

IN HER MOVING and essential book *After Every War,* the Irish poet Eavan Boland has gathered together and translated the work of nine German-speaking women poets, all of whom wrote in the decades surrounding World War II. The title comes from the Polish poet Wislawa Szymborska, who notices with a kind of wry domestic wisdom that "[a]fter every war somebody must clean up."

The poets in this collection recognize the hard personal truths of warfare. They are both witnesses and participants. Some I've lived with for years, such as Nelly Sachs (1891–1970), Ingeborg Bachmann (1926–1973), and Else Lasker-Schüler (1869–1945), whom her friend Gottfried Benn called "the greatest lyric poet Germany ever had." Others are personal revelations, such as Elisabeth Langgässer (1899–1950), who is represented by a single devastating poem ("Spring 1946"), and Rose Ausländer (1901–1988), who sounds the ground note for the book with her poem "Motherland":

> My Fatherland is dead.
> They buried it
> in fire
>
> I live
> in my Motherland—
> Word

These poets—the others are Gertrud Kolmar (1894–1943), Marie Luise Kaschnitz (b. 1901), Hilde Domin (b. 1909), and Dagmar Nick (b. 1926)—were all deeply shaped by the cataclysm of World War II. Boland has chosen a small but crucial selection of their overall work, a kind of personal anthology, that shows them to be war poets with a difference. The difference comes from being both poets and women, with all that entails. "I had to do it—suddenly, I had to sing. / I had no idea why," Else Lasker-Schüler cries out in her poem "In the Evening": "But when the evening came I wept. I wept bitterly." These poets have a particular angle of witness that comes from powerlessness, from being vulnerable, injured, marginal, excluded. Most were exiles. Several of them were Jewish, which means they suffered the Holocaust. Dispossession is a key theme. They recognized what they had lost. "I am one who cannot live among my own kind," Ingeborg Bachmann declares in "Exile." "A stranger / always carries / his native land in his arms," Nelly Sachs observes in "If Someone Comes."

Here is Hilde Domin's "Exile":

The mouth dying
The mouth twisted
The mouth trying
to say the word right
in a strange language.

There is something deeply compelling, as Boland puts it, "in the
way the world of the public poet encounters the hidden life of the
woman in these poems." The interplay is endlessly fascinating. I'm
struck by the personal way these poets confront history, test and in-
terrogate language, especially their mother tongue, question the effi-
cacy of poetry, and repeatedly defend the importance of private
feeling. They are dark elegists who view large historical events through
a focused individual lens. Their voices seem to me as necessary today
as when they wrote in the aftermath of World War II.

Here is Rose Ausländer's transfiguring elegy for her mother, "My
Nightingale," which now takes its place, along with Lasker-Schüler's
"My Blue Piano," on my shortlist of the most radiant mid-twentieth-
century poems.

My Nightingale

My mother was a doe in another time.
Her honey-brown eyes
and her loveliness
survive from that moment.

Here she was—
half an angel and half humankind—
the center was *mother.*
When I asked her once what she would have wanted to be
she made this answer to me: a nightingale.

Now she is a nightingale.
Every night, night after night, I hear her
in the garden of my sleepless dream.

She is singing the Zion of her ancestors.
She is singing the long-ago Austria.
She is singing the hills and beech-woods
of Bukowina.
My nightingale
sings lullabies to me
night after night
in the garden of my sleepless dream.

26.

MAX JACOB

Here I am in Paradise! Me, a feeble, rotting pumpkin?
In Paradise? Impossible!

MAX JACOB (1876–1944) has always seemed an oddly irresistible and contradictory figure. I'm drawn to the genuine wit and zany artistry of this dyed-in-the-wool modernist who palled around with Picasso and Apollinare, and played a key role in the development of Cubism and Surrealism. Born in Quimper, Brittany, Jacob once said that he joined the artistic community in Montparnasse "to sin disgracefully." He was a verbal cutup and comedian, a serious occultist and student of Kabbalah, a dandy, a self-lacerating homosexual, and a Jew who had a vision of Christ and subsequently converted to Catholicism. His clowning around tended to cover up his genuine mysticism and spiritual torment.

Jacob was a renegade from the middle class who lived in extreme poverty in Paris and worked at all manner of jobs. His groundbreaking work *Le cornet à dés* (*The Dice Cup*) established him as the re-inventor of the prose poem and a worthy successor to Rimbaud. Jacob treated art as a game ("Too bad for him who makes a duty of it," he declared), and he enjoyed toying with reality, undermining sentimentality, and playfully mistaking one thing for another, as in his characteristic poem "The Beggar Woman of Naples," which consists of a single paragraph. Here it is translated by John Ashbery:

> When I lived in Naples there was always a beggar woman at the gate of my palace, to whom I would toss some coins before climbing into my carriage. One day, surprised at never being thanked, I looked at the beggar woman. Now, as I looked at her,

I saw that what I had taken for a beggar woman was a wooden case painted green which contained some red earth and a few half-rotten bananas . . .

In life as in work, Jacob's ironic wit continually vied with his devotional spirit. Until 1921, he ricocheted between a wild bohemianism and an extravagant, self-mocking, theatrical penitence. "If I had sinned terribly the night before, next morning, well before dawn, you could see me crawling on my knees through the Stations of the Cross," he confessed. "I choke, I weep, I strike my face, my breast, my arms and legs, my hands. I bleed, I make the Sign of the Cross with my tears. At the end, God is taken in."

Jacob eventually moved to the small village of Saint-Benoit-sur-Loire, close to a Benedictine church. One of the ironies of his situation was that he was forced to wear the yellow star, and thus publicly identify himself as a Jew. The cutting dialogue tells all in this tiny prose poem from *Derniers poèmes:*

THE YELLOW STAR AGAIN

"Are those beets your dog's eating?"
"No, it's a Jew who fell down in the snow."
"They could find some other place to faint instead of my sidewalk."

(TRANSLATED BY WILLIAM KULIK)

Jacob was arrested by the Nazis in February 1944, and died of bronchial pneumonia in a concentration camp at Drancy, near Paris. "The path of my fate is, I'm afraid, unwavering. / I'll soon be at death's door," he foresaw in "Artless Lines," one of his last poems. "I'll leave gladly what others have envied me for, / an adolescent's heart treasured like a precious urn." The poem concludes with the commanding whisper of God:

Swift is the race hard the rocky place
and the flower of love died beneath our knees

while the lips cried silently in the depths of the heart.
An angel of the Lord came to me:
"Use your voice to sing to heaven!"
It was a wise spirit and beautiful too.
And since then! How often has God whispered:
"Silence is everywhere but in my eyes.
Become intoxicated with me. Look for me more and more.
Contemplate me: I promise nothing.
And think carefully: my image is in you.
Your secret happiness in the midst of sorrow.
Understand my law of suffering
transform your grief into holy ecstasy
through my eyes you must see your nature
through my heart you must weep with love."

(TRANSLATED BY WILLIAM KULIK)

27

INSOMNIA

I can't sleep; no light burns;
All round, darkness, irksome sleep.
—ALEXANDER PUSHKIN

I LIKE READING poetry late into the night. I like the way it takes me away from the day, from daylight thinking, and opens me up to something else, something stranger and more unknown. It creates a space for reverie, for night mind. Through poetry I enter a primary zone where silence reigns and the constant din of the culture momentarily stops, where I can feel what I think and think about what I'm feeling, where I can hear a solitary human voice rising out of the primordial darkness.

For this reason, I suppose, I am also partial to many "insomnia" poems, lyrics where the speaker operates as a sole consciousness. Everyone else seems to be far away or lost in "irksome sleep," dead to the world, and a sense of tremendous solitude permeates the air. In this way, each of us may be delivered a little more closely to ourselves. As the fifteenth-century Zen master Ikkyu formulated it:

> night after night after night stay up all night
> nothing but your own night

One of my favorite poems of sleeplessness is an untitled twelve-line lyric that the Russian poet Osip Mandelstam wrote in the Crimea in 1915. It appeared in the second edition of his groundbreaking first book, *Stone* (1916). Mandelstam associates so rapidly in this poem—the first line consists of three nouns, each an independent sentence—that I am reminded of Joseph Brodsky's definition of poetry as "accelerated thinking." It helps to know that the Crimea and the Black Sea have traditionally been regarded in Russian poetry as the closest possible Russian equivalents to the classical world of Greece.

> Insomnia. Homer. Taut sails.
> I've read to the middle of the list of ships:
> the strung-out flock, the stream of cranes
> that once rose above Hellas.
>
> Flight of cranes crossing strange borders,
> leaders drenched with the foam of the gods,
> where are you sailing? What would Troy be to you,
> men of Achaea, without Helen?
>
> The sea—Homer—it's all moved by love. But to whom
> shall I listen? No sound now from Homer,
> and the black sea roars like a speech
> and thunders up the bed.

(TRANSLATED BY CLARENCE BROWN AND W. S. MERWIN)

One could write a good essay about the chronic inability to sleep in Russian poetry. It would begin with Pushkin's "Lines Written at Night During Insomnia" (1830), it would include Innokenty Annensky's key cycle "Insomnia" (1904), and it would highlight Marina Tsvetaeva's restless ten-part sequence "Insomnia" (1916).

Tsvetaeva's voice in this poem is violent and mesmerizing. It is filled with warning: "Don't sleep! Be firm! Listen, the alternative / is everlasting sleep." I'm struck by the way that she pleads to be liberated from the bonds of day and throws open her doors wide into the night, eagerly relinquishing her social self in order to be inhabited by something more mysterious ("and people think perhaps I'm a daughter or wife / but in my mind is one thought only: night"). She would be broken down and artistically reborn; she would become a vehicle of nature, a vatic poet. Here are the four couplets that comprise section 8, which is a dark prayer, a joyous hymn to the night itself:

Black as an iris, as an iris sucking up the
Light—I love you, sharp-sighted night.

Let me sing you and celebrate you, O ancient mother
Of songs who bridles the earth's four winds.

Calling you, glorifying you—I am nothing but a
Shell in which the ocean is not yet silenced.

Night! Enough of looking into human eyes!
Reduce me to ashes, blackest of suns—night!

(TRANSLATED BY NINA KOSSMAN)

28

MARINA TSVETAEVA

Where does this tenderness come from?

THERE IS a ruthless authenticity to Marina Tsvetaeva's work. Tsvetaeva (1896–1941) was one the great Russian poets of the century just past, and she deserves to be as well known in the West as the three brilliant contemporaries with whom she is often associated—Boris Pasternak, Osip Mandelstam, and Anna Akhmatova. One reason Tsvetaeva is less famous here is that she wrote a type of vigorously rhythmical, densely textured rhyming lyric that is extremely aural and exceedingly difficult to translate. Joseph Brodsky suggested that "[i]f you could conjure up a combination of Hart Crane and Hopkins, that would be Tsvetaeva."

What *does* translate is Tsvetaeva's honesty, which is unflinching, and her passion, which is explosive. Here is an example of her relentless inspiration, a poem from 1934, translated by Angela Livingstone:

> Opened my veins—unhaltable,
> unrestorable—gush of life.
> Put your plates and dishes under it:
> every plate will be too shallow,
> every bowl too flat, it flows
> over the rim and spills out
> to the black earth, to feed the reed.
> Unrestorable, unhaltable,
> irretrievable—gush of verse.

Tsvetaeva called the poem "an explosion, a breaking in," and believed in taking "the comet's path, the comet's way." She pushed the upper lyric registers ("Marina often begins a poem in high C," Akhmatova once said) and wrote with a candor so extreme, an emotion so insatiable, that it blew open the links of causality, the carefully constructed social frame. She wrote against a world of weights and measures, against balance and "common sense," against chronological or calendar time. ("The eclipses of / poets are not foretold in the calendar.") In her memoir "Mother and Music," Tsvetaeva said that the reason there cannot be too much of the lyrical is because the lyrical is itself the "too much."

Tsvetaeva started writing poetry as a child and never let up. She was independent and high-minded, wildly impractical, fiercely romantic. There is something unworldly and even doomed about so much overflowing passion. "In every group I am alien," Tsvetaeva said, which was certainly borne out by her biography, a life in which she seemed to court disaster at every turn. "We are poets, which has the sound of outcast," she declared. She considered the poet an "*émigré* from the kingdom of Heaven and from the earthly paradise of nature."

Here is the last stanza of her 1923 poem "The Poet," which sets out her artistic program. The speaker, who defines herself "by nature and trade / a singing creature," seems partly bewildered, partly enraged, and ferociously proud:

> What shall I do—being a singer and first-born—
> when the blackest of all in this world is grey!
> where inspiration is kept as though in a thermos!
> with this measurelessness
> in a world of measures?

In addition to her poems, I am eager to recommend Tsvetaeva's soaring autobiographical and critical essays, all of them a vocal defense of "what is highest" in art and collected in English as *Art in the Light of Conscience* and *A Captive Spirit: Selected Prose.* Her splendid three-way correspondence with Pasternak and Rilke has also been published as *Letters: Summer 1926.*

Marina Tsvetaeva represents what is most exalted in lyric poetry. Pasternak said after her death that every day she had "performed some act of bravery . . . out of loyalty to the one country of which she was a citizen: poetry."

29

VELIMIR KHLEBNIKOV

We chant and enchant,
Oh charming enchantment!

MAKE WAY for the mind-bending experiments and verbal pyrotechnics of the Russian poet Velimir Khlebnikov (1885–1922), whose friends christened him "Velimir the First, King of Time." Khlebnikov's early Futurist work has the hijinks glow and aggressive hilarity of youth ("We rang for room service and the year 1913 arrived," he wrote, "it gave Planet Earth a valiant new race of people, the heroic Futurians"), and reading it, even in translation, often makes me burst out laughing.

In his most famous Futurist poem, "Incantation by Laughter," Khlebnikov breaks down the Russian word for laughter, *smekh,* and then devises a comical series of new words around it. His translator, Paul Schmidt, captures his ingenious strategy of building "permutations of the word *laugh* into a weird scenario full of prehistoric chortles." The words themselves seem to be laughing and exclaiming at the sound of their own formation, their strangely gleeful repetitions.

INCANTATION BY LAUGHTER

Hlahla! Uthlofan, lauflings!
Hlahla! Uthlofan, lauflings!
Who lawghen with lafe, who hlaehen lewchly,
Hlahla! Uthlofan hlouly!
Hlahla! Hloufish lauflings lafe uf beloght lauchalorum!
Hlahla! Loufenish lauflings lafe, hlohan utlaufly!
Lawfen, lawfen,
Hloh, hlouh, hlou! luifekin, luifekin,

Hlofeningum, hlofeningum.
Hlahla! Uthlofan, lauflings!
Hlahla! Uthlofan, lauflings!

Khlebnikov loved puns and palindromes, the roots of words, neologisms of all sorts. He loved obsessive wordplay and the magical
language of shamans. He found eerie wisdom in separate linguistic
sounds, such as *sh, m,* and *v.* There was something both very old and
startlingly new in his poetic practice. He believed that universal
truths are secreted in the sheer materiality of language, and he sought
to access them through spells and incantations, magic words, folk et-
ymologies, archaic sounds. He especially loved the Futurist term
zaum, a coined word that means something like "transrational" or
"beyondsense." He employed it to suggest the ways that poetic thinking transcends so-called common sense and the restrictive strictures
of rational intellect. "If we think of the soul as split between the government of intellect and a stormy population of feelings," Khlebnikov wrote in his essay "On Poetry," "then incantations and
beyondsense language are appeals over the head of the government
straight to the population of feelings, a direct cry to the predawn of
the soul . . ."

Khlebnikov's wordplay stands at one extreme of poetry. It reminds
us of the elemental truth that poems consist of consonants and vowels,
letters of the alphabet, syllables in action. They are radically sounded
things, verbal objects. He was a forward-looking utopian thinker who
rebelled against so-called authoritarian prosodies and had a Whitman-
like faith in the underlying unity of all things.

Here is one of the untitled poems that Khlebnikov wrote in the
last two years of his life, a period of desperate personal as well as collective hardship in Russia. He speaks in this lyric to his shamanistic
desire—it was always an outsider's dream, really—to transfigure the
World through the Word and thus fulfill a prophetic poetic destiny.

Russia, I give you my divine
white brain. Be me. Be Khlebnikov.
I have sunk a foundation deep in the minds

of your people, I have laid down an axis.
I have built a house on a firm foundation.
"We are Futurians."
And I did all that as a beggarman,
a thief, a man with a curse on his head.

30

JOSEPH BRODSKY

Give me another life, and I'll be singing . . .

JOSEPH BRODSKY (1940–1996) wrote a poignant poem for his fortieth birthday—May 24, 1980—that has stayed with me ever since I first encountered it as the lead piece in his book *To Urania* (1988). The poem is a revealing self-portrait, a summing up and coming to terms, an idiosyncratic credo by a Russian poet who liked to refer to himself as a Calvinist, which he characterized as "a man keeping strict accounts with himself, with his conscience and consciousness." A Calvinist, according to Brodsky's quirky, self-styled definition, "is someone who is constantly declaring Judgment Day against himself— as if in the absence of (or impatient for) the Almighty." By this reckoning, Dostoevsky also counted as a Calvinist, and so did Marina Tsvetaeva, one of Brodsky's favorite poets, whom he once called "the falsetto of time" and "Job in a skirt."

Brodsky translated his birthday poem himself, hence its driving music and compulsive wordplay. I can still close my eyes and hear him reading it aloud in that special hypnotizing chant, a sort of rabbinical keening, a soaring singsong, that was very much his own. "This isn't a man," Nadezhda Mandelstam once exclaimed, "it's a wind orchestra!" The aphoristic form, a capsule autobiography accelerating at lyric speed, seems especially well suited to Brodsky's particular temperament, to his keen intelligence and ironic wit, to his determined, almost classical stoicism in the face of a grief that threatened to swamp him.

Brodsky's summary poem was written from the far side of exile. He may have had little actual choice in the matter, but he nonetheless felt an enormous undertow of guilt for abandoning his native country. (Brodsky went into involuntary exile in 1972, following a conviction for social parasitism, and never returned to Russia.) "Munched the bread of exile: it's stale and warty," he declares, thus referring back to a proud poem that his mentor, Anna Akhmatova, penned in 1922: "But I pity the exile's lot," she pronounced, "wormwood infects your foreign bread." Brodsky never viewed himself as a victim—he was allergic to self-pity—but he did eat the harsh bread of exile, which only increased his special solidarity with grief. He was an intimate of loss who knew what he had sacrificed.

Yet, like his great precursors Akhmatova, Mandelstam, and Tsvetaeva, Brodsky also had an Orphic gift for turning sorrow into high song. He transformed his ordeals in life into triumphs in poetry. His cosmopolitan spirit dwells in his work. Above all, I hear the intonations of his unmistakable voice and feel that the poet has outsung death.

MAY 24, 1980

I have braved, for want of wild beasts, steel cages,
carved my term and nickname on bunks and rafters,
lived by the sea, flashed aces in an oasis,
dined with the-devil-knows-whom, in tails, on truffles.
From the height of a glacier I beheld half a world, the earthly
width. Twice have drowned, thrice let knives rake my nitty-gritty.
Quit the country that bore and nursed me.
Those who forgot me would make a city.
I have waded the steppes that saw yelling Huns in saddles,
worn the clothes nowadays back in fashion in every quarter,
planted rye, tarred the roofs of pigsties and stables,
guzzled everything save dry water.
I've admitted the sentries' third eye into my wet and foul
dreams. Munched the bread of exile: it's stale and warty.
Granted my lungs all sounds except the howl;
switched to a whisper. Now I am forty.

What should I say about life? That it's long and abhors transparence.
Broken eggs make me grieve; the omelette, though, makes me vomit.
Yet until brown clay has been crammed down my larynx,
only gratitude will be gushing from it.

31

CZESLAW MILOSZ

I ask not out of sorrow, but in wonder.
—"Encounter"

The first movement is joy,
But it is taken away.
—"The Poor Poet"

What is poetry which does not save
Nations or people?
—"Dedication"

Human reason is beautiful and invincible.
—"Incantation"

The purpose of poetry is to remind us
how difficult it is to remain just one person . . .
—"Ars Poetica"

And the heart does not die when one thinks it should . . .
—"Elegy for N. N."

What was accepted in bitterness and misery turned into praise . . .
—"From the Rising of the Sun"

There are nothing but gifts on this poor, poor earth.
—"The Separate Notebooks"

SOMETIMES AT NIGHT or in the early morning, the phrases—the lines—come back to me like talismans, like hard-won messages, metaphysical truths, prayers, offerings from the deep. I was in my early twenties when I first read Czeslaw Milosz's work, which has stayed with me ever since as a touchstone of modern poetry itself. I first felt from his work the nobility and grandeur of poetry, yet also learned from him to distrust rhetoric, to question false words and sentiments. "Try to understand this simple speech as I would be ashamed of another," he avowed in "Dedication." "I swear, there is in me no wizardry of words." One felt from the beginning the purposefulness of Milosz's deceptive simplicity, his distrust of "pure poetry," his anguished irony, his humility before the perplexing plenitude of reality, the depth of his quest for clarity and truth.

Milosz's poems circulate in the bloodstream not just of Polish but also of American poetry. He offered us at every stage of his development a model of poetic—of human—integrity and seriousness. One marvels at how much of the twentieth century he forced himself to confront and internalize, how much beauty he wrung from its blood-soaked precincts. So much of his work seems haunted by survivor's guilt, the poignancy of living after what was, for so many, the world's end. Poetry served him as an offering to the dead, a form of expiation, a hope for redemption. His first obsessive subject was the grim reality of human suffering. Yet his poems are also filled with a survivor's wonder, with a sense of astonishment that the world still exists at all, that we are here to partake of it with a profound gratitude and reverence. He was submerged, as he put it, "in everything that is common to us, the living." He looked to the earth—to being here—for salvation, and kept an eye on the eternal.

Milosz's greatest poetry is written at the borders of what can be said. It makes a strong effort at expressing the unsayable. There was always in his work an element of catastrophism, a grave open-eyed lucidity about the twentieth century. His work was initiated by the apocalyptic fires of history. Milosz usefully employed the guilt so deeply ingrained in him to summon old stones, to remember those who came before him. He was weighed down by the past, fundamentally responsible to those he had outlasted, and thus bore the burden of long memory. He taught the American poet—and American poetry itself—to consider historical categories, not the idea of history vulgarized by Marxism but something deeper and more complex, more sustaining: the feeling that mankind is memory, historical memory, and that "our hope is in the historical." In both poetry and prose he gave us a series of Cassandra-like warnings about America's painful indifference to European experience, about the consequences of what happens when "nature becomes theater." In his splendid poetic argument with Robinson Jeffers, he countered Jeffers's praise of inhuman nature with his native realm where nature exists on a human scale. Milosz modeled his own obsessive concern with our collective destiny, with what he called "the riddle of Evil active in history." Like Alexsander Wat, whose memory he devotedly kept alive, he was deeply aware of our tragic fragmentation, but he didn't revel in that fragmentation so much as seek to transcend it. In our age of the most profound relativism, he offered an ongoing search for immutable values. He gave us a historical poetry inscribed under the sign of eternity.

I love Milosz's poetry for its plenitudes and multilevel polyphonies. He taught us to love lyric poetry and also to question it. He insisted that his poems were dictated by a *daimonion,* and yet he also exemplified what it means to be a philosophical poet. His poetry was fueled by suffering but informed by moments of unexpected happiness. He understood the cruelty of nature and yet remembered that the earth merits our affection. He thought deeply about the rise and fall of civilizations, and he praised the simple marvels of the earth, the sky, and the sea. "There is so much death," he wrote in "Counsels," "and that is why affection / for pig-tails, bright-colored skirts in the wind, / for paper boats no more durable than we are." He wrote of the eternal moment and the holy word: *Is.* He reminded us how difficult it is to remain just one person. He insisted on our humanity. I love his poetry most of all for its radiant moments of wonder and being, because of its tenderness toward the human. It is a permanent gift.

GIFT

A day so happy.
Fog lifted early, I worked in the garden.
Hummingbirds were stopping over honeysuckle flowers.

There was no thing on earth I wanted to possess.
I knew no one worth my envying him.
Whatever evil I had suffered, I forgot.
To think that once I was the same man did not embarrass me.
In my body I felt no pain.
When straightening up, I saw the blue sea and sails.

32

ADAM ZAGAJEWSKI

I'm truly not a child of the ocean,
as Antonio Machado wrote about himself,
but a child of air, mint, and cello . . .

ADAM ZAGAJEWSKI'S poems put us in the presence of great mysteries. They deliver us to something deep and strange and perhaps even unlimited within ourselves. They have a strong kinship to prayer, a paradoxical feeling for truth, a fiery sense of quest, and a keen longing for radiance:

A FLAME

God, give us a long winter
and quiet music, and patient mouths,
and a little pride—before
our age ends.
Give us astonishment
and a flame, high, bright.

(TRANSLATED BY CLARE CAVANAGH)

Zagajewski's poems are everywhere shadowed by death, and extremely conscious of human cruelty. They recognize the savageries— the charnel house—of history. Like all Polish poets in the twentieth century, Zagajewski understands what human beings are capable of doing to each other. "It could be Bosnia today, / Poland in September '39, France / eight months later, Germany in '45, / Somalia, Afghanistan, Egypt," he writes in his poem "Refugees." "In the Parc de Saint-Cloud . . . I pondered your words," he writes to the painter Joseph Czapski: "The world is cruel; rapacious / carnivorous, cruel."

Yet Zagajewski's poems are also filled with splendid moments of spiritual lucidity. They are spirited by what he calls "festive proclamations." "I was impaled by sharp barbs of bliss," he writes in his poem "Cruel." "I know I'm alone, but linked / firmly, to you, painfully, gladly," he declares in "Presence": "I know only the mysteries are immortal." For him, even the action of swimming becomes like prayer: "palms join and part, / join and part / almost without end." I marvel at the way his poems transport us into a realm that is majestic, boundless, and unknown.

Zagajewski was born in 1945 in the medieval city of Lvov ("There was always too much of Lvov," he writes, "no one could / comprehend its boroughs") and grew up in the ugly industrial city of Gliwice. These two places, so finely described in his prose book *Two Cities,* form two sides of his imagination: "Two cities converse with one another," he confesses: "Two cities, different, but destined for a difficult love affair, like men and women." The third formative city of his experience is Krakow, where he was a student and awakened to poetry, music, and philosophy. These student years are the subject of his luminous prose work *Another Beauty,* which Susan Sontag calls "a wise, iridescent book" that "dips in and out of many genres: coming-of-age memoir, commonplace book, aphoristic musings, vignettes, and defense of poetry—that is, a defense of the idea of literary greatness." Poetry for Zagajewski delivers us to what is highest and most exalted in ourselves. Like music, it momentarily saves us.

The collection *Without End: New and Selected Poems* brings together Zagajewski's three major books in English: *Tremor* (1985), *Canvas* (1991), and *Mysticism for Beginners* (1997). It also includes previously unpublished early work and a sublime group of new poems. Zagajewski started out in the early 1970s writing under the sign of the newborn opposition movement in Poland. He had a strong sense of the writer's social responsibility and a clear idea that "the collectivity (the nation, society, generations) is the chief protagonist and addressee of creative, artistic works." Since the mid-1970s, however, he has increasingly given sway to another side of his nature. He has given vent to the aesthetic, committed himself to the (permanent) values of art. Or as he puts it: "I have discovered there is also a 'metaphysical' part of myself that is rather anarchic—not interested in politics or in history but in poetry and music."

Zagajewski has never forgotten the importance of addressing communal concerns, the necessity of civitas, and yet he has also learned the fundamental value of privacy, of the morality of speaking only for oneself. His poem "Fire" marks one turning point in his evolution from a dissident poet:

> Probably I am an ordinary middle-class
> believer in individual rights, the word
> "freedom" is simple to me, it doesn't mean
> the freedom of any class in particular.
> Politically naïve, with an average
> education (brief moments of clear vision
> are its main nourishment), I remember
> the blazing appeal of that fire which parches
> the lips of the thirsty crowd and burns
> books and chars the skin of cities. I used to sing
> those songs and I know how great it is
> to run with others; later, by myself,
> with the taste of ashes in my mouth, I heard
> the lie's ironic voice and the choir screaming
> and when I touched my head I could feel
> the arched skull of my country, its hard edge.

(TRANSLATED BY RENATA GORCZYNSKI)

The rival claims on Zagajewski's attention have increasingly given way to deeper aesthetic and even metaphysical divisions. He is a poet of compelling dualisms ("The world is torn. Long live duality! One should praise what is inevitable," he wryly proclaims). A powerful dialectic operates in his work between reality and imagination, between history and philosophy, between the temporal and the eternal.

"Two contradictory elements meet in poetry: ecstasy and irony," Zagajewski writes in *Two Cities:* "The ecstatic element is tied to an unconditional acceptance of the world, including what is cruel and absurd. Irony, in contrast, is the artistic representation of thought, criticism, doubt." He gives weight to both elements, and yet his deepest impulse is to try to praise the mutilated world, indeed, to praise the mysteries of—and even beyond—the world itself. He is in some sense a pilgrim, a seeker, a celebrant in search of the divine, the unchanging, the absolute. His poems are filled with radiant moments of plenitude. They are spiritual emblems, hymns to the unknown, levers for transcendence.

A QUICK POEM

I was listening to Gregorian chants
in a speeding car
on a highway in France.
The trees rushed past. Monks' voices
sang praises to an unseen god
(at dawn, in a chapel trembling with cold).
Domine, exaudi orationem meam,
male voices pleaded calmly
as if salvation were just growing in the garden.
Where was I going? Where was the sun hiding?
My life lay tattered
on both sides of the road, brittle as a paper map.
With the sweet monks
I made my way toward the clouds, deep blue,
heavy, dense,
toward the future, the abyss,
gulping hard tears of hail.
Far from dawn. Far from home.
In place of walls—sheet metal.
Instead of a vigil—a flight.
Travel instead of remembrance.
A quick poem instead of a hymn.

A small, tired star raced
up ahead
and the highway's asphalt shone,
showing where the earth was,
where the horizon's razor lay in wait,
and the black spider of evening
and night, widow of so many dreams.

(TRANSLATED BY CLARE CAVANAGH)

33

EDVARD KOCBEK

I feel now, as never before, that
a poem is the condensed power of all human
abilities, and that its ideal lies
in the power of language to transcend itself.

EDVARD KOCBEK (1904–1981) is a major Slovenian poet. *Nothing Is Lost,* his selected poems, is eloquently translated by Michael Scammell and Veno Taufer. This marvelous body of work spans more than forty years and confirms that Kocbek belongs in the company of other notable Eastern European poets, such as Vladimir Holan, Vasko Popa, and Zbigniew Herbert. He combined a keen, almost pantheistic feeling for nature with a powerful historical consciousness ("History rambles through nature," he wrote in the poem "Pentagram," "man is mysteriously hawk-eyed"). I admire his independent imagination ("As a writer I am completely independent, no force on earth can tell me what to do") and deep faith in poetry.

Kocbek was born in what is now eastern Slovenia but was at the time part of the Austro-Hungarian empire. The poems in his first book, *Earth* (1934), are deeply rooted in his native region. Reading them now, one feels that his pastoral sensibility and vital intimacy with nature, which at times seems mystical, was always infused with a painful sense of time, an agonized feeling of cosmic sorrow.

EARTH, I GET EVERYTHING FROM YOU

Earth, I get everything from you, earth
to you I return, my flesh smells of holy
sacrifice and mortal sorrow, long will I
look upward by day and by night.

Earth, our grave, how lovely you are, earth,
I am a sweet dark grain among grains, bewildered
by your depths, birds chirrup over our heads,
one of them will peck us up.

Kocbek had a complicated political history. He fought with the
Communist-led partisans in World War II and played a key role in the
new Slovenian government until he published unsparingly honest excerpts from his war diaries (*Comradeship,* 1949) and a book of short
stories (*Fear and Courage,* 1951) that realistically portrayed the war
crimes that were committed on all sides. The self-incriminating por-
trayal enraged the Communist authorities and brought about his official disgrace and downfall. He lived under virtual house arrest for
many years in Yugloslavia, which accounts for the nearly thirty-year
gap between his first and second books. *Dread* appeared in 1963 and
reestablished Kocbek as a major literary presence with a gift, as
Scammell puts it, "for personalizing the political and politicizing the
personal."

There is a strong sense of existential dread in Kocbek's work and
a recurring dialogue between faith and skepticism ("Faith and unfaith
burned with a single flame"). As Charles Simic formulates it in his
lucid foreword to the book, "Kocbek is a connoisseur of philosophical paradoxes and impossible moral predicaments." He defied dogmas
("The law of freedom of the human mind," he explained, "is like the
quiet defense of ancient rights") and took responsibility for his own
actions. Freedom was his watchword. Here is the revealing but unfinished poem that he was working on at the time of his death:

I HAVEN'T DONE PLAYING WITH WORDS

I haven't done playing with words
that have meaning, now I would like to give myself up
to the dangerous game of words that mean nothing
and are a mystery to themselves. Freedom is
the terrible freedom of nothingness. Which side

shall I choose now that the decisive moment
has come? Till now I have played, but from now on,
hidden in the earth, I shall utter
unknown words through the eons, perhaps
through all eternity . . .

34

TOMAŽ ŠALAMUN

I have a racket, air to breathe, clumsiness to protect
my soul and brilliance and Maruška and Ana and friends
to sleep with, my body and poetry.

TOMAŽ ŠALAMUN's book *Feast* is a work of exuberant whimsy and fierce rebellion. There is something deeply irreverent about the work of this Slovenian writer who came of age in the 1960s, something freewheeling and stubbornly off-the-cuff—disruptive, enraged, uncanny—in his raids and flights, in his urgent associations. He would refashion a recalcitrant historical world to the heart's desire. "O God, for the day to come when I / can mold the world with my Slovenianness," he calls out at the end of one poem: "Able to play strong, dense games." His poems constitute at once a series of playful and ironic counterstrikes against history and a joyful messianic lyric.

Šalamun's poems embody his faith in reveries and dreams ("A man must be judged by his dreams," he declares in his self-portrait "I"), but one also feels in them the pressure, the dark undertow, of human cruelty and suffering. The headlines cry out ("Death glues a newspaper," he observes wryly); Balkan wars hover in the background ("Human lives are fluff," he announces bitterly in "War": "Lines of refugees, houses in flames"). There are downdrafts of grief in these upward-sailing lyrics. Joy and suffering coexist in our world; they are simultaneous. The poem "Words" makes clear that Šalamun remembers—he seems helpless to forget—that someone is entering hell at the very moment he is glimpsing paradise:

> Let them serve you champagne in bed,
> the chilled one, as you awaken, still hot.
> Rasputin smelled too much. Foscolo and

Leopardi, too—they built the steps for
Nietzsche—swim in the *Gai savoir.* Will tundra
suffer cynically? Will the ice roar

when the little balls jet into the heart
of the Romanovs, like steam? The knight
combs his hair. He woke up lost in thought.

The sun strikes deep into the wells of the sky:
depends on how you look at it—for someone it is the hour
to be shot at dawn, for me the infinite gift

of red, of violet and blush-graying white
above the bridge across the Loire. Yesterday
I had to write something for George Lambert Ristin,

he is very curious. The lights in town are not
extinguished yet, the duality flies above the sea gulls.
The sea gulls show their acne. They have long beaks,

they're trained for the mud beneath the marsh,
just as some canaries can dot and stipple. They're all
flying. Little frogs, snails, shells, Krombergs and

adoratus. A Malagasian reinstated the slivers of ships.
Small blacks climb on the shipwrecks, they saved
themselves from drudgery. The bourgeoisie

of Nantes ate slavery. They tramped over the ruins
with their wheelbarrows. Blessed little ribbons cut up
by little girls, the scissors returned to the baskets

lined with plush. Hangars are like skyscrapers.
The crunching of Scotch tape is related to the sun.
It creeps in silence. Strikes the window.

(TRANSLATED BY CHRISTOPHER MERRILL AND THE AUTHOR)

Robert Hass has pointed out that Šalamun's tradition has been the disruptive, visionary side of European experimental art. With Blake, Šalamun would say that "Energy is eternal delight." He is an heir to Rimbaud (especially the young seer of *Illuminations,* who asserted, "A Poet makes himself a visionary through a long, boundless, and systematized disorganization of all the senses") and Lautréamont; to the Russian Futurists and the German Expressionists; to Khlebnikov and Apollinaire; to the French Surrealists who believed in what André Breton termed "mad love." I also hear something of the improvisatory delight and dailiness of the New York poets in these lyrics ("I breathe and a poem jumps up," he says in a line that echoes Frank O'Hara).

Šalamun has blended and assimilated his European and American influences into a poetry all his own, without losing his sense of gratitude and wonder. Freedom is the first condition of his poetry—the freedom of the anarchic single voice, of the idiosyncratic personal testimony. Šalamun's poetry derails rational logic and lyric elegance in order to delineate a strange reality. He refers often to the "infinite gift" of sunlight, to a blinding vision that is a portal to other realms. "There is another world, and it is in this one," Paul Eluard asserted, and Šalamun repeatedly points to the existence—the intangible reality—of that other world. His "strong, dense games" are a way of gaining access to its mysteries. As he testifies in the concluding lines of "Feast":

> Along this window, in this window
> there are innumerable other civilizations,
> innumerable other cosmological systems.
> Thus suffering does not matter,
> layers do.
>
> This is what I show here.

I welcome you to Tomaž Šalamun's delightful and eclectic table. It is spread with impromptu secrets and timed surprises. It is overflowing with associations. Throw open a window, pull up a chair, and enjoy the imaginative feast.

35

RADMILA LAZIĆ

I'll laugh everywhere, weep wherever I can.

"LIFE IS CANDIED fruit and vinegar," the poet Radmila Lazić declares in *A Wake for the Living,* translated from the Serbian with great panache by Charles Simic. "I add them to my verses in equal amounts." There is something bittersweet about Lazić's utterly convincing work, which has the texture of lived experience.

A Wake for the Living brings together a representative selection from Lazić's six collections of poetry. It is the first English translation of her work. Born in 1949, Lazić has a jaunty wit, a restless and irreverent intelligence, and a startling way of stalking the truth. She writes with the refreshing honesty—the unsettling boldness—of a woman at midlife. She prefers autumn to spring ("I'll celebrate October and not May") and decides that "goodness is boring." "I still want to make whoopee down here!" she exclaims in her poem "Goodness." "It seems it's hell I'm getting myself ready for."

Lazić writes as a feminist with a dark sense of humor and a surreal imagination, a woman forthright about her desires ("Let me get to the nitty-gritty," the speaker announces in "Dorothy Parker Blues." "I give you the visa / To my body—my homeland") and unsentimental about marriage. She can no longer be hoodwinked by conjugal love. "Many times I fell in love forever," she ruefully recalls in one poem. "I won't share my solitude with anyone," she concludes in another. "I came to know the bliss of departure."

There is a kind of dialectic operating in Lazić's work between irony and ecstasy, between the wisdom of long experience, which teaches her that "the time of miracles is behind us," and the innocence of fresh desire, which keeps surprising her with its bright insistence. On the one hand, she has developed what she calls a "twilight metaphysics":

> It's too late to teach my heart anything.
> The alphabet of suffering
> I already know it by heart. I test it live.
> Life knows more than the Sibyl.
>
> Time has stopped. What bliss is there in flowing?
> Reality resembles a moth-eaten sweater—
> This is what poetry is like.

On the other hand, the speaker in Lazić's poems repeatedly finds herself inspired by passion, overtaken by desire, ready to give up the practical world for a lover's avid embrace. "To hell with politics, with the stock market! / Come and lie next to me," she calls out. "I give you my body on credit, / My soul on the layaway plan."

The poem "Pleasures" is characteristic of Lazić's inner dialogue and division. The whole poem consists of a single short list, the summary catalog of a speaker who has passed youth, who can settle down to a few genuine things at the end of each day. She embraces solitude. And yet she can also be overcome by longing, which suddenly sneaks up on her late at night. The poem ends with a simple rousing affirmation.

PLEASURES

> A few verses.
>
> A few lines about poetry.
>
> A few sips down the throat
>
> Of something thick and bitter.
>
> The evening lowers its weary bones.

Memory.   Silence.

The barely audible tick-tack.

If only there was a summer shower.

My head next to someone's navel. Yes!

36

PRIMO LEVI

I commend these words to you.
Engrave them on your hearts...

ONE OF THE urgent commandments of poetry, especially the poetry of history, is to remember. Americans seem to have been initiated (or reinitiated) into history in another way on the now infamous day of September 11, 2001, and, as a result, the poetry of historical consciousness—poetry with a long memory—has taken on special collective meaning for us. Our innocence seems to be something that we keep needing to give up in light of current events. We are not entirely self-determining; we, too, are bound to the rest of the world.

Here is Primo Levi's poem "Shemà," which is included in the poet Joan Murray's useful anthology *Poems to Live By in Uncertain Times.* The poem is based on the principal Jewish prayer, "Hear, [*Shemà*] O Israel: the Lord is our God, the Lord is One!" (Deuteronomy, 6:4–9). Levi returned from Auschwitz to his native Italy after World War II, vowing never to forget the horror he had witnessed. The prayer, which he had learned as a twelve-year-old boy studying for his bar mitzvah, echoed in his memory, like a clarion call. He borrowed its solemn liturgical cadence and style for the poem he wrote on January 10, 1946, which he then used as the epigraph to his first book, *If This Is a Man* (1947). It is addressed to everyone who lives in safety, and it carries a message that has been brought back from the kingdom of death.

SHEMÀ

You live secure
In your warm houses,

Who return at evening to find
Hot food and friendly faces:

> Consider whether this is a man,
> Who labours in the mud
> Who knows no peace
> Who fights for a crust of bread
> Who dies at a yes or a no.
> Consider whether this is a woman,
> Without hair or name
> With no more strength to remember
> Eyes empty and womb cold
> As a frog in winter.

Consider that this has been:
I commend these words to you.
Engrave them on your hearts
When you are in your house, when you walk on your way,
When you go to bed, when you rise.
Repeat them to your children.
Or may your house crumble,
Disease render you powerless,
Your offspring avert their faces from you.

(TRANSLATED BY RUTH FELDMAN AND BRIAN SWANN)

In this poem, Levi was especially drawing on verses six and seven of Deuteronomy:

And these words, which I command thee this day, shall be in thine heart: And thou shalt teach them diligently unto thy children, and thou shalt talk of them when thou sittest in thine house, and when thou walkest by the way, and when thou liest down, and when thou risest up.

"Whether we like it or not," Levi wrote to a friend, "we are witnesses and we carry the weight of that fact." The burden of memory is heavy, but also electrifying. "I had a torrent of urgent things I had to tell the civilized world," he declared. "I felt the tattooed number on my arm burning like a sore."

The prophetic fury behind the particular witnessing, the *remembering,* at the end of Levi's poem is immense. The poet puts a terrible curse upon anyone who forgets these people, this Adam and Eve, who have been so dehumanized that we are asked to consider "if this is a man" and "if this is a woman." It is a lasting obligation to remember their suffering. It is a human injunction, a ritual commandment. We must do everything in our powers, Levi suggests, to keep them from becoming anonymous victims; we must engrave their images on our hearts and pass on their memories to our children.

37

AVRAHAM BEN YITZHAK

As their thoughts circled a man was bitterly seeking.

AVRAHAM BEN YITZHAK (1883–1950) was one of the most enigmatic, reticent, and solitary figures in modern Hebrew poetry. He was an aristocrat of the spirit who cultivated silence and published a total of eleven poems during his lifetime. All of them are astonishing. His output may have been meager—he never published a book and he stopped writing poems by the age of forty-five—but his accomplishment is unquestionable.

Ben Yitzhak appears in Elias Canetti's memoir of the 1930s, *The Play of the Eyes.* Who was this mysterious figure who was born Abraham Sonne in Galicia (Poland), spent much of his life in Vienna, and eventually settled in Jerusalem? Canetti remembered that Sonne, who was also close to the novelist Hermann Broch, "inspired an addiction such as I had never experienced for any other intellectual":

> Sonne knew a great deal by heart . . . [H]e had memorized the whole Bible and could quote any passage in Hebrew without hesitation. But he performed these mnemonic feats with restraint and never made a show of them. . . . His way of reciting and interpreting certain short chapters came as a revelation to me; I realized that he must be a poet, and in the Hebrew language.

Sonne was a curious kind of Hebrew poet, though—a figure who seemed worthy of and in some ways comparable to his primary German models, Hölderlin, Rilke, Trakl, and Hofmannsthal, but with a painfully small oeuvre. "My heart / has been eaten by lightning," he would confess in one fragment. "As their thoughts circled a man was bitterly seeking," he wrote in another. One thinks of him as a refined, charismatic, and reclusive figure ("He had the same method in dealing with persons and things," Canetti recalled, "[and conceived] of individuals as distinct fields of knowledge"), a man of tremendous intellectual curiosity, encyclopedic learning, and lethal silences. I like Lea Goldberg's story of how a friend once joked to him, "Nu? Perhaps we can be silent now about something else?"

It is now possible to read Ben Yitzhak's *Collected Poems*—his eleven canonical lyrics, a rejected twelfth poem, and a striking group of drafts and fragments—in an edition expertly edited by Hannan Hever and brilliantly translated by Peter Cole. There is a rare purity and even nobility in Ben Yitzhak's work, which, as Hever points out, is deeply rooted in Scripture, in what the poet called "the voice of ancient song." Cole captures the biblical rhythms and allusions with terrific dexterity. He finds a voice for Ben Yitzhak's modernist psalms, his twentieth-century lamentations, his prophetic silences.

Here is Ben Yitzhak's last published poem, "Blessed Are They Who Sow and Do Not Reap. . . ." In *The Modern Hebrew Poem Itself,* Dan Pagis argues that it "affirms the poet's conviction and confidence in silence as the only true mode of self-expression."

BLESSED ARE THEY WHO SOW AND DO NOT REAP . . .

Blessed are they who sow and do not reap—
they shall wander in extremity.

Blessed are the generous
whose glory in youth has enhanced the extravagant
brightness of days—
who shed their accoutrements at the crossroads.

Blessed are the proud whose pride overflows
the banks of their souls
to become the modesty of whiteness
in the wake of a rainbow's ascent through a cloud.

Blessed are they who know
their hearts will cry out from the wilderness
          and that quiet will blossom from their lips.

Blessed are these
for they will be gathered to the heart of the world,
          wrapped in the mantle of oblivion
—their destiny's offering unuttered to the end.

38.

KADYA MOLODOWSKY

I am a wandering girl,
My heart is practiced in longing.

THE YIDDISH POET Kadya Molodowsky (1894–1975) published six books of poetry in her lifetime. Molodowsky is best known for her children's poems, but I am especially compelled by the adult work of this rebellious and learned modernist, who viewed herself as an exiled outsider. As she put it in "My Ultimate Biography": "In endless wanderings, across arid ways, / No matter how fast trains approach and retreat, / I'm always outside, walking by watchfully / on permanently battered, bare feet."

Molodowsky was born in Bereza Kartuska, a shtetl in White Russia. She participated fully in Yiddish literary culture, first in Poland, where she taught school and lived until 1935, and then in America, where she settled in New York City and supported herself by writing for the Yiddish press. My grandfather, who loved Yiddish poetry, was a devoted reader of the literary journal *Svive* (Surroundings), which she founded and edited for nearly thirty years. He would be pleased, as I am, by the bilingual edition, *Paper Bridges: Selected Poems of Kadya Molodowsky,* translated and edited by Kathryn Hellerstein (Wayne State University Press, 1999).

Molodowsky entered poetry by listening to the inner voices of women:

> The women of our family will come to me in dreams at night and
>   say:
> Modestly we carried a pure blood across generations,
> Bringing it to you like well-guarded wine from the kosher
> Cellars of our hearts.
>
> —"WOMEN-POEMS"

She showed great sympathy for "all impoverished women who scour burnt pots ("Poor Women") and posed her own modernity against traditional female roles.

Molodowsky published her single most gripping book in New York in 1946. As she explained this collection of *khurbm-lider,* poems lamenting the destruction:

> I saw in succession before my eyes a Jewish world that had been destroyed, Jewish cities, destruction and pain. I gave this book the name *Only King David Remained,* in order to say that the Jewish people was no more, all that remained was King David alone with his sorrow-crown on his head. The book begins with the poem, *"Eyl khanun"* ("Merciful God"):

> Merciful God,
> Choose another people,
> Elect another.
> We are tired of death and dying,
> We have no more prayers.
> Choose another people,
> Elect another.
> We have no more blood
> To be a sacrifice.
> Our house has become a desert.
> The earth is insufficient for our graves,
> No more laments for us,
> No more dirges
> In the old, holy books.

> Merciful God,
> Sanctify another country,
> Another mountain.
> We have strewn all the fields and every stone
> With ash, with holy ash.
> With the aged,
> With the youthful,

And with babies, we have paid
For every letter of your Ten Commandments.

Merciful God,
Raise your fiery brow,
And see the peoples of the world—
Give them the prophecies and the Days of Awe.
Your word is babbled in every language—
Teach them the deeds,
The ways of temptation.

Merciful God,
Give us simple garments
Of shepherds with their sheep,
Blacksmiths at their hammers,
Laundry-washers, skin-flayers,
And even the more base.
And do us one more favor:
Merciful God,
Deprive us of the Divine Presence of genius.

39

YEHUDA AMICHAI

Once you were my guardian,
Now I am your guard.

AFTER MY father died, one of the first poems I wanted to reread was Yehuda Amichai's "Letter of Recommendation." I first read this lyric in the Israeli poet's book *Amen* in 1977, and it has remained with me ever since as a model of sacred passion, of unabashed feeling and precise tenderness.

LETTER OF RECOMMENDATION

On summer nights I sleep naked
in Jerusalem on my bed,
which stands on the brink
of a deep valley
without rolling down into it.

During the day I walk about,
the Ten Commandments on my lips
like an old song someone is humming to himself.

Oh, touch me, touch me, you good woman!
This is not a scar you feel under my shirt.
It's a letter of recommendation, folded,
from my father:
"He is still a good boy and full of love."

I remember my father waking me up
for early prayers. He did it caressing
my forehead, not tearing the blanket away.

Since then I love him even more.
And because of this
let him be woken up
gently and with love
on the Day of Resurrection.

(TRANSLATED BY YEHUDA AMICHAI AND TED HUGHES)

Amichai's poems keep what he calls "the route to childhood open." They speak with warmth, nostalgia, and reverence for his dead father. Playful wit doesn't work against the feeling in this poetry, but in tandem with it. Unlike many contemporary poets here and abroad, Amichai doesn't fear showing too much emotion in his work, and he often lets his love songs ("Oh, touch me, touch me, you good woman!") turn into memorial poems and prayers for the dead. I love the human scale—the vulnerable presence—in Amichai's poetry, and I can't help feeling that the example of a sweet, gentle, and religious Jewish father stands as an implicit challenge to other more traditional hyperaggressive societal models of fatherhood and masculinity.

Do we become like parents to the dead? In "My Father's Memorial Day," Amichai visits not just his father's graveside but all those buried with him in a single row, a group of people yoked together by death, "his life's graduation class." I'm struck by the complete confidence he has in the mutual, ongoing love that persists between his father and him ("My father still loves me, and I / Love him always, so I don't weep") and the way the poem then opens out into a lyric that tries to do justice to the genuine human sadness of the cemetery itself. Amichai's feeling extends to embrace the suffering of others ("I have lit a weeping in my eyes"). He concludes with a kind of ritual mourning—a parental feeling—for someone else's child:

My Father's Memorial Day

On my father's memorial day
I went out to see his mates—
All those buried with him in one row,
His life's graduation class.

I already remember most of their names,
Like a parent collecting his little son
From school, all of his friends.

My father still loves me, and I
Love him always, so I don't weep.
But in order to do justice to this place
I have lit a weeping in my eyes
With the help of a nearby grave—
A child's. "Our little Yossy, who was
Four when he died."

(TRANSLATED BY YEHUDA AMICHAI AND TED HUGHES)

40

AHARON SHABTAI

My lips mutter: Palestine! Do not die on me!

DESPERATE TIMES call for desperate measures. The Hebrew poet Aharon Shabtai, an erudite classicist and literary troublemaker, wrote a shocking book of poems that is powered by political rage against the Israeli government. The very title of the volume, *J'Accuse,* is terrifically charged, since it evokes Zola's famous denunciation of anti-Semitism in the French government during the Dreyfus affair. Shabtai now turns the historical accusation against his own government, which he will not forgive for its crimes against the Palestinian people.

The poems of this book, which are terse, unhappy, and scornful, actually derive from two different collections and cover a six-year period dating from the 1996 election of Benjamin Netanyahu as prime minister. The first third comes from Shabtai's 1999 collection, *Politika,* the rest from his most recent book, *Artzenu (Our Country).* The collection nonetheless reads as a furious whole. It is not for the fainthearted. It is an upsetting and provocative book.

In his excellent introduction, the translator Peter Cole compares Shabtai to the classical figure of Archilochus the Scold. He points out that Shabtai moves "with often disturbing ease between the poles of praise and scorn, lyric flight and biological matter-of-factness." One thing that remains constant is Shabtai's unwavering identification with his dispossessed Arab neighbors. He burns with righteous fury against what he calls "the new Jew," who "rises at night, / puts his uniform on, / kisses his wife and child, / and, in two or three hours, / destroys / a quarter in one of Gaza's ghettos."

The poem "War," which is addressed to Ehud Barak, sets the uncompromising tone:

> I, too, have declared war:
> You'll need to divert part of the force
> deployed to wipe out the Arabs—
> to drive them out of their homes
> and expropriate the land—
> and set it against me.
> You've got tanks and planes,
> and soldiers by the battalion;
> you've got the rams' horns in your hands
> with which to rouse the masses;
> you've got men to interrogate and torture;
> you've got cells for detention.
> I have only this heart
> with which I give shelter
> to an Arab child.
> Aim your weapon at it:
> even if you blow it apart
> it will always,
> always mock you.

The playful, celebratory side of Shabtai's work is expressed in the joyous last poem of the book, "I Love Passover":

> I love Passover,
> since that's when you'll be back.
> Like every year,
> we'll take the car to Kiryat Motzkin
> and, over glasses of wine
> and bowls of *charoset,*
> Zvi will tell us
> of the March of Death.
> Then we'll return to Tel Aviv,

and as you drive in the dark,
the car's windows
will fog up,
and I'll put my hand on your knee.
At home, we'll get into bed
and celebrate our own
private Seder.
I see myself putting
my lips to your belly
and thinking of honey,
while in the street below
our angel passes.

41

TAHA MUHAMMAD ALI

And so
it has taken me
all of sixty years
to understand
that water is the finest drink,
and bread the most delicious food,
and that art is worthless
unless it plants
a measure of splendor in people's hearts.

So writes the Palestinian poet Taha Muhammad Ali in a deeply humane collection entitled *Never Mind*, which includes twenty poems and a short story (Ibis Editions, 2000). Translated by Peter Cole, Yahya Hijazi, and Gabriel Levin, it is Ali's first book of poetry to appear in English, and I am grateful for its large embrace.

Ali speaks with an emotional forthrightness and unflinching honesty that at times reminds me of the Turkish poet Nazim Hikmet, at times of the Israeli poet Yehuda Amichai. He writes in a literary Arabic grounded in the vernacular and rooted in local custom. He is less didactic than many poets on the contemporary Palestinian literary scene, and he has developed a style that seems both ancient and new, deceptively simple and movingly direct.

Ali was born in 1931 in the Galilee village of Saffuriya, and, indeed, there is an element of the village storyteller in his work. Along with most of Saffuriya's residents, he fled to Lebanon during the Arab-Israeli war in 1948, only to return a year later and settle with his family in Nazareth, where he has lived ever since. He is an autodidact who owns a souvenir shop, which is now mostly run by his sons, and he somewhat ironically describes himself as "a camel fleeing the slaughterhouses, /

galloping toward the East, / pursued by processions / of knives and as-
sessors, / women wielding / mortar and pestle for chop meat!"

Here is a poem that I feel ought to be required reading in Washington. It tells about a character named Abd El-Hadi, a sort of holy
fool, an innocent dreamer who wouldn't hurt anyone or anything. He
knows nothing of his so-called enemies, and would even serve them a
meal—labneh is a kind of cheese made with yogurt—if they suddenly appeared.

ABD EL-HADI FIGHTS A SUPERPOWER

In his life
he neither wrote nor read.
In his life he
didn't cut down a single tree,
didn't slit the throat
of a single calf.
In his life he did not speak
of the *New York Times*
behind its back,
didn't raise
his voice to a soul
except in his saying:
"Come in please,
by God, you can't refuse."

. . .

Nevertheless—
his case is hopeless,
his situation
desperate.
His God-given rights are a grain of salt
tossed into the sea.

Ladies and gentlemen of the jury:
about his enemies

my client knows not a thing.
And I can assure you,
were he to encounter
the entire crew
of the aircraft carrier *Enterprise,*
he'd serve them eggs
and labneh
fresh from the bag.

42.

VÉNUS KHOURY-GHATA

You say when you happen to die
the darkness is only frightening at night
when the fearful dead hold their black breath

VÉNUS KHOURY-GHATA is a Lebanese poet and novelist who lives in France and chooses to write in French. It's a complex linguistic and emotional decision, since it means living a double life between her maternal Arabic and her adopted French ("I'm a bigamist," she declares simply). She travels between languages. She characterizes the Francophone writer as "someone who leaves a language he lives in for one which lives in him." Yet one wonders if she has ever entirely left the language of her origins, since she has also said that she writes in Arabic "by means of French."

The French language has given Khoury-Ghata the psychological space and necessary distance to write about her war-torn native realm. She has been nourished by two sources and bridges literary traditions. On one hand, she has been influenced by such classic French figures as Pascal and Racine, who, she says, "taught me to tighten a sentence till it wept," by the "insatiable Rabelais," and the "melancholy Baudelaire." On the other hand, she is also known for bringing the rhythms of spoken Arabic and the sounds of Arabic poetry into French verse. She carries the rich language of her childhood to the more austere language of her education. "I stuff the French language with loukoum," she annouces gleefully, "I teach it to belly dance."

The American poet Marilyn Hacker has faithfully translated two books of Khoury-Ghata's into English: *Here There Was Once a Country* (2001) and *She Says* (2003), which consists of two extended sequences, "Words" and "She Says." There is an element of fable, a quasi-surreal, mythic quality to everything Khoury-Ghata writes. Death hovers everywhere in the background. Her poetry is marked by the specter of two hundred thousand people who died in Lebanon during the civil war that scarred her youth. "I felt guilty about transforming the dead into words, lining them up like lead soldiers on my pages," she has said, "but I was incapable of turning to another subject."

I'm especially moved by the section "Early Childhood" in *Here There Was Once a Country*. "The country was so narrow at that time / the dead and the living slept five in a bed with their troubles," Khoury-Ghata writes. "It was God's business to blush at such a situation." A poet was being formed. "One must lift the dawn up to see the poet seated atop the landscape."

> Here there was once a country
> fire withdrew from women's fingers
> bread deserted the ploughed furrows
> and the cold devoured all children who wore daffodils on their
>   shoulders
>
> Here there was once a wall
> which reproduced itself in prosperous times
> became rectangle square but never circle
> so as not to humiliate the fountains
> which held the rights to day's roundness
>
> Here there was once a hunter
> who knocked down his house to go into the forest
> and verify that his shots pierced the eardrums of the rocks
>
> Here there was once a pebble
> which turned into a gravestone at the mere sight of a passer-by
>
> Here there was once an infinitely white night
> an infinitely black tree

which pulled its bark up to its chin
when noon lengthened shadows down to the ravine

Here there was once an echo of another echo
and the horns of great cattle which melted when even a wing
      passed overhead

43.

PROTEST POETRY

That was not a country.
But it could erase the scrolls of our destiny.
—SAADI YOUSSEF

PROTEST POETRY is the most earnest of genres. It doesn't have much of a sense of humor—it doesn't have time for one. It is timely, oppositional, urgent. It is born from outrage and linked to social action. But Thomas Lux's poem "The People of the Other Village," which was written in opposition to the Gulf War, breaks the mold with its cutting wit and black humor. Lux strategically turns the protest poem into a dark parable of tribalism. Each of the examples of escalating violence and revenge has a kind of comic awfulness. I find myself especially haunted by the primal truth of the refrain: "We do this, they do that." The poem first appeared in Lux's book *Split Horizon* (1994).

THE PEOPLE OF THE OTHER VILLAGE

hate the people of this village
and would nail our hats
to our heads for refusing in their presence to remove them
or staple our hands to our foreheads
for refusing to salute them
if we did not hurt them first: mail them packages of rats,
mix their flour at night with broken glass.
We do this, they do that.
They peel the larynx from one of our brothers' throats.
We devein one of their sisters.
The quicksand pits they built were good.
Our amputation teams were better.

We trained some birds to steal their wheat.
They sent to us exploding ambassadors of peace.
They do this, we do that.
We canceled our sheep imports.
They no longer bought our blankets.
We mocked their greatest poet
and when that had no effect
we parodied the way they dance
which did cause pain, so they, in turn, said our God
was leprous, hairless.
We do this, they do that.
Ten thousand (10,000) years, ten thousand
(10,000) brutal, beautiful years.

I've been reading with enormous interest the selected poems of Saadi Youssef, *Without an Alphabet, Without a Face,* which has been excellently translated from the Arabic by the poet Khaled Mattawa. Youssef was born in Iraq in 1934, but since 1979 has lived in exile in a vast range of countries (Algeria, Lebanon, France, Greece, Cyprus, Yugoslavia, and England), all of which come into his work. He has lived what he calls "a life of forced departures," which has deepened rather than stunted his humanity.

Mattawa points out in a helpful introduction that Youssef "prefers whispering to declaiming." Whispering does seem to capture both the intimacy and the urgency of this poet's usual voice. One of the louder poems in Youssef's work is his long poem "America, America," which was written in 1995 in direct response to the hardship and suffering faced by the Iraqis under sanctions instigated by the United States. Here is its strongest (and most Whitmanesque) section:

I too love jeans and jazz and *Treasure Island*
and John Silver's parrot and the balconies of New Orleans.
I love Mark Twain and the Mississippi steamboats and Abraham
   Lincoln's dogs.
I love the fields of wheat and corn and the smell of Virginia
   tobacco.

But I am not American.

Is that enough for the Phantom pilot to turn me back to the Stone
  Age?

I need neither oil nor America herself, neither the elephant nor the
  donkey.

Leave me, pilot, leave my house roofed with palm fronds and this
  wooden bridge.

I need neither your Golden Gate nor your skyscrapers.

I need the village, not New York.

Why did you come to me from your Nevada desert, soldier armed
  to the teeth?

Why did you come all the way to distant Basra, where fish used to
  swim by our doorsteps?

Pigs do not forage here.

I have only these water buffaloes lazily chewing on water lilies.

Leave me alone, soldier.

Leave me my floating cane hut and my fishing spear.

Leave me my migrating birds and the green plumes.

Take your roaring iron birds and your Tomahawk missiles. I am
  not your foe.

I am the one who wades up to the knees in rice paddies.

Leave me to my curse.

I do not need your day of doom.

44.

ISHIKAWA TAKUBOKU

When I breathe,
This sound in my chest
Lonelier than the winter wind

THUS DECLARES Ishikawa Takuboku (1886–1912) in the opening poem of *Sad Toys* (translated by Sanford Goldstein and Seishi Shinoda), a collection of 194 tanka that he wrote in the last eighteen months of his life. I have an abiding affection for this tanka reformer whose life was devastated by poverty and illness—he died of tuberculosis at the age of twenty-six—but who never lost his sense of the deeply humane purposes of poetry. "First of all, a poet must be a human being," he said. "Second, he must be a human being. Third, he must be a human being."

> At my words "Christ was a man,"
> The sorrow I felt
> Seeing my sister's eyes pitying *me*. (#192)

The classic Japanese tanka is a thirty-one-syllable poem in five units. In Japanese, tanka is traditionally printed in one or two lines, but in English we usually divide it into a quintet (5-7-5-7-7). Identified for centuries with the court, it served as the foundation of virtually all Japanese poetry written between 850 and 1900. Takuboku retained the thirty-one-syllable count, but turned the tanka into an irregular three-line form that suited his mercurial temperament and modern sensibility. This was perhaps the most radical change in the form in its long history, and it paved the way for free verse to enter Japanese poetry.

> An old newspaper!
> Why, they're praising my poems—
> Though only in two lines or three . . . (#73)

Takuboku blended a formal with a colloquial diction. He called his tanka "sad toys," which suggests that his own poetry is a melancholy form of play. For example, "Setting the doll I bought for my child / By her bed where she naps, / I enjoy myself alone." (#191)

Perhaps Takuboku's greatest innovation was to open up the codified subject matter of the tanka to a wide range of daily experiences, high and low moments. He turned the tanka sequence into an emotional diary, an accurate reflection of his inner life. He connected his work to naturalistic trends in the Japanese novel and deemed the new poetry "poems to eat." "Poetry must not be what is called poetry," he declared. "It must be an exact report, an honest diary, of the changes in a man's emotional life."

> Suddenly forgetting my illness one day,
> I bellowed forth that imitation of a cow!—
> My wife and child out . . . (#181)

Some of Takuboku's most natural and touching poems are the tanka he wrote for his daughter Kyōko. After convalescing from a serious illness, for example, he laments lost time: "Four months of illness— / O this sadness in seeing my child / So much taller even in that time" (#153). He ponders his own complex feeling on seeing his daughter growing up: "Why this sadness each day / In seeing the healthy growth / Of my child?" (#154).

A few of the most freighted poems seem addressed to his daughter but spoken to himself, as in a diary, and overheard by the reader. I am delighted by #160—

> Once in a while
> Praising my kid
> Singing at the top of her voice!

—and haunted by #157: "May you never resemble your father, / Nor your father's father! / Thus thinks your father, my child."

One of my favorite poems (#161) memorializes a tender, unspoken, and unexpected moment of connection between father and daughter:

> What prompted her—
> Flinging aside that toy—
> To gently come and sit by me?

45

LAM THI MY DA, XUAN QUYNH

The poetry of earth is never dead...
—JOHN KEATS

HERE IS an understated and beautiful little four-line poem by the contemporary Vietnamese poet Lam Thi My Da, which suggests that war may test the truth of Keats's claim but does not refute it. Like a tiny metaphysical poem by Marvell or Donne, the quatrain creates an argument that hinges on the word *but* at the start of the second line:

GARDEN FRAGRANCE

Last night a bomb exploded on the veranda
But sounds of birds sweeten the earth this morning.
I hear the fragrant trees, look in the garden,
Find two silent clusters of ripe guavas.

Summer reaches its culmination in the richness of August, a moment in the turning year that looks forward with great anticipation to the coming harvest. I am moved by Lam Thi My Da's 1971 poem "Night Harvest," a sonnet in which she mingles the harvesting of rice with the experience of falling bombs. This is a dark communal harvest, since the men are away at war, and the remaining harvesters in the village are all women. Yet their twelve white hats brighten the night, and the tone of the poem is playful, stoic, and completely unafraid.

NIGHT HARVEST

The white circles of conical hats have come out
Like the quiet skies of our childhood,
Like an egret's spreading wings in the night:
White circles evoking the open sky.

The golds of rice and cluster-bombs blend together.
Even delayed-fuse bombs bring no fear:
Our spirits have known many years of war.
Come, sisters, let us gather the harvest.

Each of us wears her own small moon
Glittering on a carpet of gold rice.
We are the harvesters of my village,
Twelve white hats bright in the long night.

We are not frightened by bullets and bombs in the air—
Only by dew wetting our lime-scented hair.

An especially fine poem is a radiant piece by the Vietnamese poet Xuan Quynh (1942–1988), whose work is represented in the ground-breaking anthology *6 Vietnamese Poets,* edited by Nguyen Ba Chung and Kevin Bowen. The editors call Xuan Quynh "the quintessential woman poet of the rear in the North," and yet her work also breaks free of its original circumstances:

SUMMER

It's the season of birdsong.
The sky is deep blue, sunlight is everywhere.
The soil climbs the tree; the sap tends the fruits.
Man's footsteps break new paths.

It's the season in which nothing can hide.
The whole world is dressed in light.
The sea aqua, the white sails full.
And bitterness turns into poetry.

It's the season of hopes and dreams,
Of man's ancient and innumerable cravings.
Winds turn to storms, rains into rivers and seas.
A simple glance might light the spark of love.

It's the season of twilights.
The paper kite parts the high open sky,
The crickets stay awake in the warm night singing,
The moor hen breaks the noon's silence.

O summer, have you gone?
O desires of youth, are you here or not?
The earth still holds the deep blue of the sea,
And the sweet fruit, the faint color of blossoms.

46

MIGUEL HERNÁNDEZ

I call myself clay though Miguel is my name.

MIGUEL HERNÁNDEZ (1910–1942) was one of the most openhearted and heartbreaking Spanish-language poets of the twentieth century. Although less well-known in the United States, he is a figure comparable to, say, Federico García Lorca, César Vallejo, and Pablo Neruda. "I have plenty of heart," Hernández claimed in one poem, "I who have a bigger heart than anyone, / and having that, I am the bitterest also." It was true: he was one of the great martyred poets of the Spanish Civil War.

Ted Genoways's triumphant bilingual edition *The Selected Poems of Miguel Hernández* gives us a rich opportunity to experience Hernández's emotionally charged poetry, which is so filled with human difficulties, so full of the earth and the spirit of freedom. The book divides into three parts: The Early Poems (1923–1936), the War Poems (1936–1939), and the Prison Poems (1939–1942).

Hernández was a shepherd boy from the village of Orihuela in eastern Spain who, under the guidance of a local priest, educated himself in the poetry of the Spanish Golden Age. I am amazed by the sonnets in his second book, *The Unending Lightning* (1936), the culmination of his early manner, where the poet's volcanic feelings collide with the classical restraints of the traditional form, as in "My heart can't go on any longer":

> My heart can't go on any longer
> putting up with its love-mad and murky storm,

and it raises to my tongue the blood-filled
noisy thing that weighs it down.

Now my tongue, slow and long, is a heart,
and my heart is a tongue, long and slow. . . .
You want to count up the pain? Go out and count
the sweet grains of the bitter sand.

My heart can't stand this sadness anymore:
it flies in my blood, along with the floating
ghost of a drowned man, and goes down all alone.

And yesterday, you wrote from your heart
that you have a touch of homesickness—
half for my body, half for the grave.

(TRANSLATED BY TIMOTHY BALAND)

Hernández's embrace of impure poetry, to use Neruda's term, of
larger free-verse rhythms and more surrealistic imagery, coincided with
his deepening concern for current events and a growing commitment
to the anti-Fascist cause. He became a soldier-poet, at times didactic,
as in *Wind of the People* (1937), but also struggling to hold on to his
humanity, as in *Man Is a Hunter* (1939). "Help me to be a man," he
pleaded in his poem "Hunger": "don't let me be a beast, / starving, enraged, forever cornered. / A common animal, with working blood, /
I give you the humanity that this song foretells."

It seems impossible to come away unmoved by the work Hernández wrote when he was dying of tuberculosis in a Spanish prison.
There is so much suffering nobility in poems such as "War" ("All the
mothers in the world / hide their wombs"), "Waltz Poem of Those in
Love and Inseparable Forever," "Imagination's Tomb," and "Lullabies
of the Onion," the masterpiece that he wrote to his infant son ("I
woke from childhood," he advised, "don't you ever"). This work culminated in *Songbook and Balladbook of Absences* (1941). I leave you with

the last lines that Hernández wrote on the wall above his cot in the Alicante prison infirmary. They are an affectionate farewell greeting, a brotherly good-bye to the earth itself, the sign that, as Vicente Aleixandre put it, "the light never went out in him, not even in the last moment, the light that, more than anything else, made him die tragically with his eyes open."

> Adíos, brothers, comrades, friends,
> let me take leave of the sun and of the fields.

47

CÉSAR VALLEJO

I was born on a day
that God was sick.

CÉSAR VALLEJO'S POEMS have an anguished power, a rebellious lexical energy, and a wild, freewheeling emotionalism. Sympathy for the suffering of others is a current that runs through all of his work. At times, one feels as if he has descended into the welter of the unconscious and returned bearing messages from this other world. Yet his own voice comes through as that of the most vulnerable, agonized, and compassionate of speakers—a witness urgently testifying to the experience of human pain.

Vallejo was born on March 16, 1892, in a small Andean mining town in northern Peru. He had Indian and Spanish blood on both sides. His poetry shows tremendous feeling for his mother, the emotional center of his religious childhood; for his father, a notary who wanted him to become a priest; and for his ten older brothers and sisters. He graduated from the University of Trujillo in 1915, with a thesis on romanticism in Spanish poetry.

Vallejo supported himself by teaching in primary schools. He read widely, worked furiously at his poems, and belonged to the vanguard Colonida group. He also suffered several traumatic love affairs, after one of which he attempted suicide. In 1919, the year after his mother's death, he published his first collection of poems, *Los heraldos negros*, which Rebecca Seiferle has now scrupulously translated as *The Black Heralds*.

THE BLACK HERALDS

There are blows in life, so powerful . . . I don't know!
Blows like God's hatred; as if before them,

the undertow of everything suffered
were to well up in the soul . . . I don't know!

They're few; but they exist . . . They open dark furrows
in the most ferocious face and the most powerful loins.
Perhaps they're wooden horses of barbaric Attilas,
or black messengers that Death sends to us.

They're profound lapses of the soul's Christs,
of some adorable faith that Destiny blasphemes.
Those bloodthirsty blows are cracklings of some
bread that in the oven's door burns up on us.

And man . . . Poor . . . poor man! He turns his eyes, as
when a slap on the shoulder calls us by name;
he turns his crazed eyes, and everything he's lived
wells up, like a pool of guilt, in his gaze.

There are blows in life, so powerful . . . I don't know!

The black riders come with messages of destruction that leave the
speaker reeling and desolate. In these poems of alienated romanticism,
Vallejo grapples with the anachronism of his past as well as the tragic
incompatibilities of his divided heritage. Faced with these contradictions, he speaks of his own harsh solitude and inexplicable longings.
Seiferle is wonderfully alert to the indigenous elements in Vallejo's
work, though I don't agree with her polemical assertion that Vallejo
has been "colonized" by such previous translators as James Wright,
Robert Bly, Thomas Merton, and Clayton Eshleman, who have served
the poet well. One of Vallejo's recurring subjects is the void left in the
soul when the Logos has become uncertain and Christianity has lost
its stable meaning. Suddenly bereft of a common spiritual vocabulary,
the poet seeks to create an authentic language of his own in a fallen
world.

In 1920, Vallejo returned home for a visit and got inadvertently
mixed up in a political feud. Though innocent, he went into hiding

for three months and then was incarcerated for 105 days, one of the gravest experiences of his life. During this period, he wrote many of the poems for his second book, *Trilce* (1922), which both Seiferle and Eshleman have translated with great daring. Its seventy-seven poems, which bear numbers for titles, are hermetic; the syntax disregards grammatical rules and logical narrative. Language is put under intense pressure; surreal images float loose from their context and poetic forms are radically broken down and reconstituted. Neologisms abound. There is a cabalistic obsession with numbers in a world where reality is fragmented and death omnipresent. Vallejo's dire poverty, his bitter sense of orphanhood ("Give way to the new odd number / potent with orphanhood") and brooding exile from childhood, his rage over social inequities—all make their way into an astonishing work that fell, as the author declared, into a total void. He published no more collections of poetry in his lifetime.

In 1923, Vallejo left Peru for good and settled in Paris, where he met his future wife, Georgette Phillipart, a woman of strong socialist convictions, and eked out the barest subsistence. Several times he nearly starved to death. In the late 1920s, he underwent a crisis of conscience and became consumed by the quest for a better social order. In 1931, he published two books: *Tungsten,* a social realist novel, and *Russia in 1931,* a travel book. His political activism peaked with his involvement in the doomed Republican cause in the Spanish Civil War. He wrote descriptive accounts of the conflict as well as a play, *The Tired Stone,* and the fifteen magnificent poems that became *Spain, Take This Cup from Me.* One of my favorites is the poem "Masa" ("Mass"), dated November 10, 1937:

> When the battle was over,
> and the fighter was dead, a man came toward him
> and said to him: "Do not die; I love you so!"
> But the corpse, it was sad! went on dying.
>
> And two came near, and told him again and again:
> "Do not leave us! Courage! Return to life!"
> But the corpse, it was sad! went on dying.

Twenty arrived, a hundred, a thousand, five hundred thousand,
shouting: "So much love, and it can do nothing against death!"
But the corpse, it was sad! went on dying.

Millions of persons stood around him,
all speaking the same thing: "Stay here, brother!"
But the corpse, it was sad! went on dying.

Then, all the men on the earth
stood around him; the corpse looked at them sadly, deeply moved;
he sat up slowly,
put his arm around the first man; started to walk . . .

(TRANSLATED BY ROBERT BLY)

Vallejo died on April 15, 1938. In the last fifteen years of his life, he wrote 110 poems that are his crowning achievement. The year after his death his widow published *Poemas humanos* (*Human Poems*), which brought together his undated lyric and prose poems written between 1923 and 1936, as well as dated poems from 1936 to 1938. Recent scholarship suggests that Vallejo intended three separate collections: *Payroll of Bones, Sermon on Barbarism,* and the Spanish Civil War Verses. Human feeling is the convulsive subject of these apocalyptic books. The poems speak to the difficulty of maintaining a human face in an alienated industrial world where people wander among objects like strangers and language no longer represents reality. All are shot through with sadness as, disaffected and dislocated, Vallejo struggles to speak as clearly as possible. The poems are haunted by premonitions of the poet's death ("I will die in Paris, on a rainy day, / on some day I can already remember"), by his sense of the torment of others ("I know there is someone / looking for me day and night inside her hand, / and coming upon me, each moment in her shoes"), by his grief over the impending fate of Spain and the destiny of Europe. Finally, Vallejo emerges as a prophet pleading for social justice, as a grief-stricken Whitmanian singer moving through a brutal universe:

And don't bother telling me anything,
that a man can kill perfectly,
because a man,
sweating ink, does what he can, don't bother telling me . . .

(TRANSLATED BY ROBERT BLY)

48.

SUFFERING

*This afternoon it rains as never before; and I
don't feel like staying alive, heart.*
—César Vallejo

THERE ARE POEMS that tremble with human presence, that put the suffering of a single human being squarely in front of us. Such poems have a dynamic simplicity that rivets our attention. They have the power to disturb and even shame us.

Here is a poem by the contemporary Haitian Creole poet Woudòf Milè (Rudolph Muller) that presents a teenage girl loitering helplessly on an urban street corner at night:

A 16-YEAR-OLD GIRL WHO'S STANDING

A 16-year-old girl
who's standing
on the corner of Grand and Miracle Streets
at 11 in the evening
in a tired little dress

A 16-year-old girl
who's standing like an i
under an arcade
She's not waiting for a bus
she's not waiting for anyone
it's just that at her house
her hungry mother
is about to die

she'd rather be standing there
at 11 in the evening
in the cold under the Grand Street
arcade.

The suffering of people at the margins of urban society can drive
some people mad. That's the situation the Peruvian poet César Vallejo
found himself confronting in Paris between 1923 and 1938, when his
devotion to modernism, as well as his deep interest in philosophy, suddenly seemed beside the point in light of so much naked poverty and
suffering. Compassion for others is one of the key hallmarks of Vallejo's
radical lyrics. I've been haunted for years by what I would call his desolate afternoon poems, which are especially striking because they are
filled with the agon of helplessness before the suffering of others. I think
of "Agape," which is haunted by the notion of Christian or sacrificial
love ("Today nobody has come; / and today I have died so little in the
afternoon"), and of this untitled poem, which no one ever forgets:

A man walks by with a baguette on his shoulder
Am I going to write, after that, about my double?

Another sits, scratches, extracts a louse from his armpit, kills it
How dare one speak about psychoanalysis?

Another has entered my chest with a stick in hand
To talk then about Socrates with the doctor?

A cripple passes by holding a child's hand
After that I'm going to read André Breton?

Another trembles from cold, coughs, spits blood
Will it ever be possible to allude to the deep Self?

Another searches in the muck for bones, rinds
How to write, after that, about the infinite?

A bricklayer falls from a roof, dies and no longer eats lunch
To innovate, then, the trope, the metaphor?

A merchant cheats a customer out of a gram
To speak, after that, about the fourth dimension?

A banker falsifies his balance sheet
With what face to cry in the theater?

An outcast sleeps with his foot on his back
To speak, after that, to anyone about Picasso?

Someone goes to a burial sobbing
How then become a member of the Academy?

Someone cleans a rifle in his kitchen
How dare one speak about the beyond?

Someone passes by counting with his fingers
How speak of the non-self without screaming?

(TRANSLATED BY CLAYTON ESHLEMAN)

49

SELF-NAMING

When I was born, one of the crooked
angels who live in shadow, said:
Carlos, go on! Be gauche *in life.*
—CARLOS DRUMMOND DE ANDRADE, "SEVEN-SIDED POEM"

IT'S USUALLY funny and more than a little ironic when a poet narcissistically uses his or her own name in the title or body of a poem, drawing attention to the conventional divide between author and subject, writer and speaker. To do so is always to split oneself off, to say with Rimbaud, *"Je est un autre"* ("I is another").

There's often a dark undertow, a self-lacerating quality, to the self-styled humor, as when the Brazilian poet Carlos Drummond de Andrade lectures himself to hold on and calm down at the beginning of his poem "Don't Kill Yourself":

Carlos, keep calm, love
is what you're seeing now:
today a kiss, tomorrow no kiss,
day after tomorrow's Sunday
and nobody knows what will happen
Monday.

It's useless to resist
or to commit suicide.
Don't kill yourself. Don't kill yourself!
Keep all of yourself for the nuptials
coming nobody knows when,
that is, if they ever come.

De Andrade's whole poem, acutely translated by Elizabeth Bishop, is a lesson in talking himself down from a love affair that is causing "an ineffable racket" inside him. It's a staying action against despair as he counsels himself to be stoic: "Love in the dark, no, love / in the daylight, is always sad, / sad, Carlos, my boy, / but tell it to nobody, / nobody knows nor shall know."

The French surrealist Robert Desnos playfully uses his own name in "The Voice of Robert Desnos," and the Italian Giuseppe Ungaretti talks to himself in the midst of a thick fog in his key World War I lyric "Pilgrimage":

> Ungaretti
> man of pain
> all you need is an illusion
> to give you courage.

I adore the Hungarian Attila József's wry love poem to himself, which is entitled "Atilla József" and begins "I really love you, / believe me. It is something I inherited / from my mother. / She was a good woman. After all, / she was the one who brought me / into this world."

The American poet Paul Zimmer has made a lifework out of the tactic in *The Zimmer Poems,* and Charles Simic, an American writer with an Eastern European sensibility, uses it to terrific textual effect in his early poem "Charles Simic" ("Charles Simic is a sentence"). But the most serious and shocking instance of a poet referring to himself in the third person comes at the turning point in the Peruvian poet César Vallejo's magnificent sonnet "Black Stone Lying on a White Stone." There's a complex, startling use of tenses in this devastating and unprecedented self-elegy in which he predicts (and undergoes) his own death:

> I will die in Paris on a rainy day,
> on some day I can already remember.
> I will die in Paris—and I don't step aside—
> perhaps on a Thursday, as today is Thursday, in autumn.

It will be a Thursday, because today, Thursday, setting down
these lines, I have put my upper arm bones on
wrong, and never so much as today have I found myself
with all the road ahead of me, alone.

César Vallejo is dead. Everyone beat him,
although he never does anything to them;
they beat him hard with a stick and hard also

with a rope. These are the witnesses:
the Thursdays, and the bones of my arms,
the solitude, and the rain, and the roads . . .

(TRANSLATED BY ROBERT BLY)

50

PABLO NERUDA

Let us uncork all our bottled up happiness.

PABLO NERUDA was a magnificent poet of Chile, of Latin America, and finally of the Americas, who well may be, in the words of Gabriel García Márquez, "the greatest poet of the twentieth century—in any language." Beloved by Chileans of all ages and classes, he is known throughout the world—an iconic figure comparable to, say, Pablo Picasso or Charlie Chaplin. He is one of the most widely read and cherished poets in history. On the anniversary of Neruda's birth, no celebration would be more fitting than to go down to the shore and read aloud his poems. He loved the playful anarchy of the sea— creative, destructive, ceaselessly moving. He loved the marriage of wind, water, and sand, and found inspiration in the crashing fury and freedom of the waves, the seabirds on the coast, the endlessness of blue sky. "I need the sea because it teaches me," he wrote: "I move in / the university of the waves." He loved how the sea forever renewed itself, a renewal echoed in his work as well as in his life. He felt that creating poetry was like constantly being born. So let us head for the sea to recite his poems and come back refreshed, deepened and enlarged.

Neruda was born Neftalí Ricardo Reyes y Basoalto in 1904 in Parral, in central Chile. His father was a railroad worker, his mother a primary school teacher. The first heartbreak of his life was that he never knew his mother, who died less than two months after he was born. As he wrote in "The Birth":

> And that's where I'm from, that
> Parral of the trembling earth,

a land laden with grapes
which came to life
out of my dead mother.

(TRANSLATED BY ALASTAIR REID)

All his life, Neruda linked womanhood to the regeneration of earth and the cyclical processes of nature. It was one of his most emotionally motivated, earnestly held associations.

The family moved to the frontier town of Temuco in southern Chile, where Neruda was raised in a land of powerful solitude, luxuriant nature, and endless rain. "My father is buried in one of the rainiest cemeteries in the world," he wrote sadly. He adored his stepmother, whom he called *la mamadre* ("the more-mother"), and when he was fourteen wrote his first lyric for her. "And it was at that age," he wrote later, "poetry arrived / in search of me." As a teenager, he took the pseudonym "Pablo Neruda" to conceal the publication of his first poems from his disapproving father, and he later adopted the name legally. But he quickly found approval elsewhere. He brought his work to the new principal of the local girls' school, the famed poet Gabriela Mistral, who told him: "I was sick, but I began to read your poems and I've gotten better, because I am sure that here there is indeed a true poet."

Neruda's professional life began early. He moved to the capital city of Santiago and published his first collection, *Book of Twilight*, in 1923. He followed it a year later with the astounding *Twenty Love Poems and a Song of Despair*, which instantly catapulted him to fame and is still loved throughout Latin America. It is the first poetry in Spanish that unabashedly celebrates erotic love in sensuous, earthly terms. "Love poems were breaking out all over my body," he later recalled.

I read these poems in W. S. Merwin's stimulating translation when I was nineteen and immediately recognized the adolescent lover, at once a child and an adult, being schooled in the art of longing and obsession. "Tonight I can write the saddest lines," Neruda declared in the twentieth love poem. "I no longer love her, that's certain, but maybe I love her. / Love is so short, forgetting is so long." I still think of the first poem in this collection as an initiation, an introductory text to the poetry of desire:

BODY OF A WOMAN

Body of a woman, white hills, white thighs,
you look like a world, lying in surrender.
My rough peasant's body digs in you
and makes the son leap from the depth of the earth.

I was alone like a tunnel. The birds fled from me,
and night swamped me with its crushing invasion.
To survive myself I forged you like a weapon,
like an arrow in my bow, a stone in my sling.

But the hour of vengeance falls, and I love you.
Body of skin, of moss, of eager and firm milk.
Oh the goblets of the breast! Oh the eyes of absence!
Oh the roses of the pubis! Oh your voice, slow and sad!

Body of my woman, I will persist in your grace.
My thirst, my boundless desire, my shifting road!
Dark river-beds where the eternal thirst flows
and weariness follows, and the infinite ache.

(TRANSLATED BY W. S. MERWIN)

Neruda benefited from a tradition among Latin American governments of subsidizing authors through appointments to the foreign service. He served in cities around the world, an experience that profoundly shaped his vision; but he always returned to Chile with a renewed sense of wonder and called himself "a Chilean ever and always."

Neruda's first post, which he chose at random, was in Rangoon, Burma, where he was cut off from his language, his culture, and his history. Profoundly estranged from everything around him ("Really, don't you find yourself surrounded by destructions, deaths, ruined things . . . blocked by difficulties and impossibilities?" he wrote to a friend), he began to write the harsh, ferociously surreal poems that would bloom into the three disconsolate volumes of *Residence on Earth* (1925–45). These poems reflect ancient terrors and modern anxieties, a near-religious desolation; he once called them "a mass of almost ritualistic verses . . . with mystery and suffering, like those created by the poets of old." "It so happens I am sick of being a man," he confesses in "Walking Around":

> I don't want to go on being a root in the dark,
> insecure, stretched out, shivering with sleep,
> going on down, into the moist guts of the earth,
> taking in and thinking, eating every day.
>
> I don't want so much misery.
> I don't want to go on as a root and a tomb,
> alone under the ground, a warehouse with corpses,
> half frozen, dying of grief.

> (TRANSLATED BY ROBERT BLY)

"Life led me through the world's farthest regions," Neruda once said, "before I reached what should have been my point of departure: Spain." He married twice during the years he served in various consular positions in Ceylon, Java, and Singapore; in Buenos Aires, where he became friends with Federico García Lorca; then in Barcelona and Madrid, where he also became friends with Rafael Alberti and Miguel Hernández.

This remarkable poetic fraternity was blown apart by the outbreak of the Spanish Civil War in 1936, and Neruda spent the next few years shuttling between Madrid, Paris, and Santiago. He was a passionate supporter of the Republican cause and wrote fiery poems denouncing the Fascists and, eventually, raging against their victory. "So you ask why his poems / don't tell us of dreams, and leaves, / and great volcanoes in his native land?" he asked in "I Explain Some Things": "Come see the blood in the streets, / come see / the blood in the streets, / come see the blood / in the streets!"

Neruda had slowly developed a vision of unalienated man, of justice and equality. "The world has changed and my poetry has changed," he said in 1939. On the night of his father's death in 1938 he began *Canto general* (General Song), which, by the time it was published in 1950, had grown into 340 poems arranged in fifteen sections. The heart of the epic is "The Heights of Macchu Picchu," his meditation on the Inca fortress hidden for centuries in the Andes Mountains. He said it marked "a new stage in my style and a new direction in my concerns." As he stood on the hallowed ground, Neruda vowed to make the stones speak on behalf of those who had built and labored on the ancient fort. "Rise to be born with me, brother," he called out:

> I come to speak through your dead mouth.
> All through the earth join all
> the silent wasted lips
> and speak from the depths to me all this long night
> as if I were anchored here with you,
> tell me everything, chain by chain,
> link by link, and step by step,
> file the knives you kept by you,
> drive them into my chest and my hand
> like a river of riving yellow light,
> like a river where buried jaguars lie,
> and let me weep, hours, days, years,
> blind ages, stellar centuries.
>
> Give me silence, water, hope.
>
> Give me struggle, iron, volcanoes.

Fasten your bodies to me like magnets.

Hasten to my veins to my mouth.

Speak through my words and my blood.

(TRANSLATED BY JOHN FELSTINER)

What had begun as a poem about Chile turned into a poem that delineated the full geological, biological, and political history of South America. It became a comprehensive song, a general chant, a Whitmanian epic of the New World, a mythification of America.

By this time, Neruda had become an ardent communist. Over the years he wrote a lot of sincerely felt, but otherwise weak, didactic poems denouncing Western imperialism. His strident praise for the Communist Party seems at best naïve, and his admiration for Stalin, whom he never disavowed, can be hard to stomach. Such figures as Octavio Paz and Czeslaw Milosz broke with him over communism. In his *Memoirs,* completed just a few days before his death, Neruda called himself "an anarchoid," and that seems closer to the truth. "I do whatever I like," he said.

Nonetheless, Neruda's social and political commitments were crucial to his life and work. He was elected senator for the Communist Party in Chile in 1945. He campaigned for Gabriel González Videla, who became president the next year, and whose government then outlawed the party. Neruda denounced him, and in 1948 he was accused of disloyalty and declared a dangerous agitator. After a warrant for his arrest was issued, Neruda went into hiding in Chile, then fled to Argentina and traveled to Italy, France, the Soviet Union, and Asia. (His brief stay on the island of Capri during his exile was fictionalized in the touching film *Il Postino.*) Throughout this period he was writing love poems for Matilde Urrutia—"Ah great love, small beloved!"—who became his third wife. These blossomed into *The Captain's Verses* (1952), which was published anonymously, and *100 Love Sonnets* (1959).

Neruda returned to Chile in the mid-1950s, and his productivity continued unabated until the end of his life. When he was invited by the editor of a Caracas newspaper to contribute weekly pieces, he accepted on the condition that the work appear in the news section and not in the literary supplement. The paper agreed. "This is how I published a long history of time, things, artisans, people, fruit, flowers, and life," Neruda recalled in his *Memoirs.* The three books that then came out in rapid succession—*Elemental Odes, New Elemental Odes,* and *Third Book of Odes* (1952–57)—were truly meant to be elemental, even elementary, to carry news of things from their birth onward, to accord material objects a life of their own, to estrange the familiar.

The list of their subjects is dizzying. Nothing ordinary was alien to Neruda, or, for that matter, ordinary—everything was magical. He wrote separate odes to tomatoes and wine, to an artichoke and a dead carob tree, to conger chowder, to a large tuna in the market, to his socks and his suit, to his native birds, to light on the sea, to the dictionary, to a village movie theater. He wrote an ode to time and another to the earth, an "Ode for Everything." "Nothing was to be omitted from my field of action," Neruda commented. The first poem, "The Invisible Man," is explicit in its sense of the poet's urgency: "what can I do, / everything asks me / to speak, / everything asks me / to sing, sing forever." These three rapturous collections present an affirmative alternative to the three despairing books of *Residence on Earth,* which Neruda came to feel were too negative. The odes are funny, fiery, and exultant, savagely new and profoundly ancient.

Neruda became a faculty member at the University of Chile in 1962, worked intensively on the 1964 and 1970 presidential campaigns for the socialist Salvador Allende, and served as the Chilean ambassador to France. He received the Nobel Prize for Literature in 1971. "There is no unassailable solitude," he said in his acceptance speech. "All roads lead to the same point: to the communication of who we are." He concluded:

> I come from a dark province, from a country separated from others by a severe geography. I was the most abandoned of poets, and my poetry was regional, sorrowful, steeped in rain. But I always had confidence in man. I never lost hope. That may be why I am here with my poetry, and with my flag.

Ill with cancer, Neruda retired to his beloved house in Isla Negra, Chile, where he had written *Isla Negra, A Notebook* (1964), a kind of autobiography in verse that explores his landscape, his roots, his formative experiences. This is supplemented by his splendid *Memoirs,* as well as by seven books of poems published posthumously. He wrote of entering "the silence into which everything falls / and, finally, we fall." Heartbroken over the coup that ousted Allende and the dark hour enveloping his country, Neruda died of cancer eleven days later—on September 23, 1973—in Santiago.

Neruda remains an immense presence in poetry. His work contains multitudes, like that of his beloved predecessor Walt Whitman. He was a poet of freedom and the sea, a wondrous love poet, the singer of an endlessly proliferating nature, a necessary voice of social consciousness. His writing is radiantly impure and obstinately humane. In his *Memoirs,* Neruda asserts:

> Poetry is a deep inner calling in man; from it came liturgy, the psalms, and also the content of religions. The poet confronted nature's phenomena and in the early ages called himself a priest, to safeguard his vocation. . . . Today's social poet is still a member of the earliest order of priests. In the old days he made his pact with the darkness, and now he must interpret the light.

51

NICANOR PARRA

Poetry has acquitted itself well
I have conducted myself horribly
Poetry ends with me.

I GET A GREAT kick out of Nicanor Parra's work. I like his caustic wit and brutal honesty. The Chilean poet coined the term *antipoemas* ("antipoems") for his fierce, astringent, sardonic lyrics. Parra has always used his flat colloquial voice and deadpan irony to take aim at poetry's high lyric pretensions. He offers a comic antidote to several generations of romantic Spanish and Latin American poets. Rimbaud coined the image of a piano at the top of the Alps for his delirious music, but Parra clearly prefers a roller coaster to represent the effect of his own hard-boiled mercurial style:

ROLLER COASTER

For half a century
Poetry was the paradise
Of the solemn fool.
Until I came
And built my roller coaster.

Go up, if you feel like it.
I'm not responsible if you come down
With your mouth and nose bleeding.

Parra's work is well represented in two books edited by Miller Williams: *Poems and Antipoems* (1967) and *Emergency Poems* (1972).

Parra reminds us that modern poetry invariably needs gate crashers to keep it honest, to put it in touch with rude reality. Immersed in life and allergic to Art for Art's sake, to pretentiousness of any kind, to overblown rhetoric and imagery, he strips the lyric down to its root values, its solid core, and tells the truth at all costs. "Doctor," he says, "the coffin cures everything."

The traditional task of the poet may be to give names to things, but the role of the antipoet is to change them. "To the lovers of belles-lettres / I offer my best wishes," Parra writes, "I am going to change the names of some things." "In poetry everything is permitted," he allows, but then wryly adds: "With only this condition, of course: / You have to improve on the blank page."

Parra drolly undermines the pastoral, the idyllic, and the amatory in his work, but he also concludes that his negative strategy is a kind of endgame. There is a recognition in Parra's work that what we say is different from what we think, and what we think is different from what we feel. This leads to radical alienation, a Kafkaesque regress so great that it causes him to disavow even his cherished assertions. He recognizes that everything is relative, nothing true. The ultimate anti-poetic act is self-negating, and in the end Parra renounces everything he has said with a final bitter flourish:

I Take Back Everything I've Said

Before I go
I'm supposed to get a last wish:
Generous reader
            burn this book
It's not at all what I wanted to say
In spite of the fact that it was written with blood
It's not what I wanted to say.

No lot could be sadder than mine
I was defeated by my own shadow:
The words take vengeance against me.

Forgive me, reader, good reader
If I cannot leave you
With a faithful gesture. I leave you
With a forced and sad smile.

Maybe that's all I am
But listen to my last word:
I take back everything I've said.
With the greatest bitterness in the world
I take back everything I've said.

ALFONSINA STORNI

I am like the she-wolf.
I broke with the pack
And fled to the mountains
Tired of the plain.

I have a son, the outcome of love without marriage,
For I couldn't be like the others, another ox
With its neck in a yoke; I hold my proud head high!
I plow through the underbrush with my own hands.

NEAR THE END of her life, the Argentine poet Alfonsina Storni (1892–1938) wrote a dramatic series of poems that she called "anti-sonnets," which appeared in her moving posthumous volume *Mascarilla y trebol* (*Mask and Clover*). These poems abandoned rhyme but maintained a traditional structure of fourteen lines: two quatrains, or four-line stanzas, and two tercets, or three-line stanzas. They are argumentative poems that take the traditional subject of the sonnet, romantic love, and radically dismantle it.

Storni treats the god of love with a bracing lyricism and dark cynicism in her allegorical poem *"A Eros"* ("To Eros"), which introduces her final work. She had always been a radical and unconventional figure. Now the woman who broke with the pack has come down to the sea with a lifetime of experience behind her. Her head is still high. Picture her in her mid-forties strolling along a sandy beach, suddenly catching a doll-like figure of Eros by the throat. Eros tries to wound her, but she is undeterred and cuts him open to uncover his inner workings. She even finds his secret trapdoor. Then she tosses him back into the sea.

To Eros

I caught you by the neck
on the shore of the sea, while you shot
arrows from your quiver to wound me
and on the ground I saw your flowered crown.

I disemboweled your stomach like a doll's
and examined your deceitful wheels,
and deeply hidden in your golden pulleys
I found a trapdoor that said: sex.

On the beach I held you, now a sad heap,
up to the sun, accomplice of your deeds,
before a chorus of frightened sirens.

Your deceitful godmother, the moon
was climbing through the crest of the dawn,
and I threw you into the mouth of the waves.

(TRANSLATED BY KAY SHORT)

Mask and Clover concludes with a passionate homage to poetry, the antisonnet "A madona poesia" ("To My Lady of Poetry"). The poet serves a larger god. Storri's final book, then, commences with a lyric that uncovers the deceit of romantic love, but it closes with a romantic reaffirmation of the religious purity of her stubborn and furious art. Love may have been corrupted, but poetry remains intensely pure.

To My Lady of Poetry

I throw myself here at your feet, sinful,
my dark face against your blue earth,
you the virgin among armies of palm trees
that never grow old as humans do.

I don't dare look at your pure eyes
or dare touch your miraculous hand:
I look behind me and a river of rashness
urges me guiltlessly on against you.

With a promise to mend my ways through your
divine grace, I humbly place on your
hem a little green branch,

for I couldn't have possibly lived
cut off from your shadow, since you blinded me
at birth with your fierce branding iron.

(TRANSLATED BY KAY SHORT)

53

JORGE LUIS BORGES

*I, who had always thought of Paradise
in form and image as a library.*

WE TEND TO THINK of Jorge Luis Borges (1899–1986) as a writer of fictions, as the author of mind-bending metaphysical parables that cross the boundaries between the short story and the essay. But Borges always identified himself first as a reader, then as a poet, and finally as a prose writer. He found the borders between genres permeable and lived in the magic space, the imaginary world, created by books. "If I were asked to name the chief event in my life, I should say my father's library," he said in 1970. "In fact, sometimes I think I have never strayed outside that library."

Borges was so incited, so inflamed by what he read, so beholden to what he encountered, that it demanded from him an answer in kind, a creative response. He was an Argentine polyglot who learned English even before he learned Spanish (in a sense, he grew up in the dual world of his father's library of unlimited English books and his mother's sensuous Hispanic garden). As a teenager in Geneva during World War I he also learned Latin and German, which he considered the language of the philosophers, and in old age he devoted himself to studying old Germanic languages. One could say that reading others spurred Borges into writing poetry, which was for him something so intimate, so essential, it could not be defined without oversimplifying it. "It would be like attempting to define the color yellow, love, the fall of leaves in autumn," he said. He loved Plato's characterization of the poet as "that light substance, winged and sacred."

One of the persistent motifs in Borges's work is that our egos persist, but that selfhood is a passing illusion; that we are all in the end one, that in reading Shakespeare we somehow become Shakespeare. "For many years I believed that literature, which is almost infinite, is one man," he said. "I want to give thanks, " he wrote in "Another Poem of Gifts,"

> For the fact that the poem is inexhaustible
> And becomes one with the sum of all created things
> And will never reach its last verse
> And varies according to its writers . . .

Borges's first book of poems, *Fervor of Buenos Aires* (1921), was inspired by his native city and written under the sign of a vanguard imagist sect called the Ultraist movement (in Spanish, *Ultraísmo*), a group of Spanish poets who believed in the supreme power of metaphor and the liberating music of free verse. "I feel that all during my lifetime I have been rewriting that one book," he confessed. He wrote poetry throughout the 1920s, but then it mysteriously deserted him as he went on to create a new kind of narrative prose, the astonishing works that registered his greatness: *Inquisitions* (1925), *Universal History of Infamy* (1935), *The Garden of Forking Paths* (1941), *Ficciones* (1944), and *A New Refutation of Time* (1987), among others. (The first English-language collections of Borges's writing, *Labyrinths* and *Ficciones,* appeared in 1962.)

Borges suffered from hereditarily weak eyesight and eventually became the sixth generation of his family to go blind. This was an especially tragic fate for the reader and writer who was also the director of Argentina's National Library. In "Poem of the Gifts," written in the 1950s, he speaks of God's splendid irony in granting him at one time 800,000 books and total darkness. The conclusion of the poem underscores the tragedy of a man who has been denied access to what he most loved:

> Painfully probing the dark, I grope toward
> The void of the twilight with the point of my faltering
> Cane—I for whom Paradise was always a metaphor,
> An image of libraries.

The fabulist returned to poetry in the 1950s with a more direct and straightforward style, a beguiling and deceptive simplicity. He dictated his poems to classical meters and chanted them aloud at readings. He wrote about the flow of rivers and the nature of time, his ardor for Buenos Aires, the culture of his ancestors, his study of Old Norse and Anglo-Saxon, the contradictions of temporal experience, the power of certain sunsets and certain dawns, the immanence of a revelation always about to arrive. His poems show how much he loved to read the narrative language of storytelling (of Rudyard Kipling, G. K. Chesterton, and Robert Louis Stevenson, of *Gilgamesh* and *Beowulf*), and the magical language of lyric poetry (of runes, riddles, and spells, of Walt Whitman at his most incantatory and Ralph Waldo Emerson at his most oracular), and the investigatory language of metaphysical speculation (from Spinoza to Kafka, from Schopenhauer to Berkeley, Swedenborg, and Unamuno). Borges was a rapturous writer, a literary alchemist who emerged as an explorer of labyrinths, an adventurer in the fantastic, a poet of mysterious intimacies who probed the infinite postponements and cycles of time, the shimmering mirrors of fiction and reality, the symbols of unreality, the illusions of identity, the disintegration of the self into the universe, into the realm of the Archetypes and the Splendors.

The Enigmas

I who am singing these lines today
Will be tomorrow the enigmatic corpse
Who dwells in a realm, magical and barren,
Without a before or an after or a when.
So say the mystics. I say I believe
Myself undeserving of Heaven or of Hell,
But make no predictions. Each man's tale
Shifts like the watery forms of Proteus.
What errant labyrinth, what blinding flash
Of splendor and glory shall become my fate
When the end of this adventure presents me with

The curious experience of death?
I want to drink its crystal-pure oblivion,
To be forever; but never to have been.

(TRANSLATED BY JOHN UPDIKE)

54

OCTAVIO PAZ

Words are bridges.

OCTAVIO PAZ PRACTICED poetry like a secret religion. He dwelt in its mysteries, he invoked its sacraments, he read its entrails, he inscribed its revelations. Writing was for him a primordial act, and he stared down at the blank page as if it were an abyss until it sent him reeling over the brink of language. The poems he brought back are filled with ancient wonder and strangeness, hermetic knowledge, a dizzying sense of the sacred. They are magically, and sometimes violently, uprooted from silence. They are drawn from a deep well. Here is his three-line poem *"Escritura"* ("Writing"): *"Yo dibujo estas letras / como el día dibuja sus imágenes / y sopla sobre ellas y no vuelve":*

> I draw these letters
> as the day draws its images
> and blows over them
> > > and does not return

(TRANSLATED BY ELIOT WEINBERGER)

Paz started writing poems as a teenager and never let up until the end of his life. Lyric poetry was for him a core activity, at the root of his being, and for nearly seventy years he was driven by invisible demons to try to connect to himself and to others through the sensuality, the rhythmic fervor, of words. Inspiration was for him not a static entity, but a forward thrust, an aspiration, the act of "going beyond ourselves to the encounter of ourselves." Paz wrote poetry with a sharp awareness of being himself and, simultaneously, someone or something else. He called this "the other voice." He experienced the merging of voices as a submersion, a type of flooding. "We still keep alive the sensation of some minutes so full they were time overflowing, a high tide that broke the dikes of temporal succession," he writes in *The Bow and the Lyre,* a sustained defense of poetry Shelley himself might have cherished. "For the poem is a means of access to pure time, an immersion in the original waters of existence." He also defined the poetic experience as "an opening up of the wellsprings of being. An instant and never. An instant and forever."

Paz was—and in his work he remains—a seeker, and the quest for a moment to abolish linear or successive time is one of the driving forces of his aesthetic, a defining feature of his pilgrimage. Poetry is a wayward siren song calling him to a perpetual present, to an erotic consecration of instants, and to a superabundance of time and being. "Poetry is in love with the instant and seeks to relive it in the poem, thus separating it from sequential time and turning it into a fixed present," he says in his Nobel lecture, "In Search of the Present."

The fixed present, the endless instant, the eternal moment—the experience is for Paz something to be attained, like reality, like being itself. "Door of being, dawn and wake me," he prays near the conclusion of his circular masterpiece "Sunstone":

> allow me to see the face of this day,
> allow me to see the face of this night,
> all communicates, all is transformed,
> arch of blood, bridge of the pulse,
> take me to the other side of this night,
> where I am you, we are us,
> the kingdom where pronouns are intertwined,
>
> door of being: open your being
> and wake, learn to be . . .

If you can get to the present, there are presences, Paz suggests, and he trusts poetry's capacity to deliver those presences through images incarnated in words, through words flowing in rhythm. "The instant dissolves in the succession of other nameless instants. In order to *save it* we must *convert it* into a rhythm," he writes in *Alternating Current,* where he also defines rhythm as "the reincarnation of the instant." Rhythm serves the poet as a means of access—a reliable guide—to originary or pure time.

Paz needed lyric poetry as a primary mode of crossing, of rendering the self diaphanous, of becoming "a wind that stops / turns on itself and is gone" ("The Face and the Wind"). The words themselves become a way of seeking others that also links him back to the spaces opening up inside himself. "Between now and now, / between what I am and you are, / the word *bridge,*" he declares in his short poem "The Bridge":

> Entering it
> you enter yourself:
> the world connects
> and closes like a ring.

Language becomes a form of practical magic as the word becomes a bridge, a juncture, a span of connection. "Everything is a door / everything a bridge," he proclaims in "Sleepless Night." Words are transfiguring and have a threshold power. They are portals to the other side. The refrain "Words are bridges" reverberates through his poetic cantata "Letter of Testimony." They are a form of a linkage, a way of reaching out, reaching across, that is also a means of reaching in: "Let yourself be carried by these words / toward yourself."

For Paz, the words become the only way of attaining himself, attaining a truer identity than social identity—a shadowy, psychic truth, a mode of being. "I'm not finished with myself yet," he declares in his prose poem "The Besieged." "I am the shadow my words cast," he concludes in "A Draft of Shadows." It's as if he doesn't have that real self, that hidden or shadow identity, without the word, the poetic act. The word *bridge,* the word-bridge, becomes the site of a poetic crossing into true being. As he expresses it in "Pillars":

Between the end and the beginning
a moment without time,
a delicate arch of blood,
a bridge over the void.

I'm struck by how many of Paz's poems seem to unfold and take place in liminal spaces, in pauses and intervals, odd crossings, interrupted movements. He finds a poetic space opening up in gaps and ruptures, in the realm of the betwixt and between. Consider all the arches and bridges in his poems, the shadowy tunnels and endless interior corridors, the elemental passageways, the vertiginous heights. Paz is a poet of crossings and thresholds, of portals to the other side. His inspired poetic gift opened up deep wellsprings of being and delivered eternal pauses, what Virginia Woolf calls "Moments of Being." It is "Within a Moment: The Pulsation of the Artery," William Blake writes, "When the Poets Work is Done." I find such a luminous moment of revelation in "Between Going and Staying":

Between going and staying the day wavers,
in love with its own transparency.

The circular afternoon is now a bay
where the world in stillness rocks.

All is visible and all elusive,
all is near and can't be touched.

Paper, book, pencil, glass,
rest in the shade of their names.

Time throbbing in my temples repeats
the same unchanging syllable of blood.

The light turns the indifferent wall
into a ghostly theater of reflections.

I find myself in the middle of an eye,
watching myself in its blank stare.

The moment scatters. Motionless,
I stay and go: I am a pause.

(TRANSLATED BY ELIOT WEINBERGER)

55

JULIA DE BURGOS

Rio Grande de Loiza!... Great river. Great flood of tears.
The greatest of all our island's tears
save those greater that come from the eyes
of my soul for my enslaved people.

JULIA DE BURGOS (1914–1953) is the bedrock of Puerto Rican poetry. For the past few years, I've been living with and marveling at the work in *Song of the Simple Truth,* an excellent bilingual edition of her complete poems (*Obra poética completa*) compiled and translated by Jack Agüeros and published by Curbstone Press (1997).

I am eager to recommend the highly lyrical, turbulent, commemorative, socially conscious poems of this key Spanish-language poet who published only two books in her lifetime, who was an heir to Walt Whitman, Pablo Neruda (she knew his *Twenty Love Poems* by heart), and Alfonsina Storni, who, she said, had the "tragic sense of life." She was a proto-feminist ("the desire to follow men warped in me"), a Puerto Rican *independentista,* and a devoted internationalist. De Burgos was painfully well-acquainted with poverty and deeply interested in social and political problems. She also insisted on thinking for herself. "The madness of my soul / cannot repose," she declares in the poem "My Soul": "it lives . . . / in the silence / of the free thinker, who lives alone . . ."

De Burgos's best-known poem, "Rio Grande de Loiza," links her childhood river ("My wellspring, my river / since the maternal petal lifted me to the world") to the sources of her art ("and my childhood was all a poem in the river, / and a river in the poem of my first dreams") and the grief of her native island. One of my favorite poems of hers, "To Julia de Burgos," splits herself off into the intimate who writes and the social person who bears her name. It is reminiscent of Borges's marvelous prose piece "Borges and I." De Burgos's strategy of attack is to divide herself in two: "You are like your world, selfish," she declares, "not me / who gambles everything betting on what I am." She shows how one part of herself can be claimed by the world, while the other, truer, part can be entirely free ("You are the cold doll of social lies, / and me, the virile starburst of the human truth"). Her poetry comes from this inner spirit—"I belong to nobody."

The spirit of freedom and independence flashes through de Burgos's work. She was destined to build something that cannot be ruined, something of her own that lasts.

SEAWALL

I'm going to make a seawall
with my small happiness . . .
I don't want the sea to know
that pains go through my breast.

I don't want the sea to touch
the shore of my earth . . .
I have run out of dreams,
crazy from shadows in the sand.

I don't want the sea to look
at blue mourning in my path . . .
(My eyelids were auroras
when the storm crossed!)

I don't want the sea to cry
a new rainstorm at my door . . .
All the eyes of the wind
already cry me as dead.

I'm going to make a seawall
with my small happiness,
light happiness of knowing myself,
mind the hand that closes.

I don't want the sea to arrive
at the thirst of my poem,
blind in the middle of light,
broken in the middle of an absence.

56

CONTEMPORARY MEXICAN POETS

The poet's country is words
and his dominions blank pages
—ALBERTO BLANCO, "METAMORPHOSIS OF A CHAIR"

WHAT HAVE THE POETS of Mexico been up to lately? Anyone eager to know or even just curious will be delighted by Mónica de la Torre and Michael Wiegers's capacious anthology, *Reversible Monuments: Contemporary Mexican Poetry* (Copper Canyon Press, 2002). This multilingual labor of love, which presents the original poems *en face* alongside their translations into English, includes a substantial selection of work by thirty-one poets born after World War II. To our great benefit, it also represents several indigenous poets, who write in such languages as Zapotec, Tzeltal, and Mozatec. *Reversible Monuments* flows north across the Americas and takes a rightful place beside Octavio Paz and Samuel Beckett's groundbreaking compilation *An Anthology of Mexican Poetry* (1958) and Mark Strand's landmark book *New Poetry of Mexico* (1970).

Octavio Paz's encyclopedic knowledge of world literature set the gold standard for Mexican poetry, and the post-Paz generation is fittingly diverse and international in perspective. In a useful introduction, Eliot Weinberger points out that this is indeed the first generation of Mexican poets as a whole to bring such a wide international sensibility to their work. It is no accident that many are notable translators.

The way that literatures cross-pollinate is always intriguing. I'm struck by the concentrated intensity of Pure López Colomé, who seems indebted to Paul Celan, and the long, dreamy, sensuous river poems of José Rivas, reminiscent of St. John Perse. I'm moved by

Francisco Hernández's long poem inspired by the music and madness of Robert Schumann ("I see the music of Robert Schumann / like one sees a book, a coin, / or a lamp") and Tedi López Mills's meditative lyrics about reading other writers, such as Virgil ("and the year does not matter") and Guillaume Apollinaire ("And your voice faithful as a shadow"). Her elegant poem to Joseph Brodsky ("And Never Did . . .") begins by playfully establishing a series of crucial northern and southern differences:

> I don't know the Baltic marshes,
> metal shattered by northern cold,
> dementia of hoarfrost on nocturnal windowpanes.
>
> The Tartar masses flattened like new grass are alien to me
> and the wind's campaign among gray shoals
> I've watched only from tropical esplanades
> burning, not freezing, with its lashing of sand.
>
> No snow ever settled on my pen,
> nor exile on my body anywhere but in sleep,
> and I barely imagine the dominant rhymes
> —I'm told—of Russian in the war of your lips
> against the false syllabication and imprecise echo
> of another language declaimed.
>
> But the mania for remembrance is the same . . .

(TRANSLATED BY ESTHER ALLEN)

One of the most surprising poets is Pedro Pérez Conde, who writes under the magical pseudonym Búffalo Conde and has been paraphrasing sections of *The Song of Songs* into the Tzeltal language. The result is a deliciously hybrid and transplanted work that brings together two ancient worlds, two majestic landscapes:

Flower of Gold

Fountain in the orchard of my beloved,
watermill sanctified in my honor,
that flows from the fields where the buffalo rests:
come here my legendary Beloved.

"I've come to my field, oh beloved, my companion;
I've drank of my water and my juice, my wife:
now you should drink plentifully of this juice, my beloved."
It is the voice of my husband that calls.

(TRANSLATED BY MICHAEL WIEGERS)

57

SLEEP AND POETRY

What is it? And to what shall I compare it?
It has a glory, and nought else can share it.
The thought thereof is awful, sweet, and holy . . .
—JOHN KEATS, "SLEEP AND POETRY"

EVERY NIGHT we enter another world, the kingdom of sleep, which no one entirely understands. We lie down and penetrate this startling realm as if it's a completely ordinary experience, yet it turns out to be one of the strangest things most of us ever do. Where do we go when we sleep? Where are we rushing with such urgency? Dreaming is a kind of obscure underground thinking, which has its own inexorable laws, its own governance, and sleep is a mysterious shadow country—awful, sweet, and holy—that each of us enters alone.

Mary Ruefle creates a sense of ritual occasion for this entry into the unconscious—an eerie land in a timeless zone—in her poem "Before Bed" from her book *Cold Pluto:*

I bathe at night. I dress in white. The sheets are clean,
for sleep is an important occasion.
And since I cannot bear a tick, the small clock
is placed under the bed
like a carefully lost invitation.
I am going to a coronation. And I'm not just
one of the crowd, I am walking down the aisle
of a great church and somebody carries my head
on a pillow. When we reach the end I pick it up,
hold it high, say a few words of farewell.
Then I put it on somebody else's head.
And though you could say I've never worn it

myself, I play an important role,
I plan the details that allow the rest of the country
to sleep, to dream of the day they'll be the one.
But I keep the secrets of how it is done.

"The dream is an involuntary kind of poetry," British psychologist Charles Rycroft writes in his book *The Innocence of Dreams* (Pantheon, 1979). So, too, the poem is a voluntary form of dreaming. The poem is a made thing—a magical entity—coaxed along by rational intellect, but depth-charged by the irrational. In his stimulating anthology *Night Errands: How Poets Use Dreams* (University of Pittsburgh Press, 1998), Roderick Townley suggests that writing poetry takes not just craft but a particular kind of bravery, "a willingness to enter the dark world of the unconscious and confront whatever lives there." He calls poets "our designated dreamers."

One of my own newest designated dreamers is the Argentine poet María Negroni, whose volume *Night Journey*, translated by Anne Twitty, takes the wordless logic of dreams and turns it into her own precise, oracular music. This book is pervaded by the spooky sense of a woman traveling in many directions, most of them unrequested, journeying through shadows and mirrors, navigating the mysteries by shuttling between life and death:

THEORY OF A GOOD DEATH

In the bluish climate of a stony city, they are
burying me. I watch and say:
Leave her alone. Can't you see she's alive? Don't
you see her face twitching?
"It's true," someone says. "It's not time for her to
die yet. She hasn't practiced enough. Love's
exactions have not been written on her soul; there
are still a few partitions between her and life.
Something must advance to its center like a
question. Must dare petition and surrender. Must

thrust a signpost into her sand image, to see what
the mouth makes of silence. She has to live."
So they let me live. The stranger is still talking but
I can't understand him. He says something about
the Good Death: a secret, an indispensable error,
loving face-to-face, something like that. Then he
evaporates into a stronghold of shadow and I, half-
troubled, half-content, board a train and abandon
the last city on earth.

58

SCOTTISH POETRY: NORMAN MACCAIG

The rose of all the world is not for me.
I want for my part
Only the little white rose of Scotland
That smells sharp and sweet—and breaks the heart.
—HUGH MACDIARMID, "THE LITTLE WHITE ROSE"

WHEN I WAS twenty-two years old, I spent four months living in Edinburgh and studying Scottish literature on my own. The poet Norman MacCaig kindly took me under his wing—he was already something of an iconic presence in his native city—and introduced me around. Every Friday afternoon I'd head over to his hospitable flat for a short crash course in Scottish poetry. We worked our way up from the three great "makars" who created a golden age of Scottish verse—Robert Henryson (c. 1420–c. 1506), William Dunbar (c. 1460–c. 1520), and Gavin Douglas, Bishop of Dunkeld (c. 1474–c. 1522)—to such admired contemporaries as Robert Garioch, who wrote in Scots, and Sorley MacLean (Somhairle MacGill-Eain), who set the benchmark for contemporary Gaelic poetry. Mr. MacCaig had a way of making it all vitally, even buzzingly, present.

Afterward, we'd retire to a pub where I peppered him with questions about his close friend Christopher Murray Grieve (Hugh MacDiarmid), who had revolutionized Scottish poetry, and listened to tales about his raucous contemporaries. "Scotland small?" MacCaig would ask incredulously after he had downed a couple of whiskeys. "Our multiform, our infinite Scotland *small*?" He was quoting MacDiarmid's *Lucky Poet:* " 'Nothing but heather!'—How marvelously descriptive! And incomplete!" He smoked and said it took him "two fags" to complete a poem. For my part, I could wryly amuse him by reciting in my Chicago accent the envoi to his own "Ballade of Good Whiskey":

> Chris! (whether perpendicular or flat
> Or moving rather horribly aslant)
> Here is a toast that you won't scunner at—
> Glenfiddich, Bruichladdich and Glengrant!

Norman MacCaig (1910–1996) published sixteen books of poetry during his lifetime. He had a sturdy, humane, nonacademic way of thinking about poetry. His poems, which are written in a limpid English, have a sly wit and tonic honesty. MacCaig kept strict accounts with himself and wore his erudition lightly. I still see Scotland through his eyes, whether he is writing about the cityscapes of Edinburgh or the rural area around Lochinver in Sutherland, where he spent his summers. ("Time adds one malice to another one," he declared: "So many summers, and I have lived them too.") He wrote with a hard won, classically achieved clarity, "a long haul to lucidity" (Sorley MacLean), that was balanced by what Robert Louis Stevenson called a "strong Scots accent of the mind."

Here is a sharply observant, playful, and bracing memorial poem by a true maker:

PRAISE OF A COLLIE

> She was a small dog, neat and fluid—
> Even her conversation was tiny:
> She greeted you with *bow,* never *bow-wow.*
>
> Her sons stood monumentally over her
> But did what she told them. Each grew grizzled
> Till it seemed he was his own mother's grandfather.
>
> Once, gathering sheep on a showery day,
> I remarked how dry she was. Pollóchan said, 'Ah,
> It would take a very accurate drop to hit Lassie.'

She sailed in the dinghy like a proper sea-dog.
Where's a burn?—she's first on the other side.
She flowed through fences like a piece of black wind.

But suddenly she was old and sick and crippled . . .
I grieved for Pollóchan when he took her a stroll
And put his gun to the back of her head.

59

P. K. PAGE

It has to be loved the way a laundress loves her linens,
the way she moves her hands caressing the fine muslins
knowing their warp and woof,
like a lover coaxing, or a mother praising.
It has to be loved as if it were embroidered
with flowers and birds and two joined hearts upon it.
It has to be stretched and stroked.
It has to be celebrated.
O this great beloved world and all the creatures in it.
It has to be spread out, the skin of this planet.

P. K. PAGE is one of the finest and most exuberant Canadian poets. She is a kind of high-spirited, socially conscious Elizabeth Bishop, a celebratory writer with a keen eye, a roving intelligence, and a compassionate sensibility. "It is the writer's duty to describe," she declares as a statement of principle: "Nothing less will do." It is also this particular writer's inclination to praise. "It has to be made bright," she writes, "the skin of this planet / till it shines in the sun like gold leaf."

Page has the expansive descriptive powers of a writer who caresses the world. At times she reminds me of the English poet Charles Tomlinson, who has made a lifework out of affirming that "seeing is believing." Like Tomlinson, Page is a graphic artist and brings a strong visual sensibility to her writings. For her, the analogy between poetry and painting is exact and exacting:

> Just as the painter must, from two make three
> or conjure light, build pigments layer on layer
> to form an artefact, so I must probe
> with measuring mind and eye to mix a blue
> mainly composed of air.

Page's chronicle of the external world ("not my life only," she insists, "our / whole planetary life") is informed by a deep environmental understanding of "Planet Earth," which is what she first chose as the title of her new and selected poems. The poet Eric Ormsby has instead entitled it *Cosmologies* and carefully culled it from her two-volume collected poems published in Canada, *Hidden Room.* The planetary ethic is the same; the earth demands our great protective awareness. It needs us to care for it. "Art and the planet tell us. Change your life."

Page belongs to an important generation of Canadian poets that includes A. M. Klein, F. R. Scott, and A. J. M. Smith. She has an intricate formal sense and moves with dazzling ease between traditional forms and free verse. What characterizes all her work is her deep attentiveness to what Pablo Neruda called "the holy surfaces." Landscapes fascinate her. She is highly conscious of cruelty and thus no sentimentalist, yet there is an almost mystical way that she observes the country or gazes up at the sky. "The very stars are justified," she asserts in "Star-Gazer": "I have proofread / and proofread / the beautiful script. / / There are no / errors."

For P. K. Page, an entranced observer who has been writing celebratory lyrics for more than fifty years, the world can be read and studied like a strange and marvelous script. It is filled with mysterious presences.

THE DISGUISES

You, my Lord, were dressed in astonishing disguises:
as a Chinese emperor, ten feet tall,
as a milk-skinned woman
parading in exquisite stuffs.

You were ambiguous and secret
and hidden in other faces.

How did we know you were there at all?
Your ineffable presence
perfumed the air like an avenue of lilacs.

60

KATHLEEN RAINE

Because I love
All night the river flows into my sleep,
Ten thousand living things are sleeping in my arms,
And sleeping wake, and flowing are at rest.

KATHLEEN RAINE, who died in July 2003 at the age of ninety-five, was an enigmatic and mystical nature poet of great rectitude and serious-ness. She was a devoted scholar of Neoplatonism and agreed with William Blake, her first master in poetry, that "One Power alone makes a poet—Imagination, The Divine Vision." She believed with W. B. Yeats, her second master in poetry, that "poetry and religion are the same thing." Raine was at home in Eastern traditions and consid-ered India the "supreme civilization of the Imagination." All her work is a passionate testimonial to spiritual values in a materialist age. It is a quest for a lost Eden, a timeless kingdom glimpsed in childhood. "Nature sees, sees itself, is both seer and seen," she writes in her poem "Seventh Day": "This is the divine repose, that watches / The ever-changing light and shadow, rock and sky and ocean."

Raine may be the last English poet who could claim full-fledged membership in the English holy tradition. She embraced spiritual mysteries and explored Celtic culture, astronomy, and magic. "I wanted," she said, "to get away from the Sherlock Holmes misconcep-tion that everything has a rational explanation." In addition to her *Collected Poems,* I am eager to recommend her three volumes of auto-biography: *Farewell Happy Fields* (1973), *The Loud Unknown* (1975), and *The Lion's Mouth* (1977). Her esoteric scholarly investigations in-clude *Blake and Tradition* (1968–69), *From Blake to "A Vision"* (1979), and *Blake and the New Age* (1979).

My favorite poems of Raine's are a group of "spells" that she wrote under the influence of old Celtic folk poetry. The repetitions in these haunting poems are meant to "Spell away sorrow, / Charm away grief" ("Spell Against Sorrow"). They aim to inspire and even induce bliss. These spells seek transcendence and testify to the circular unity of creation.

SPELL OF CREATION

Within the flower there lies a seed,
Within the seed there springs a tree,
Within the tree there spreads a wood.

In the wood there burns a fire,
And in the fire there melts a stone,
Within the stone a ring of iron.

Within the ring there lies an O
Within the O there looks an eye,
In the eye there swims a sea,

And in the sea reflected sky,
And in the sky there shines the sun,
Within the sun a bird of gold.

Within the bird there beats a heart,
And from the heart there flows a song,
And in the song there sings a word.

In the word there speaks a world,
A word of joy, a world of grief,
From joy and grief there springs my love.

Oh love, my love, there springs a world,
And on the world there shines a sun
And in the sun there burns a fire,

Within the fire consumes my heart
And in my heart there beats a bird,
And in the bird there wakes an eye,

Within the eye, earth, sea and sky,
Earth, sky and sea within an O
Lie like the seed within the flower.

61.

WENDY COPE

God decided he was tired
Of his spinning toys.

IN 1986, MY FRIEND Amy Clampitt went to England and brought me back a copy of Wendy Cope's first book, *Making Cocoa for Kingsley Amis.* We read it together and soon we were keeled over with laughter at Cope's hilarious parodies of other writers. My favorite are still her group of "Waste Land Limericks," which follow the five-part structure of Eliot's poem. There's something wickedly clever about the way Cope takes the great despairing poem of high modernism and summarizes it by way of Edward Lear, using an English stanza form whose exclusive purpose is light verse:

WASTE LAND LIMERICKS

I

In April one seldom feels cheerful;
Dry stones, sun and dust make me fearful;
Clairvoyants distress me,
Commuters depress me—
Met Stetson and gave him an earful.

II

She sat on a mighty fine chair,
Sparks flew as she tidied her hair;
She asks many questions,
I make few suggestions—
Bad as Albert and Lil—what a pair!

III

The Thames runs, bones rattle, rats creep;
Tiresias fancies a peep—
A typist is laid,
A record is played—
Wei la la. After this it gets deep.

IV

A Phoenician called Phlebas forgot
About birds and his business—the lot.
Which is no surprise,
Since he'd met his demise
And been left in the ocean to rot.

V

No water. Dry rocks and dry throats,
Then thunder, a shower of quotes
From the Sanskrit and Dante.
Da. Damyata. Shantih.
I hope you'll make sense of the notes.

Among other things, Cope invents a poet named Jason Strugnell, the subject of a BBC program, *Shall I Call Thee Bard?* I especially like Strugnell's Shakespearean sonnets, such as #1 ("The expense of spirits is a crying shame, / So is the cost of wine"), #4 ("Not only marble, but the plastic toys / From cornflake packets will outlive this rhyme"), and #6 ("Let me not to the marriage of true swine / Admit impediments. With his big car / He's won your heart, and you have punctured mine."). Here is the triple proof that Strugnell also has an English feeling for Japanese haiku:

(i)

The cherry blossom
In my neighbor's garden—Oh!
It looks really nice.

(ii)

The leaves have fallen
And the snow has fallen and
Soon my hair also . . .

(iii)

November evening:
The moon is up, rooks settle,
The pubs are open.

62.

THOM GUNN

The sniff of the real, that's
what I'd like to get . . .

THOM GUNN, who died in April 2004 at the age of seventy-four, was a lively Anglo-American poet with a warm heart and a cool head, a rare combination. His rigorous intelligence and sympathetic imagination are everywhere in evidence in his twelve books of poems. Poetry on both sides of the Atlantic has been enriched by his *Collected Poems,* which brings together nearly four decades of work from his assured first book, *Fighting Terms* (1954), to his sunlit middle collection *Moly* (1971), to his magisterial book of elegies, *The Man with Night Sweats* (1992). His final collection, *Boss Cupid* (2000), suggests that this excellent verse technician was, in the end, a provocative gay love poet.

Gunn was a transplanted British writer who identified strongly with San Francisco, his adopted hometown. He studied with the poetic rationalist Yvor Winters at Stanford (the Library of America recently published his excellent edition of Winters's *Selected Poems*), who ingrained in him a permanent sense of the rigor and balance of the Elizabethan plain style. As he wrote in a tribute poem to Winters:

> You keep both Rule and Energy in view,
> Much power in each, most in the balanced two:
> Ferocity existing in the fence
> Built by an exercised intelligence.

What Gunn concluded about his former teacher is also eminently true of himself: "For all his respect for the rules of poetry, it is not the Augustan decorum he came to admire but the Elizabethan, the energy of Nashe, Greville, Gascoigne, and Donne, plain speakers of little politeness."

Gunn was very much at home in the traditional meters of English poetry, though he also liked to experiment with syllabic stanzas and looser free-verse rhythms, with what he called "openness." He had "little politeness," and part of the shock of his work is the way he employed a plain style and traditional English meters to write about the contemporary urban life he found in California—about drugs and panhandlers, gay bars and tattoo parlors. There is a powerful dialectic, a high tension, running throughout his work between raw anarchistic energy and powerful intellectual control. His poems enact an ongoing struggle to keep Rule and Energy in right relation, proper balance.

Gunn insisted on the continuity between England and America, between meter and free verse, between epiphanic vision and everyday consciousness. His existential rebelliousness was tempered by a sense of our common humanity. I would say that his Elizabethan manner reached its peak in his sequence of elegies for friends who died during the AIDS epidemic of the late 1980s. Here is a memorial lyric for his friend Larry Hoyt, whose life was too early stilled:

STILL LIFE

I shall not soon forget
The grayish-yellow skin
To which the face had set:
Lids tight: nothing of his,
No tremor from within,
Played on the surfaces.

He still found breath, and yet
It was an obscure knack.
I shall not soon forget
The angle of his head,
Arrested and reared back
On the crisp field of bed,

Back from what he could neither
Accept, as one opposed,
Nor, as a life-long breather,
Consentingly let go,
The tube his mouth enclosed
In an astonished O.

63

ROBERT FROST AND EDWARD THOMAS

the only brother I ever had . . .
—ROBERT FROST

ROBERT FROST didn't love many people, but one of the few he did love was Edward Thomas (1878–1917), a splendid English poet who has been underappreciated on our side of the Atlantic. The two met in England in 1913 and made a lasting bond. Frost recognized the lyric element in Thomas's prose writings about nature and persuaded him to start writing poetry. ("Did anyone ever begin at 36 in the shade?" Thomas wondered.) Thomas also began writing under the stimulus of World War I—Frost said the war "made some kind of new man and a poet out of him." Frost penned a touching elegy for him, which begins:

> I slumbered with your poems on my breast
> Spread open as I dropped them half-read through
> Like dove wings on a figure on a tomb,
> To see, if in a dream they brought of you,
>
> I might not have the chance I missed in life
> Through some delay, and call you to your face
> First soldier, and then poet, and then both,
> Who died a soldier-poet of your race.

Edward Thomas wrote 142 poems between December 1914 and April 1917, when he died in Flanders. He never saw a book of his poems in print. His poetry was triggered by his genuine love of the English countryside, his feeling for the unfathomable mysteries of nature. Prone to depression, he always delighted in what he called "this

England." His friend Walter de la Mare remembered that "England's roads and heaths and woods, its secret haunts and solitudes, its houses, its people—themselves resembling its thorns and juniper—its very flints and dust, were his freedom and his peace." Like Thomas Hardy, Thomas loved the oldest English poetry, traditional ballads and folk songs, which come down to us, he said, "imploring a new lease of life on the sweet earth."

Thomas wrote "The Owl" in February 1915, three months before enlisting. I love the dramatic clarity, the rhythmic poise, and the spiritual balance of this impassioned poem, which was first published under the title "Those Others."

The Owl

Downhill I came, hungry, and yet not starved;
Cold, yet had heat within me that was proof
Against the North wind; tired, yet so that rest
Had seemed the sweetest thing under a roof.

Then at the inn I had food, fire, and rest,
Knowing how hungry, cold, and tired was I.
All of the night was quite barred out except
An owl's cry, a most melancholy cry

Shaken out long and clear upon the hill,
No merry note, nor cause of merriment,
But one telling me plain what I escaped
And others could not, that night, as in I went.

And salted was my food, and my repose,
Salted and sobered, too, by the bird's voice
Speaking for all who lay under the stars,
Soldiers and poor, unable to rejoice.

I'm moved by the scrupulous emotional precision of this poem about coming to a place of rest after a long winter tramp in the country.

The speaker recognizes that he entered the inn hungry but not starved, cold but not frozen, tired but not so exhausted that rest was impossible. The owl's melancholy cry splits the poem in half. The first part is given over to a feeling of gratitude, the second to the speaker's recognition of his own privilege, of what he managed to escape but others could not. I especially like how Thomas savors the word *salted,* which means "flavored" but also carries connotations of bitterness and tears, of open wounds. "The Owl" sounds a deep nocturnal note, and it demonstrates what de la Mare called Thomas's "compassionate and suffering heart."

64

AGHA SHAHID ALI

You've forgiven everyone, Shahid, even God—
Then how could someone like you not live forever?

AGHA SHAHID ALI, who died in December 2001 at the age of fifty-two, was a widely admired, much loved Kashmiri-American poet. He was born in New Delhi, grew up in Kashmir, and taught poetry in the United States. He was thoroughly bilingual (in English and Urdu) and bicultural, and called himself "a multiple-exile," a theme that reverberates through his eight books of poems. It crescendos in his two recent collections, both superb: *The Country without a Post Office* (1997) and *Rooms Are Never Finished* (2002). His work is by turns stately, anguished, dislocated, extravagant, high-spirited, and heartbreaking.

Ali was a great proponent of the *ghazal* (pronounced "ghuzzle"), a form that goes back to seventh-century Arabia and has been widely practiced throughout Eastern literature ever since. He instigated and edited a book entitled *Ravishing Disunities: Real Ghazals in English* (2000), which is a gift to American poetry. Like many others, I had illuminating conversations with him about the use of the form by the Persian (Farsi) poet Ḥāfeẓ (1325–1389) and the Urdu master Ghālib (1797–1869); by the German Goethe, who popularized it in the West; the Spaniard Lorca, who viewed it as a testament to the Muslim element in his native Andalusia; and the South Asian Faiz, whom he translated with great acuity (*The Rebel's Silhouette: Selected Poems*).

Ali was himself a splendid practitioner of the form, which consists of at least five thematically autonomous couplets, each with the same rhyme plus a refrain. The poet often signs off with his or her own name in the final signature couplet. The form is driven, he suggested, by a constant sense of longing. He liked to point out that one definition of the word *ghazal* is "the cry of the gazelle when it is cornered in a hunt and knows it will die." This definition gives special resonance to Ali's own ghazals, which are both playful and grief-stricken, animated by the feeling of love and dedicated to the idea of the beloved. Ali found equal power and feeling in the Arabic form of the *qasida,* which was used so evocatively by his beloved García Lorca. Here, then, is a poem of ravishing disunity, of radiant disjunction, that stands as a true self-elegy for a poet who will be much missed:

ARABIC

The only language of loss left in the world is Arabic—
These words were said to me in a language not Arabic.

Ancestors, you've left me a plot in the family graveyard—
Why must I look, in your eyes, for prayers in Arabic?

Majnoon, his clothes ripped, still weeps for Laila.
O, this is the madness of the desert, his crazy Arabic.

Who listens to Ishmael? Even now he cries out:
Abraham, throw away your knives, recite a psalm in Arabic.

From exile Mahmoud Darwish writes to the world:
You'll all pass between the fleeting words of Arabic.

The sky is stunned, it's become a ceiling of stone.
I tell you it must weep. So kneel, pray for rain in Arabic.

At an exhibition of Mughal miniatures, such delicate calligraphy:
Kashmiri paisleys tied into the golden hair of Arabic.

The Koran prophesied a fire of men and stones.
Well, it's all now come true, as it was said in the Arabic.

When Lorca died, they left the balconies open and saw:
his *qasidas* braided, on the horizon, into knots of Arabic.

Memory is no longer confused, it has a homeland—
Says Shammas: Territorialize each confusion in a graceful Arabic.

Where there were homes in Deir Yassein, you'll see dense forests—
That village was razed. There's no sign of Arabic.

I, too, O Amichai, saw the dresses of beautiful women.
And everything else, just like you, in Death, Hebrew, and Arabic.

They ask me to tell them what Shahid means—
Listen: It means "The Beloved" in Persian, "witness" in Arabic.

65

REETIKA VAZIRANI

Our person is a covered entrance to infinity
choked with the tatters of tradition
—Mina Loy

Reetika Vazirani (1962–2003) was born in India and raised in Maryland. She published two books of poems, *White Elephants* (1996) and *World Hotel* (2002), in her short life. Her poetry shows so much cosmopolitan energy and panache, so much formal dexterity and control—her work abounds with sonnets, sestinas, and villanelles—that it is possible for readers to miss its underlying sense of dislocation and homelessness.

"It's me, I'm not home," she declared jauntily in one poem, though the phrase also had a deadly accuracy. She could be playful and even jokey, but the lightness masked a darker rootlessness, a deeper pain.

It's Me, I'm Not Home

It's late in the city and I'm asleep.
You will call again? Did I hear
(please leave a message after the beep)

Chekhov? A loves B. I clap
for joy. B loves C. C won't answer.
In the city it's late, I'm asleep,

and if your face nears me like a familiar map
of homelessness: old world, new hemisphere
(it's me leave a message after the beep),

then romance flies in the final lap
of the relay, I pass the baton you disappear
into the city, it's late and I'm asleep

with marriages again, they tend to drop
by, faithful to us for about a year,
leave a message after the beep,

I'll leave a key for you, play the tape
when you come in, or pick up the receiver.
It's late in the city and I'm asleep.
Please leave a message after the beep.

There is something strangely unsettled and uprooted in Vazirani's poetry, so much of which is about emigration, about traveling between cultures, being caught between worlds. She took on and inhabited many other voices, but all of them sound displaced and even lost. Everyone in her poems is always setting out for somewhere else, for a different life, but no one ever truly arrives. It's as if all states are liminal, all relocations temporary. Vazirani was haunted by family voices, inherited stories. Her speakers are always obsessively looking back. One might even say that her work exists in a subtle but permanent state of culture shock. She said: "Culture shock is not your reflex upon leaving the dock; it is when you have been a law-abiding citizen for more than ten years: when someone asks your name and the name of your religion and your first thought is I don't know."

Vazirani's work is formally well-mannered and even law-abiding, but it is also radically conflicted and self-aware. One of her models was Derek Walcott, another Antonio Machado, a third Jean Rhys. (Think of Rhys as a poet of color.) Vazirani's sense of ethnic identity was one of constant stimulation and flux. The past was a heavy burden that had to be reinvented, the future a perpetual blank. "We say *America you are / magnificent,* and we mean / we are heartbroken," she wrote in one poem: "pack lightly we move so fast." "The earth / is solitary and uncontrolled," she wrote in another, "a watery eye is its only home."

Reetika was a friend, and ever since her untimely death in mid-July 2003, I have been walking around with her three-line poem "Lullaby" on my lips. It is beautiful and inconsolable, a lullaby that wounds.

LULLABY

I would not sing you to sleep.
I would press my lips to your ear
and hope the terror in my heart stirs you.

PART 2

"IT IS NOT UPON you alone the dark patches fall, / The dark threw its patches down upon me also," Walt Whitman declares in "Crossing Brooklyn Ferry," one of his finest poems. Whitman is well-known as our swaggering national bard, epic chanter of democracy, but he also had a wayward, solitary, and self-accusing side. He recognized the voice that was both great and small within us. He identified with the least attractive traits in others, and he took himself to account. He charged in and convicted himself:

> I am he who knew what it was to be evil,
> I too knotted the old knot of contrariety,
> Blabb'd, blush'd, resented, lied, stole, grudg'd,
> Had guile, anger, lust, hot wishes I dared not speak,
> Was wayward, vain, greedy, shallow, sly, cowardly, malignant,
> The wolf, the snake, the hog, not wanting in me,
> The cheating look, the frivolous word, the adulterous wish, not
>   wanting,
> Refusals, hates, postponements, meanness, laziness, none of these
>   wanting . . .

It is the self-critical, brutally honest side not just of Whitman, our representative voice, but of American poetry itself that has especially compelled me.

September 11 in some ways forced America into a midlife confrontation with vulnerability, fragility, mortality. Our great openness has been sorely tested, our notorious innocence challenged. Americans found themselves connected to the world in new, unexpected, and sometimes terrifying ways. Many people subsequently turned to poetry for guidance and solace. Poetry has been particularly useful because it is sustained by true depths of feeling. It is unsettling because it tells the truth about our inner lives. It is consoling for the same reason. We also have roles as citizens, and poetry can help us to comprehend them. "It is difficult to get the news from poems," William Carlos Williams puts it, "yet men die miserably every day / for lack / of what is found there."

I began writing the column "Poet's Choice" soon after September II and embraced the task of choosing poems that speak to our disquieting condition. There are many American poems in the following pages that respond to suffering, that hit a note of lamentation. Yet Americans always seem to light out for new territory, to build from the rubble, and our poetry recognizes the powerful countercurrent of determination in our national character. I also quote local poems that praise the sacredness of daily life. We look for things to affirm, then affirm them. "Poetry dwells in possibility," as Emily Dickinson recognized.

This American half of the book is intensely personal to me. One of my tasks has been to memorialize poets, some of them friends, who have died over the past few years. We are buoyed by their work. Another has been to introduce a wide range of new voices who speak to our future. There are, above all, a group of strong poets here writing from the very midst of life. They think about their parents and their children, their country and its place in the world. They sing of loves lost and found, they advocate for social justice. They question themselves and account for their spiritual journeys. They leave an intense verbal record of our planet. Here is a poetry filled with psalms and laments, elegies and odes, lyrics that look backward and remember, lyrics that look forward and hope, poems that grieve, poems that celebrate.

66.

READING

READING

My eye frees what the page imprisons:
the white the white and the black the black.
—Ibn 'Ammar of Silves

Reading has been a deeply liberating experience for me. Like many of us, I feel as if it has given me most of my interior life and delivered me to myself. It has also taken me to extraordinary places where I otherwise never would have traveled. As a result, I've always liked poems that take reading as their ostensible subject and treat it with the genuine intensity it deserves.

In his book *Flesh and Blood* (1987), which has the feeling of a contemporary sonnet sequence, C. K. Williams includes six poems about reading that are structured as urban parables. Each one takes the general idea of reading and yokes it to a specific story: a man fixing a flat tire in bitterly cold weather suddenly stops to read a newspaper found in the trunk of his car, or a cop who usually stands in the hallway with a "menacingly vacant expression" gets completely absorbed by a political pamphlet. There's a voyeuristic element to these rapid, notational, ethnographic poems, a sense of invasive scrutiny, as if the poet had discovered a person doing something almost illicit, something intensely private, in a public setting. Here he trains his gaze on a woman reading on a bus:

Reading: The Bus

As she reads, she rolls something around in her mouth, hard candy
    it must be, from how long it lasts.
She's short, roundish, gray-haired, pleasantly pugnacious-looking,
    like Grace Paley, and her book,

219

Paint Good and Fast, must be fascinating: she hasn't lifted her eyes
    since Thirty-fourth Street,
even when the corner of a page sticks so that she has to pause a bit
    to lick her index finger . . .
No, now she does, she must have felt me thinking about her: she
    blinks, squints out the window,
violently arches her eyebrows as though what she'd just read had
    really to be nailed down,
and, stretching, she unzips a pocket of her blue backpack,
    rummages through it, and comes out with,
yes, hard candy, red and white, a little sackful, one of which she
    offers with a smile to me.

Wallace Stevens's "The House Was Quiet and the World Was Calm" takes up the plenitude of reading late on a summer night. I think of this lyric from *Transport to Summer* (1947) as a work of tremendous spiritual poise and attainment that accesses the transaction between the reader, the book, the house, the night, and the world. It's as if all the terms are algebraically lined up. The poem establishes a correspondence between the inner realm of the house and the outer one of the cosmos. The quietness of the dwelling and the calmness of the universe are a kind of subject rhyme. This is a twofold proposition: the house was quiet *and* the world was calm. The poem has to be set at night because it suppresses the ordinary or quotidian world and creates a realm of autonomous solitude. It has to be a summer night because summer is the season of plenitude. Reading is re-created here as a physical activity and mental action. It is an act of attention, a quest, the fulfillment of a desire.

THE HOUSE WAS QUIET AND THE WORLD WAS CALM

    The house was quiet and the world was calm.
    The reader became the book; and summer night

    Was like the conscious being of the book.
    The house was quiet and the world was calm.

The words were spoken as if there was no book,
Except that the reader leaned above the page,

Wanted to lean, wanted much most to be
The scholar to whom his book is true, to whom

The summer night is like a perfection of thought.
The house was quiet because it had to be.

The quiet was part of the meaning, part of the mind:
The access of perfection to the page.

And the world was calm. The truth in a calm world,
In which there is no other meaning, itself

Is calm, itself is summer and night, itself
Is the reader leaning late and reading there.

67.

BIRTH

I did it with my body!

THERE'S AN AUDACIOUS moment in John Berryman's long poem "Homage to Mistress Bradstreet" in which he dramatizes Anne Bradstreet giving birth to her first child in 1633. Berryman had to take a giant imaginative leap in order to create an idiom wherein the seventeenth-century American poet could speak of her labor even as she was having it. Here she is, describing the birth itself:

So squeezed, wince you I scream? I love you & hate
off with you. Ages! *Useless.* Below my waist
he has me in Hell's vise.
Stalling. He let go. Come back: brace
me somewhere. No. No. Yes! everything down
hardens I press with horrible joy down
my back cracks like a wrist
shame I am voiding oh behind it is too late

hide me forever I work thrust I must free
now I all muscles & bones concentrate
what is living from dying?
Simon I must leave you so untidy
Monster you are killing me Be sure
I'll have you later Women do endure
I can *can* no longer
and it passes the wretched trap whelming and I am me

drencht & powerful. I did it with my body!

Berryman's poem comes to mind because in a fine anthology, *Birth: A Literary Companion* (University of Iowa Press, 2002), Kristin Kovacic and Lynne Barrett identify a genre they call "birth literature." They deliver an imaginative guidebook, a kind of spiritual Baedeker, to the daunting country of parenthood. The poems and stories are arranged chronologically from early pregnancy to late infancy. The centerpiece of the book is a section called "Notes from the Delivery Room." It contains Lee Upton's witty and ferocious poem "Women's Labors," which plays off the cliché that a woman's work is never done and ends with a feeling of true timelessness, absolute freedom:

> You might want to be amused at the work
> that is never done—or at our most difficult
> labor, our work soonest ended.
>
> In some work we are with most women,
> crossing a bridge in our labor.
> You will forgive me if I resort to Homer.
>
> When the master returns,
> the handmaidens are ordered
> to clean up after the dead suitors,
>
> washing blood from the tables,
> the blood and water running from their sponges.
> And then a cable is drawn about their waists,
>
> and they are lifted from the ground
> to perish in a great bunch together.
> Even Homer must have pitied them:
>
> a knot of slaves who only yesterday
> laughed, believing the master
> would always be missing.

How could I not pity them more—
slaves no one will defend.
If you are a woman in labor

waves break at the spine,
and a giant cable is drawn about your body.
You are held in the air for a very long time.

At last, later, you may be—
as I was—handed a daughter.
And for hours it seems there are no gods to claim us.

It is an illusion of course. But
even after the bracelet is clamped
upon the infant's wrist,

it seems we belong to no one.
We are out of history's singular lens.
For hours we serve no state, no master.

68

THE POET AS MOTHER

I'm a riddle in nine syllables,
An elephant, a ponderous house,
A melon strolling on two tendrils.
—SYLVIA PLATH, "METAPHORS"

IN "PORTRAIT OF the Artist as Mother," the concluding sequence of her book *Four Testimonies,* Kate Daniels explores with haunting exactitude her dual roles as both a poet and a mother. The poignant twenty-poem sequence begins appropriately enough with "Genesis 1: 28" ("In the dank clarity of the Green Line tunnel, / we hatched our plan—to grow a creature / from those nights of love, those afternoons / of thick scents, those liquid mornings") and it concludes with a mother's grateful meditation on coming home to her own growing children. The poem "Prayer for My Children" begins with a singer's defiant bravado in the first stanza—*Je regret rien*—that turns into something sweeter and more maternal in the explanatory second section, which hinges on the word *because.*

PRAYER FOR MY CHILDREN

I regret nothing.
My cruelties, my betrayals
of others I once thought
I loved. All the unlived
years, the unwritten
poems, the wasted nights
spent weeping and drinking.

No, I regret nothing
because what I've lived

has led me here, to this room
with its marvelous riches,
its simple wealth—
these three heads shining
beneath the Japanese lamp, laboring
over crayons and paper.
These three who love me
exactly as I am, precisely
at the center of my ill-built being.
Who rear up eagerly when I enter,
and fall down weeping when I leave.
Whose eyes are my eyes.
Hair, my hair.
Whose bodies I cover
with kisses and blankets.
Whose first meal was my own body.
Whose last, please God, I will not live
to serve, or share.

I've been struck by the way that in recent years so many female poets
have claimed motherhood as one of the natural rights (rites) and subjects
of their poetry. There is a kind of underground ancestry for this claim.
Anne Bradstreet, the Puritan mother of American poetry, initiated the
subject with her splendid poem "Before the Birth of One of Her Children," which expresses her fear of death in childbirth. Poets write from
the body, and in her last major poems, "Hermetic Definition" and "Winter Love," H. D. mystically identifies the art of writing with the act of
giving birth, a connection also made by Sylvia Plath in "Metaphors."

Labor may also turn into joy. There's a jaunty, verbally packed
poem about nursing in Kathleen Ossip's delightful first book, *The
Search Engine,* which won the APR/Honickman first book prize:

NURSLING

Over there, a fly buzzed—bad.
All ours: the bra, the breast, the breeze.

Starlet of the reciprocal gaze.
Something about her rhymed like mad.

And ours the sigh, the suck, the sing.
We forgave everything we could.
Ravenous palmist. I'm gone for good.
At last I gauged the brash, brash spring.

The skin fiend folded like a fawn.
Torso Magellan. Time's own nub.
Here at the center of the dimmest bulb.
A mouth hovered before latching on.

69.

ALLEN GROSSMAN

Persons write poetry for their mothers.

IN HIS WONDERFULLY stimulating critical book *The Sighted Singer: Two Works on Poetry for Readers and Writers,* Allen Grossman suggests that his poetry continues, in a very literal way, the speech of his mother. He insists that his poems pick up at the exact place where his mother's voice leaves off. They complete the sentences, the thoughts, she started to utter but could not herself conclude.

I would add to this that Grossman's poetry seems haunted by the Freudian idea that a son's poetic work should fulfill his mother's spoken (and unspoken) desires. He prolongs her will. He carries out her dreams. He inscribes her phantasmal longings for a golden world, remaking them in the process. Or as he formulates it: "My poetry is a direct consequence of a motive as intimate and necessary to me as life itself, to construct a world consistent with the desire of a world which I encountered in the heart and soul of my mother."

One key implication of Grossman's thinking is that poetry originates not with ourselves but with our mothers, who first gave us speech, the texture of sounds, our mother tongue. They gave us the words that became our world and, in the process, they sentenced us to ourselves. We are beholden to those who came before us, who gave us life itself. Poetry has a deep maternal source in a language that fundamentally voices itself through us.

Grossman believes that poetry sustains its power because it is the speech not of just one person, but of a force that is even greater than the individual. The maternal origin points to the "source of the world, the deep source of art, the point of intersection between nothing and something; both for myself as an individual, as the mother is, and myself as the member of a cosmos which did itself have a beginning." The mother is both an individual person and a larger principle of origin. He thus considers it a commonplace that people—"persons"—write poetry for their mothers.

Grossman's explicitly maternal poem "The Runner" is striking for the way the absent mother summoned up by thought becomes in the end an uncanny figure, an irrepressible shadow presence. The poem asserts a confidence in the continuity of things, a confidence that is expressed as an ongoingness, "a hope in the everlasting and never-ending relationship between this man and his mother."

THE RUNNER

The man was thinking about his mother
And about the moon.

It was a mild night.
He was running under the stars. The moon
Had not risen,

but he did not doubt it would
Rise as he ran.

Small things crossed the road
Or turned uneasily on it. His mother
Was far away, like a cloud on a mountain
With rainy breasts. The man was not a runner
But he ran with strength.

After a while, the moon
Did rise among the undiminished stars,
And he read as he ran the stone night-scripture
Of the moon by its own light.

Then his mother
Came and ran beside him, smelling of rain;
And they ran on all night, together,
Like a man and his shadow.

70

STANLEY KUNITZ

To find the father is to find oneself.

THE QUEST FOR the lost father is one of the driving motifs of Stanley Kunitz's work. It gives his poetry an elemental shock, a grounding truth, and takes on archetypal status. As he first put it in *Intellectual Things* (1930): "Let sons learn from their lipless fathers how / Man enters hell without a golden bough" ("The Lesson").

Kunitz never knew his father, who committed suicide six weeks before his son was born. It was a grave and heartbreaking prenatal loss. His mother obliterated every trace of her dead husband ("my mother's breast was thorny, / and father I had none," Kunitz has one character sing out), and her silence created an irresolvable sense of mystery that permeated his childhood.

Kunitz took up his central subject in earnest in his groundbreaking second book, *Passport to War* (1944). The key poems are "Night Letter" ("Pardon," I plead, clutching the fragile sleeve / Of my poor father's ghost returned to howl / His wrongs"), "Father and Son" ("'Father,' I cried, 'Return! You know / the way. I'll wipe the mud stains from your clothes; / No trace, I promise, will remain'"), "The Hemorrhage," "The Harsh Judgment," and "The Guilty Man," which concludes with an address:

> Father, the darkness of the self goes out
> And spreads contagion on the flowing air.
> I walk obscurely in a cloud of dark:
> Yea, when I kneeled, the dark kneeled down with me.

Touch me: my folds and my defenses fall;
I stand within myself, myself my shield.

Kunitz's sense of a search for a father who can never be found reached its apex in *The Testing-Tree* (1971), which I still consider one of his finest and most translucent books. "The Portrait" is hauntingly explicit:

> My mother never forgave my father
> for killing himself,
> especially at such an awkward time
> and in a public park,
> that spring
> when I was waiting to be born.
> She locked his name
> in her deepest cabinet
> and would not let him out,
> though I could hear him thumping.
> When I came down from the attic
> with the pastel portrait in my hand
> of a long-lipped stranger
> with a brave moustache
> and deep brown level eyes,
> she ripped it into shreds
> without a single word
> and slapped me hard.
> In my sixty-fourth year
> I can feel my cheek
> still burning.

"To find the father is to find oneself," Kunitz once told an interviewer. "And to become a father is to reenact an archetypal mystery. That's to become part of a majestic drama." Kunitz best enacts the paternal drama in his nine-part poem "Journal for My Daughter." "Your turn. Grass of confusion," he declares at the outset: "You say you had a father once: / his name was absence. / He left, but did not let you go." Yet the poet lets go of his role as a lost son long enough to waken to another role, a glittering new world of responsibility. I especially love the way the final section of the poem turns to Coleridge:

> The night when Coleridge,
> heavy-hearted,
> bore his crying child outside,
> he noted
> that those brimming eyes
> caught the reflection
> of the starry sky,
> and each suspended tear
> made a sparkling moon.

71

CHILDHOOD

. . . that double-headed monster of damnation and salvation—Time.
—SAMUEL BECKETT, *PROUST*

EVER SINCE William Wordsworth, childhood has been a crucial, dangerous, and perhaps inevitable subject for poetry. Rainer Maria Rilke, for example, asserted that childhood is one of poetry's two inexhaustible sources (the other was dreams). I've always been partial to poems that travel a long way back into unconscious memories, that return to the deep, as opposed to the recent, past, such as Randall Jarrell's "Thinking of the Lost World" and Elizabeth Bishop's masterpiece "In the Waiting Room." These poems are empowered by what Marcel Proust called involuntary memory, that which is spontaneously given back to us, as if by magic, unconsciously. Involuntary memory is triggered by something that has talismanic power: a petite madeleine, a chord of music, the sight of a boy breaking down in tears.

Time may be the subject of most poems, but it takes on particular poignancy in poems of childhood, which are so often about what is lost and found. There is always a strategic decision about tense in such poems. Thus, some begin in the past and stay there, such as Theodore Roethke's anthology piece "My Papa's Waltz"; some begin in the present and then turn to the past, such as Gerald Stern's startling one-sentence lyric "The Dancing"; and some begin in the present, turn to the past, and then come back to the present, such as Robert Hayden's haunting crisis lyric "The Whipping":

> The old woman across the way
> is whipping the boy again

and shouting to the neighborhood
    her goodness and his wrongs.

Wildly he crashes through elephant ears,
    pleads in dusty zinnias,
while she in spite of crippling fat
    pursues and corners him.

She strikes and strikes the shrilly circling
    boy till the stick breaks
in her hand. His tears are rainy weather
    to woundlike memories:

My head gripped in bony vise
    of knees, the writhing struggle
to wrench free, the blows, the fear
    worse than blows that hateful

Words could bring, the face that I
    no longer knew or loved. . . .
Well, it is over now, it is over,
    and the boy sobs in his room,

And the woman leans muttering against
    a tree, exhausted, purged—
avenged in part for lifelong hidings
    she has had to bear.

    "The Whipping" enacts a mental transport. The central memory is triggered by the speaker watching a boy being beaten across the way. He sees the boy struggling to escape, crying out, and suddenly he is involuntarily catapulted back into his own past, into the unbearable experience of being bludgeoned and screamed at by a loved one who becomes disfigured by rage. When he returns to the present tense ("Well, it is over now, it is over") he is talking about both the boy in his room and himself as a child.

Hayden complicates the moral resonance at the end of the poem with the suggestion that the woman (the neighbor in the present and, by implication, the adult in his own past) has been avenging a lifetime of secret hurts. This doesn't justify or excuse her behavior, but it does help to explain it. Hayden could only come to such an understanding through the writing of the poem itself. Some recognition and wisdom was delivered to him—and thus to us—by his descent into "that double-headed monster."

72

NAOMI NYE

as a kid he didn't pluck the wings off flies
tie tin cans to cats' tails
lock beetles in matchboxes
or stomp anthills
he grew up
and all those things were done to him
I sat at his deathbed
he said to read him a poem
about the sun and the sea . . .
    —Nazim Hikmet, "The Optimist"

THE POET Naomi Shihab Nye resolutely holds on to the upbeat, un-cynical notion that lyric poetry nourishes intimacy and fosters understanding, that human connections are more powerful and enduring than cultural differences. A high-spirited and indefatigable anthologist of work for preteens and young adults, Nye writes and edits with a cosmopolitan sensibility fueled by a pragmatic American optimism, which is one of our birthrights. "We must remember," she insists, "that the one flag we all share is the beautiful flag of childhood that flies with hope in every country. This is the one flag we should work to serve no matter who we are or where we live."

In 1998, Nye assembled a handsome collection of poems and paintings from the Middle East entitled *The Space Between Our Footsteps,* which has been abridged into a collection of poems called *The Flag of Childhood.* It is designated for eight- to twelve-year-olds and contains sixty poems, "a galaxy of seeds," which are very much worth planting.

Some of the lyrics are directly addressed to children or even to the condition of childhood itself; the title, for example, comes from the Palestinian poet Mohammed Shehadeh's "Letters to Childhood":

Forgive me, my child,
if the name I gave you
is not the name
you would have chosen . . .

All the children of the world,
in all my abodes
you are the roses in my courtyard,
the green and the fresh,
the sun and the stars,
you are the beautiful hands,
the ones who raise the flag of childhood high.

I give my life to you.
To you I write my poems.

(TRANSLATED BY AZIZ SHIBAB)

Other poems are reminiscences and memorials to what has been irretrievably lost: "Do you remember our childhood?" the singer Hamza El Din asks in "Childhood. 1948." Some of the most moving poems are addressed to the poet's own childhood self, an innocent who lives within the maturated adult and eerily returns to confront him. Hence the Syrian poet Adonis's "Beginning Speech":

That child I was
came to me once
an unfamiliar face

He said nothing—we walked
each glancing in silence at the other
One step
an alien river
    flowing.

Our common origins
  brought us together
and we separated
a forest written by the earth
and told by the seasons

Child that I once was, advance,
What now brings us together?
And what have we to say each other?

(TRANSLATED BY LENA JAYYUSI AND JOHN HEATH-STUBBS)

73.

GRANDPARENTS

GRANDFATHER

Grandfather
   advised me:
      Learn a trade.
I learned
   to sit at desk
      and condense.
No layoff
   from this
      condensery.
—LORINE NIEDECKER

THERE IS a special bond, some particular resonance, in the relationship between grandparents and grandchildren, who stand on two different sides of life. They touch each other across the decades and connect from the margins. This became evident almost a decade ago in Jason Shinder's anthology of twentieth-century American poems about grandparents entitled *Eternal Light.* It reminds us how many unlikely poems about parents and grandparents had found their way into modern and contemporary American poetry.

Some of the homegrown American moderns defied T. S. Eliot's modernist credo about impersonality and wrote personal poems of intimate relationship. These poems are entirely without sentimentality. They aren't particularly sweet and have nothing in common with greeting cards. One thinks of William Carlos Williams's "The Last Words of My English Grandmother," which exists in two strikingly different versions; of Hart Crane's "My Grandmother's Love Letters"; of Kenneth Patchen's "For the Mother of My Mother's Mother"; and of Lorine Niedecker's deceptive little poem "Grandfather," which is really an ironic pretext for a lyric about the homemade art and craft of writing poetry.

It's notable that many poems about grandparents are really poems about lineage and history, about the quest for origins, about memory and forgetfulness. Some are unnerving and come with great shocks. Thus Jane Kenyon couldn't help but wonder, in "Staying at Grandma's," "If she loved me why did she say that / two women would be grinding at the mill, / that God would come out of the clouds / when they were least expecting him, / choose one to be with him in heaven / and leave the other there alone?"

I like James Wright's sonnet "My Grandmother's Ghost," Adrienne Rich's poem of foremothers "Grandmothers," Philip Levine's "Zaydee," Lucille Clifton's "Daughters" ("woman, i am / lucille, which stands for light, / daughter of thelma, daughter / of georgia, daughter of / dazzling you"), and Garrett Kaoru Hongo's poem about how he got his middle name ("Issei: First-Generation Japanese American"). I like Richard Wilbur's "Blackberries for Amelia," in which he speaks movingly from a grandfather's point of view: "And there will come the moment to be quick / And save some from the birds, and I shall need / Two pails, old clothes in which to stain and bleed, / And a grandchild to talk with while we pick."

Poetry often gives us a rich complex of emotions, such as the joy mixed with nostalgia and grief in Li-Young Lee's poem "I Ask My Mother to Sing" from his first book, *Rose* (1986):

> She begins, and my grandmother joins her.
> Mother and daughter sing like young girls.
> If my father were alive, he would play
> his accordion and sway like a boat.
>
> I've never been in Peking, or the Summer Palace,
> nor stood on the great Stone Boat to watch
> the rain begin on Kuen Ming Lake, the picnickers
> running away in the grass.

But I love to hear it sung;
how the waterlilies fill with rain until
they overturn, spilling water into water,
then rock back, and fill with more.

Both women have begun to cry.
But neither stops her song.

74

JOHN GREENLEAF WHITTIER

. . . the Broad Church of Humanity

JOHN GREENLEAF WHITTIER's *Selected Poems*, edited by Brenda Wine-apple, will come as a revelation to anyone who was force-fed Whittier in school and never turned back to him. I had an eighth-grade teacher who recited "Snow-bound" with such dull zeal that I decided it was the most boring poem in American literature. Wineapple had a similar experience. "Later I realized I had been too young for the poem," she writes in a marvelous introduction, "and now I suspect that all the schoolchildren subjected to Whittier's assurances are themselves too callow to understand, never mind care, how memory fends off the mindlessness of winter." We had no idea Whittier was summoning a lost rural world against encroaching blankness, a world whiting out, "coldness visible."

I wish someone had pointed out to us that the nineteenth-century New England poet of place was also a fiery abolitionist and socially engaged protest poet. He was a Quaker with a wide reach and a deep social conscience. "Although I am a Quaker by birthright and sincere convictions," he said, "I am no sectarian in the strict sense of the term. My sympathies are with the Broad Church of Humanity."

Whittier is well-known as the popular Yankee storyteller of "Skipper Ireson's Ride," "Barbara Frietchie," and "Telling the Bees," but I wish more readers also knew his powerful abolitionist poems. He despised slavery, the scourge of our country ("I hate slavery in all its forms, degrees and influences," he wrote), and was threatened by mobs more than a few times. His best anti-slavery poems include the sardonic ballad "The Hunters of Men," "Songs of Slaves in the Desert," and "Ichabod!," a mournful lament and furious attack on Daniel Webster for supporting the Compromise of 1850, which included a new Fugitive Slave Law. Ichabod means "inglorious" in Hebrew, and Whittier applies it to Webster for betraying the anti-slavery cause.

Ichabod!

So fallen! so lost! the light withdrawn
    Which once he wore!
The glory from his gray hairs gone
    Forevermore!

Revile him not—the Tempter hath
    A snare for all;
And pitying tears, not scorn and wrath,
    Befit his fall!

Oh! dumb be passion's stormy rage,
    When he who might
Have lighted up and led his age,
    Falls back in night.

Scorn! Would the angels laugh, to mark
    A bright soul driven,
Fiend-goaded, down the endless dark,
    From hope and heaven!

Let not the land, once proud of him,
    Insult him now,
Nor brand with deeper shame his dim,
    Dishonored brow.

But let its humbled sons, instead,
    From sea to lake,
A long lament, as for the dead,
    In sadness make.

Of all we loved and honored, nought
   Save power remains—
A fallen angel's pride of thought,
   Still strong in chains.

All else is gone; from those great eyes
   The soul has fled:
When faith is lost, when honor dies,
   The man is dead!

Then, pay the reverence of old days
   To his dead fame;
Walk backward, with averted gaze,
   And hide the shame!

75

BASEBALL

Upon the race-course, or enjoying picnics or jigs or a good game of base-ball . . .
—WALT WHITMAN, "SONG OF MYSELF," 1855

SUMMER MEANS baseball, and American poets have been enjoying a good game for 150 years. Everyone knows and has probably recited Ernest L. Thayer's ballad of humiliating failure, "Casey at the Bat." (I remember booming out its bump-a-long rhythm at a fifth-grade assembly, literally shouting, "Oh, somewhere in this favored land the sun is shining bright; / The band is playing somewhere, and somewhere hearts are light, / And somewhere men are laughing, and somewhere children shout; / But there is no joy in Mudville—mighty Casey has struck out.") Not many baseball fans also know that baseball tends to be the favored sport of most American poets.

There are more American poems about baseball than any other sport. The nature of the game gives writers space to think and remember. It connects people to childhood. For many of us, it's a nostalgic link to our fathers. So, too, baseball, as John Crowe Ransom once suggested, has the quality of the pastoral. It sets up an ideal green island with its own rules and ritually shelters us from the encroaching outside world.

Among the moderns, Marianne Moore loved baseball and compared it to writing: "You can never tell with either / how it will go / or what you will do." William Carlos Williams's "At the Ball Game" vividly portrays a baseball crowd. Carl Sandburg's "Hits and Runs" recalls a sixteen-inning minor-league game ended by darkness ("and the umpire's voice fought in the dust for a song"). Robert Frost wrote an essay in which he declared one of his "unfulfilled promises" was to write "an epic poem about a ball batted so hard by Babe Ruth that it never came back, but got to going round and round the world like a satellite." Frost said he was "never more at home in America than at a baseball game."

Donald Hall has written the best essay about poetry and baseball, "The Poet's Game," included in *Fathers Playing Catch with Sons*. Hall thinks of baseball as "a country all to itself," and has written fine poems to inhabit it, such as "The Baseball Players" and "Old Timers' Day" ("On a green field / we observe the ruin / of even the bravest / body").

My shortlist of favorite baseball poems includes May Swenson's quirky "Analysis of Baseball," Robert Francis's study of a pitcher, Michael Collier's "The Wave," B. H. Fairchild's "Body and Soul," Robert Pinsky's "The Night Game," Michael Harper's "Archives," Linda Pastan's sly lyric "Baseball," and Richard Hugo's class-driven "Missoula Softball Tournament." The strongest poems about baseball are invariably also about something else. Here is Hugo's poignant, self-accusing villanelle "The Freaks at Spurgin Road Field," which brings up a subject that is part of the American unconscious:

> The dim boy claps because the others clap.
> The polite word, handicapped, is muttered in the stands.
> Isn't it wrong, the way the mind moves back.
>
> One whole day I sit, contrite, dirt, L. A.
> Union Station, '46, sweating through last night.
> The dim boy claps because the others clap.
>
> Score, 5 to 3. Pitcher fading badly in the heat.
> Isn't it wrong to be or not be spastic?
> Isn't it wrong, the way the mind moves back.
>
> I'm laughing at a neighbor girl beaten to scream
> by a savage father and I'm ashamed to look.
> The dim boy claps because the others clap.

The score is always close, the rally always short.
I've left more wreckage than a quake.
Isn't it wrong, the way the mind moves back.

The afflicted never cheer in unison.
Isn't it wrong, the way the mind moves back
to stammering pastures where the picnic should have worked.
The dim boy claps because the others clap.

76

THE AMERICAN PROSE POEM

The other harmony of prose
—John Dryden

THE PROSE POEM is a poem written in prose rather than verse, which makes it a weird hybrid, an anomalous genre. It avails itself of the elements of prose while foregrounding the devices of poetry. Prose poems work by the sentence rather than the line, the paragraph instead of the stanza, and yet they insistently define themselves as poems, which gives them an air of rebelliousness, a sense of breaking loose from old-fashioned strictures. Still, these compulsively modern creatures may look like prose, but they think metaphorically, like poetry.

The French writer Aloysius Bertrand established the prose poem as a genre in *Gaspard de la Nuit* (1842), a book that influenced Baudelaire's *Petits poèmes en prose* (1869). Baudelaire used prose poems to rebel against the straitjacket of classical French versification. He was a master of the French alexandrine who sought liberation from it by borrowing from the realistic novel. He exploded overarching formal expectations even as he maintained a balletic sense of phrasing. He had high ambitions for the medium and wrote to a friend: "Who among us has not, in his ambitious moments, dreamed of the miracle of a poetic prose, musical without meter or rhyme, supple enough and rugged enough to adapt itself to the lyrical impulses of the soul, the undulations of the psyche, the jolts of consciousness?" Baudelaire's prose poems—along with Rimbaud's *Les Illuminations* (1886) and Mallarmé's *Divigations* (1897)—created a mixed form (part social, part transcendental) that has been widely practiced ever since.

The prose poem, which often seems like a French import, has had a strong underground American life, as David Lehman demonstrates in his striking and inclusive anthology *Great American Prose Poems.* The collection, which has an incisive introduction, begins with Emerson ("Woods, A Prose Sonnet") and Poe ("Shadow—A Parable"), picks up speed with the experimental moderns, such as Gertrude Stein (*Tender Buttons*) and William Carlos Williams (*Kora in Hell*), and hits a high mark in the 1960s and 1970s with quasi-surrealist work by W. S. Merwin, John Ashbery, James Wright, and Mark Strand, among others. "The prose poem is the result of two contradictory impulses, prose and poetry, and therefore cannot exist, but it does," as Charles Simic cleverly puts it. "This is the sole instance we have of squaring the circle."

Great American Prose Poems is filled with surprises, such as Emma Lazarus's "The Exodus (August 3, 1942)" and Thornton Wilder's "Sentences." Here is a favorite by Russell Edson, who has devoted himself exclusively to writing parable-like prose poems for almost forty years. Edson has always sought what he calls "a poetry freed from the definition of poetry, and a prose free of the necessities of fiction." I first discovered "A Performance at Hog Theater" in his book *The Childhood of an Equestrian* (1973), which has now been incorporated into his retrospective volume *The Tunnel: Selected Poems* (1994). Edson's subterranean laughter often works by crossing the boundaries between human beings and animals.

A PERFORMANCE AT HOG THEATER

There was once a hog theater where hogs performed as men, had men been hogs.

One hog said, I will be a hog in a field which has found a mouse which is being eaten by the same hog which is in the field and which has found the mouse, which I am performing as my contribution to the performer's art.

Oh let's just be hogs, cried an old hog.

And so the hogs streamed out of the theater crying, only hogs, only hogs . . .

77

WILLIAM CARLOS WILLIAMS

It is difficult
to get the news from poems
yet men die miserably every day
for lack
of what is found there.

THERE IS a deceptively modest little poem by William Carlos Williams called "The Banner Bearer." One sentence long, twelve lines and thirty-two words in its entirety, "The Banner Bearer" is a good example of the short poems that Williams wrote in the 1930s and 1940s as part of his ongoing, experimental search for a new American measure:

> In the rain, the lonesome
> dog, idiosyn-
> cratically, with each
> quadribeat, throws
>
> out the left fore-
> foot beyond
> the right intent, in
> his stride,
>
> on some obscure
> insistence—from bridge-
> ward going
> into new territory.

Rhythmically speaking, this poem has an eccentric but sure sense of pacing and motion, a sly timing, an idiosyncratic certainty. I like the way the rhythm of each individual line builds into the rhythm of each quatrain, the way the rhythm of the stanzas enlarges into the fresh, offbeat music of the poem itself. In a way, Williams uses enjambment to enact both doubt and certainty, the mind hesitant and determined. He establishes and then blocks the integrity of individual lines (each new line hesitating over and qualifying the last, somehow pushing the poem forward) until the lineation itself mirrors the dog's motion, its jerky and insistent momentum. The dog seems to me an emblem and figure of the American poet—eccentric, lonesome, determined—setting off into new territory. In this sense, "The Banner Bearer" is an ars poetica. It also provides a good example of what Ezra Pound called the "volts, jerks, sulks, balks, outblurts and jump-overs" of Williams's style.

That style is very much on display in Robert Pinsky's edition of Williams's *Selected Poems* (The Library of America, 2004). Dr. Williams once noted that "free verse is a misnomer" since "all verse must be governed," and he spent much of his poetic life searching for a new governing principle and measure—an American poetry equal to American life. He provided modern American poetry with an idiom—the music of speech, what Marianne Moore calls "the accuracy of the vernacular." Time and again he argued that "we've got to *begin* by stating that we speak (here) a distinct, separate language in a present (new era) and that it is NOT English." In addition to the emancipation of American speech, he gave us a particular way of thinking by the line. Williams is a poet of relative—as opposed to absolute—order. His lineation is organic, free-flowing, controlled. He created a method of breaking lines that mirrors perception and shows the mind at work.

Emerson told the American poet to "ask the fact for the form," and Williams had an Emersonian genius for melding form and content. His search for a new line, relatively determined, was part of his search for a new subject matter. His achievement was to make his poems out of the process, the quest. It was his deep conviction that we live in a new world and need a form of poetry equal to reality.

78

AMY LOWELL

You are ice and fire.

AMY LOWELL'S POETRY has been underestimated for most of the past seventy-five years. It has been all too easily dismissed, sometimes insulted, often ignored. Lowell's name usually comes up in histories of modernism through a series of anecdotes; one hears of the obese, cigar-smoking Boston Brahmin, the literary impresario condescended to by Pound, who dubbed her assimilation of imagist poetry "Amygism," and of the omnipresent reader and lecturer, a sort of popular barker for the new modern poetry. Eliot called her a "demon saleswoman." Van Wyck Brooks wrote that "she whizzed and she whirred, and she rustled and rumbled, and she glistened and sparkled and blazed and blared." In his poem "Dinner Call," her friend John Brooks Wheelwright teased that she was "the Biggest Traveling One-Man Show since Buffalo Bill caught the Midnight Flyer to Contact Mark Twain." Otherwise, this modernist dynamo has been relegated to literary footnotes.

Until recently, most anthologies of American poetry have tended to pick out one of Lowell's best-known pieces, usually "Patterns," and left it at that. The feminist literary scholars Adrienne Munich and Melissa Bradshaw have set out to rectify the situation in two valuable books. One is a much needed *Selected Poems,* which provides a solid, representative sampling of Lowell's work; the other is a collection of essays—*Amy Lowell, American Modern*—by a wide, transatlantic group of literary critics and scholars. Taken together, these companion volumes should help bring into focus a key body of modern work.

Lowell (1874–1925) was an autodidact who started writing poetry in her late twenties—a performance by the Italian actress Eleonora

Duse inspired her calling—and soon was making up for lost time with a vigorous self-education in poetry. She published six books of poems between 1912 and 1925. Three additional collections appeared after her untimely death. She also should be remembered for her dynamic essays, mostly defenses of the new poetry, as well as her passionate two-volume biography of John Keats.

Munich and Bradshaw have divided Lowell's work into four categories, from the most traditional to the most experimental. Her greatest contribution to our poetry is her exuberant work in free verse, or what she preferred to call "Cadenced Verse." "Cadence is rhythm," Lowell wrote. "Modern *vers libre*, far from being non-rhythmical as some people have supposed is entirely based upon rhythm. Its rhythms differ from those of metre by being less obvious and more subtle, but rhythm is, nevertheless, the very ground and root of its structure."

Lowell is most moving as a poet of Eros. She was in love with the actress Ada Dwyer Russell, whom she first met in 1909. As Lillian Faderman points out in a revealing essay in *American Modern*, Lowell's lesbian love poems "comprise one of the most detailed records in literature of an emotional and erotic relationship between two women." I especially recommend such telling short lyrics as "Aubade," "The Giver of Stars," "Venus Transiens" ("Tell me / Was Venus more beautiful / Than you are"), "A Decade," "Opal," "Madonna of the Evening Flowers," and "The Taxi":

> When I go away from you
> The world beats dead
> Like a slackened drum.
> I call out for you against the jutted stars
> And shout into the ridges of the wind.
> Streets coming fast,
> One after the other,
> Wedge you away from me,
> And the lamps of the city prick my eyes
> So that I can no longer see your face.
> Why should I leave you,
> To wound myself upon the sharp edges of the night?

79

GEORGE OPPEN

True seeing is an act of love.

GEORGE OPPEN (1908–1984) is widely known as an Objectivist poet, but he was also an American solitary, akin to Edward Hopper. There is enormous human loneliness at the heart of Oppen's scrupulously crafted poems, which are devoted to precision, accuracy, and clarity. "I have not and never did have any motive of poetry / But to achieve clarity," he declared in "Route."

The massive solitude in Oppen's work, wholly devoid of Romantic despair, seems an intrinsic part of his recognition that the earth itself can never be known. "The self is no mystery," he writes, "the mystery is / That there is something for us to stand on." Oppen treats matter as impenetrable; it cannot be reduced to "meaning" or recovered through language. "Words cannot be wholly transparent," he says, "and that is the 'heartlessness' of words." The logical steps to individual isolation are precisely set forth in "Parousia":

> Impossible to doubt the world: it can be seen
> And because it is irrevocable
>
> It cannot be understood, and I believe that fact is lethal
>
> And man may find his catastrophe,
> His Millennium of obsession.

In the failure of understanding, all the poet can affirm is, "We want to be here."

Oppen's poems participate in what he calls "the life of the mind" in order to point his readers beyond their own consciousness. The quest in his work is for clarity in relationship, for the "this in which," the determination of the human in relation to the Other. His ethical imperative is to reach for the actual, to go through what Heidegger calls "the arduous path of appearance." Oppen characteristically treats language with circumspection and distrust, questioning the ability of words to escape their contemporary abasement and once more render what it is "out there," to name the world.

Oppen's self-reflexive poetry of consciousness strives to restore meaning to language by faithfully using it to refer outward to a world of things. Power presides in his hard confrontation with the realm of external particulars. As he says in "Route": "I might at the top of my ability stand at a window / and say, look out; out there is the world."

Oppen's radiant poem "Psalm" can be found both in his generous *New Collected Poems,* capably edited by Michael Davidson, and in Robert Creeley's spare edition of *Selected Poems.* The epigraph to Oppen's poem comes from a phrase by Thomas Aquinas, *Veritas sequitur esse rei* (Truth follows from the being of things).

PSALM

Veritas sequitur . . .

In the small beauty of the forest
The wild deer bedding down—
That they are there!

Their eyes
Effortless, the soft lips
Nuzzle and the alien small teeth
Tear at the grass

The roots of it
Dangle from their mouths

Scattering earth in the strange woods.
They who are there.

                    Their paths
Nibbled thru the fields, the leaves that shade them
Hang in the distances
Of sun

                    The small nouns
Crying faith
In this in which the wild deer
Startle, and stare out.

80

YOM KIPPUR

Out of nothing I became a being,
and from a being I shall be
nothing—but until then
I rejoice, a mote in Your world,
a spark in Your seeing.
—CHARLES REZNIKOFF, "MEDITATIONS ON THE FALL AND WINTER HOLIDAYS"

YOM KIPPUR, the Day of Atonement, is the supreme festival and the most important day in the Jewish liturgical year. It is a day for "afflicting the soul" by fasting, for asking forgiveness from one another and confessing iniquity, for reconciliation with one's God. A verse in Leviticus conveys its essence: "For on this day shall atonement be made for you, to cleanse you; from all your sins shall ye be clean before the Lord."

Yom Kippur has always been a rich terrain for Jewish writers, but secular modern and contemporary American Jewish poets have given the subject a particular metaphorical resonance. They seize the holiday as an opportunity to meditate about forgiveness and unrepentance, or about the rival claims of solitude and community, or about the nature of suffering and affliction. For example, in "Yom Kippur 1984," a key poem from one of her finest collections, *Your Native Land, Your Life* (1986), Adrienne Rich pairs a definitive pronouncement from Leviticus ("For whoever does not afflict his soul throughout this day, shall be cut off from his people") with a contrary assertion by the isolationist California poet Robinson Jeffers ("I drew solitude over me, on the long shore"), and then raises a series of urgent questions about identity and difference:

What is a Jew in solitude?
What would it mean not to feel lonely or afraid

far from your own or those you have called your own?
What is a woman in solitude: a queer woman or man?
In the empty street, on the empty beach, in the desert
what in this world as it is can solitude mean?

Rich writes here as a stranger far from home, a Jew in a Christian country, a queer woman in a straight world, who finds herself alone at the far edge of the continent. She craves separateness yet needs connection. "This is the day of atonement," she declares outright, "but do my people forgive me?" "If a cloud knew loneliness and fear," she hauntingly confesses, "I would be that cloud."

My own shortlist of good contemporary Yom Kippur poems includes part two of Charles Reznikoff's "Meditations on the Fall and Winter Holidays" ("If only I could write with four pens between five fingers / and with each pen a different sentence at the same time— / but the rabbis say it is a lost art"); Robert Mezey's early poem for Philip Levine, "To a Friend on the Day of Atonement" ("Impenitent, we meet again"); Robin Becker's "Yom Kippur, Taos, New Mexico" ("Today all good Jews collect their crimes like old clothes / to be washed and given to the poor"); and Jacqueline Osherow's deeply humane "Yom Kippur Sonnet, with a Line from Lamentations":

Can a person atone for pure bewilderment?
For hyperbole? for being wrong
In a thousand categorical opinions?
For never opening her mouth, except too soon?
For ignoring, all week long, the waning moon
Retreating from its haunt above the local canyons,
Signaling her season to repent,
Then deflecting her repentance with a song?
Because the rest is just too difficult to face—
What we are—I mean—in all its meagerness—
The way we stint on any modicum of kindness—
What we allow ourselves—what we don't learn—
How each lapsed, unchanging year resigns us—
Return us, Lord, to you, and we'll return.

81

PSALMS

Praise him upon the loud cymbals: praise him upon
the high sounding cymbals.
—PSALM 150

I set these words beside the wind chime rusting in its box.
—BROOKS HAXTON, "MISSAL"

THE PSALMS are sacred songs or hymns. The term generally refers
to the Hebrew poems in the biblical *Book of Psalms,* which *The Ox-*
ford Companion to Music calls "the oldest and the greatest book of
songs now in use anywhere in the world." The psalms have been traditionally ascribed to King David, but David seems to be a compos-
ite author, a convenient fiction to bind together poems composed
over a period of more than five hundred years. Some seem to go as
far back as the ninth and tenth centuries B.C. The earliest manuscripts date from the ninth century B.C. in Hebrew, from the fourth
century B.C. in Latin, and from the second century B.C. in Greek,
when the *Book of Psalms,* spliced together from at least four previous
collections, took final form.

The Hebrew heading of the complete psalter found in several early
manuscripts (a psalter is a collection of psalms) is a word meaning "the
book of praises," and the psalms are ancient liturgical praise poems
with terrific performative power. Psalm 100 begins:

MAKE a joyful noise unto the LORD, all ye lands.
Serve the LORD with gladness: come before his presence with
    singing.
Know ye that the LORD he *is* God: *it is* he *that* hath made us, and
    not we ourselves; *we are* his people, and the sheep of his pasture.

The psalms have been a tremendous sourcebook for Western poets. As Donald Davie writes in the introduction to his splendid anthology *The Psalms in English,* "Through four centuries there is hardly a poet of even modest ambition who does not feel the need to try his hand at paraphrasing some part of Scripture, most often the psalms." One legacy of the psalms is what Coburn Freer calls "joyful religious play":

> All people that on earth do dwell,
>> Sing to the Lord with cheerful voice:
> Him serve with mirth, his praise forth tell,
>> Come ye before him, and rejoice.

(TRANSLATED BY WILLIAM KETHE, 1561)

Brooks Haxton's stimulating collection of poems *Uproar: Antiphonies to Psalms* is a book of fresh responses, of quirky commentaries, inspired by the traditional psalms. "I take psalms less as doctrine than as outcries," he writes in a telling preface, "and I cry back in these poems from whatever vantage I can find." Each of Haxton's dialectical poems takes off from a line in one of the psalms. He provides a wonderfully calibrated answering voice that is at times ironic about the faith of the psalmist, and at times grateful for it. These poems dwell, as he puts it, "on the tension in thought and feeling between skepticism and devotion."

GLOSS

He shall come down like rain upon the mown grass.
—PSALM 72

> One collector of the psalms
> in Hebrew says the wise king
> sings this psalm about himself;
> translators into the Greek say,

No, the father prophesies
the greatness of his son; some
in Aramaic say the good king
praised here as a king of kings
would be the One Annointed;
psalm and commentaries, all
from unknown hands, descend
through centuries like rain.
Into the living mind, out of a cloud
of hands, these blessings fall,
like rain upon the mown grass.

82

POETRY RESPONDS TO SUFFERING

Pain is human.
—WALLACE STEVENS

POETRY RESPONDS to suffering. It answers to it. But the sheer amount of suffering in the world, so much of it nameless, may also threaten to swamp and overwhelm the individual voice of the poet. This becomes an aesthetic as well as a moral problem, and it has particularly haunted late-Romantic poets with a modern sensibility, such as Charles Baudelaire and Wallace Stevens. In "A Postcard from the Volcano," for example, Stevens characterizes the poet as someone who sends a short but sublime message from the site of an enormous disaster. He speaks back to catastrophe:

> Children picking up our bones
> Will never know that these were once
> As quick as foxes on the hill;
>
> And that in autumn, when the grapes
> Made sharp air sharper by their smell
> These had a being, breathing frost;
>
> And least will guess that with our bones
> We left much more, left what still is
> The look of things, left what we felt
>
> At what we saw. The spring clouds blow
> Above the shuttered mansion-house,
> Beyond our gate and the windy sky

Cries out a literate despair.
We knew for long the mansion's look
And what we said of it became

A part of what it is . . . Children,
Still weaving budded aureoles,
Will speak our speech and never know,

Will say of the mansion that it seems
As if he that lived there left behind
A spirit storming in blank walls,

A dirty house in a gutted world,
A tatter of shadows peaked to white,
Smeared with the gold of the opulent sun.

Stevens's poem is a prophetic elegy for a civilization that will be destroyed. The poet's legacy, he suggests, his revenge on time, is to leave behind something that has survived—a work, a mere postcard that has nonetheless altered the very look of things, "what we felt / / At what we saw." Those who come after us will not recall its origins, he argues, but nonetheless will be changed by what the poet witnessed and named.

The question of how to transform agony into art, of how to turn pain into song, is at the heart of poem #10 in Mark Strand's luminous sequence *Dark Harbor*. Strand is one of our most Stevensian poets. The speaker in his poems is often haunted by what evades him—he has a dark sensibility of loss—and yet the poet himself has an uncanny gift for rendering fleeting and fugitive states of mind in stately language:

It is a dreadful cry that rises up,
Hoping to be heard, that comes to you
As you wake, so your day will be spent

In the futile correction of a distant longing.
All those voices calling from the depths of elsewhere,
From the abyss of an August night, from the misery

Of a northern winter, from a ship going down in the Baltic,
From heartache, from wherever you wish, calling to be saved.
And you have no choice but to follow their prompting,

Saving something of that sound, urging the harsh syllables
Of disaster into music. You stare out the window,
Watching the build-up of clouds, and the wind whipping

The branches of a willow, sending a rain of leaves
To the ground. How do you turn pain
Into its own memorial, how do you write it down,

Turning it into itself as witnessed
Through pleasure, so it can be known, even loved,
As it lives in what it could not be.

83

KENNETH REXROTH

I put your naked body
Between myself alone and death.

KENNETH REXROTH was eleven years old when his mother died from gangrene of the lung in 1916. They were exceptionally close, and during her final week she had long conferences with him in which she tried desperately to foresee all the contingencies of his future. She was eager for him to pursue his destiny as a writer and artist, but above all she wanted him to think for himself. "Somewhere in the back of my mind I suppose I remember it all," he confessed in his *Autobiographical Novel,* "and have even acted on it down the years."

Thirty-one years later, on the anniversary of her death, Rexroth paid moving tribute to the woman who had brought him into the world and instilled in him a fierce spirit of independence, who had initiated him into the creative realms that shaped his life. To my mind, this sensuous poem, which takes his mother's name for its title, shines with the quality of their affection. It seems reminiscent of D. H. Lawrence's elegies for his mother. And it is written in that translucent style Rexroth seems primarily to have learned by putting himself to school on the poets of the *Greek Anthology* and the T'ang Dynasty, especially Tu Fu, whom he revered. It first appeared in *The Signature of All Things* (1949), a book Sam Hamill rightly terms "one of the most beautifully conceived and executed volumes of poetry since Pound's *Cathay.*"

DELIA REXROTH

California rolls into
Sleepy summer, and the air

Is full of the bitter sweet
Smoke of the grass fires burning
On the San Francisco hills.
Flesh burns so, and the pyramids
Likewise, and the burning stars.
Tired tonight, in a city
Of parvenus, in the inhuman
West, in the most blood drenched year,
I took down a book of poems
That you used to like, that you
Used to sing to music I
Never found anywhere again—
Michael Field's book, *Long Ago.*
Indeed it's long ago now—
Your bronze hair and svelte body.
I guess you were a fierce lover,
A wild wife, an animal
Mother. And now life has cost
Me more years, though much less pain,
Than you had to pay for it.
And I have bought back, for and from
Myself, these poems and paintings,
Carved from the protesting bone,
The precious consequences
Of your torn and distraught life.

I am eager to recommend *The Complete Poems of Kenneth Rexroth,* which brings together sixty years of work. Rexroth was an avant-garde classicist, a cranky autodidact with a gift for languages and a hunger for world literature. I think of him especially as a personal poet who called erotic love "one of the highest forms of contemplation," as an ecological poet who celebrated the California wilderness with great perspicuity, and a social protest poet with a spiritual dimension. He was a remarkably sensitive translator of classic Chinese and Japanese poetry, and near the end of his life invented a contemporary poet from Japan, an utterly convincing young woman named Marichiko, whose love poems have a feverish intensity. Here's one of my favorites:

VII

Making love with you
Is like drinking sea water.
The more I drink
The thirstier I become,
Until nothing can slake my thirst
But to drink the entire sea.

84

MURIEL RUKEYSER

Whatever can come to a city can come to this city

.   .   .   .

Whatever can come to a woman can come to me

.   .   .   .

Whatever can happen to anyone can happen to me

MURIEL RUKEYSER (1913–1980) was one of the most engaged and en-gaging modern American poets. "Breathe-in experience, breathe-out poetry," she wrote in her first book, *Theory of Flight* (1935), and it was a method that she followed for the rest of her life. We haven't had many American poets with such a deep moral compass, such a keen historical sensibility, and such a committed social consciousness. She wrote as a woman and identified strongly with the suffering of others. As the critic Louise Kertesz puts it in *The Poetic Vision of Muriel Rukeyser:* "No woman poet made the successful fusion of personal and social themes in a modern prosody before Rukeyser."

Rukeyser's way of blending the personal and the political looks backward to Walt Whitman and forward to Grace Paley, Jane Cooper, and Adrienne Rich, who has now edited a first-rate version of Rukeyser's *Selected Poems* for the American Poets Project at the Library of America. Rukeyser's commitments were adamant and clear. She was determined to be politically aware without any sacrifice of poetic craftsmanship. "To live as a poet, woman, American, and Jew—this chalks in my position," she wrote in 1944: "If the four come together in one person, each strengthens the other."

I have always loved the clear-eyed and stubborn ethic expressed in part VII of "Letter to the Front," which first appeared in her book *Beast in View* (1944):

To be a Jew in the twentieth century
Is to be offered a gift. If you refuse,
Wishing to be invisible, you choose
Death of the spirit, the stone insanity.
Accepting, take full life. Full agonies:
Your evening deep in labyrinthine blood
Of those who resist, fail, and resist; and God
Reduced to a hostage among hostages.

The gift is torment. Not alone the still
Torture, isolation; or torture of the flesh.
That may come also. But the accepting wish,
The whole and fertile spirit as guarantee
For every human freedom, suffering to be free,
Daring to live for the impossible.

Rukeyser had a large social vision of poetry that we still desperately need. She firmly believed that American poetry—"the outcast art"—had an important place in American culture. Poetry has been an essential resource that we have often wasted in our country. "American poetry has been part of a culture in conflict," she wrote in her prose book *The Life of Poetry,* which seems to me as valuable and important today as when she first wrote it in 1949. She goes on to define two essential features of American life:

We are a people tending toward democracy at the level of hope; on another level, the economy of the nation, the empire of business within the republic, both include in their basic premise the concept of perpetual warfare. It is the history of the idea of war that is beneath our other histories. . . . But around and under and above it is another reality. . . . This history is the history of possibility.

Rukeyser understood all too well the way that warfare has been interwoven into our history, and she was determined to oppose it with a notion of democratic possibility. Keeping that possibility alive was for her part of the hard work of poetry itself. It was a kind of prophetic imperative. Hence her tiny parable of the sixth night of creation:

The Sixth Night: Waking

That first green night of their dreaming, asleep beneath the Tree, God said, "Let meanings move," and there was poetry.

85

DAILINESS

I have wished to keep the reader in the company of flesh and blood . . .
—WILLIAM WORDSWORTH, PREFACE TO LYRICAL BALLADS (1800)

EVER SINCE WORDSWORTH, there has been a strong aesthetic impulse to bring lyric poetry closer to everyday experience, to put it in touch with something humble and quotidian, to seek out what is extraordinary in ordinary life. This is accompanied by a keen interest in the local and vernacular, in the way that people actually speak, in what Robert Frost called "sentence-sounds." "They are," he said, "gathered by the ear from the vernacular and brought into books." Wordsworth himself spoke of "fitting to metrical arrangement a selection of the real language of men in a state of vivid sensation."

This Wordsworthian impulse is wonderfully expressed through Randall Jarrell's sonnetlike poem "Well Water," which has a fluent blank-verse rhythm and a sly circular motion:

> What a girl called "the dailiness of life"
> (Adding an errand to your errand. Saying,
> "Since you're up. . . ." Making you a means to
> A means to a means to) is well water
> Pumped from an old well at the bottom of the world.
> The pump you pump the water from is rusty
> And hard to move and absurd, a squirrel-wheel
> A sick squirrel turns slowly, through the sunny
> Inexorable hours. And yet sometimes
> The wheel turns of its own weight, the rusty

Pump pumps over your sweating face the clear
Water, cold, so cold! you cup your hands
And gulp from them the dailiness of life.

The hours *are* inexorable, and we might say that the poem celebrating "the dailiness of life" is often challenged and even powered by
a terrible feeling of transience, by a sense of what is passing and past.
It is deepened by the presence of death. The feeling of what we need
to cherish in ordinary life is also beautifully expressed in the title poem
of Marie Howe's *What the Living Do*. The entire book is informed by
the death of a beloved brother who, in his dying, teaches those around
him—teaches us—how to live.

WHAT THE LIVING DO

Johnny, the kitchen sink has been clogged for days, some utensil
    probably fell down there.
And the Drano won't work but smells dangerous, and the crusty
    dishes have piled up

waiting for the plumber I still haven't called. This is the everyday
    we spoke of.
It's winter again: the sky's a deep headstrong blue, and the sunlight
    pours through

the open living room windows because the heat's on too high in
    here, and I can't turn it off.
For weeks now, driving, or dropping a bag of groceries in the
    street, the bag breaking,

I've been thinking: This is what the living do. And yesterday,
    hurrying along those
wobbly bricks in the Cambridge sidewalk, spilling my coffee down
    my wrist and sleeve,

I thought it again, and again later, when buying a hairbrush: This
    is it.
Parking. Slamming the car door shut in the cold. What you called
    that yearning.

What you finally gave up. We want the spring to come and the
    winter to pass. We want
whoever to call or not call, a letter, a kiss—we want more and
    more and then more of it.

But there are moments, walking, when I catch a glimpse of myself
    in the window glass,
say, the window of the corner video store, and I'm gripped by a
    cherishing so deep

for my own blowing hair, chapped face, and unbuttoned coat that
    I'm speechless:
I am living, I remember you.

86

JOHN BERRYMAN

a human American man

JOHN BERRYMAN has one of the most idiosyncratic voices in American poetry. That voice, which is everywhere on display in a fresh *Selected Poems,* capably edited by Kevin Young, is by turns quirky and whimsical, brilliantly learned and painfully mannered, smart-alecky and anguished. Berryman combined a passionate, disruptive syntax with an irreverent blend of highbrow and lowbrow dictions—part Shakespeare, part minstrel show, part baby talk. Who could have predicted such a salty, ostentatious, and exaggerated comic style—or known that it would come to seem so intensely literary and inevitably American? Imagine Emily Dickinson crossed with Bessie Smith and Groucho Marx. The results, to use one of Berryman's favorite words, are "delicious."

No significant American poet is funnier, though the comedy is nervous and limned with sadness. ("Life, friends, is boring. We must not say so.") When I was in school my friends and I followed the antic doings of the ironic hero of *The Dream Songs*—huffy, unappeasable Henry ("an old Pussycat")—the way popular-culture addicts followed the soaps, episode by episode. We were amazed by the way that "Homage to Mistress Bradstreet" created an imaginary dialogue between two poets across the centuries. Who else would have turned to a Puritan writer he was summoning out of the past and declared, "I *want* to take you for my lover"? We didn't yet recognize the dark truth of Berryman's underlying subject, which was, as he said, "the almost insuperable difficulty of writing high verse in a land that cared and cares so little for it."

We were stunned, too, by *Berryman's Sonnets,* which showed the poet under obsessive emotional pressure "crumpling a syntax with a sudden need." The critics blasted *Love & Fame* and *Delusions, etc.,* but we regaled one another with "It is supernal what a youth can take" and "All the black same I dance my blue head off." We applauded when he fought back with "Defensio in Extremis":

> I said: Mighty men have encamped against me,
> and they have questioned not only the skill of my defences
> but my sincerity.
> Now, Father, let them have it.

In his last books Berryman spoke with unadorned directness and a certain exhibitionist glee in his wayward past. He wrote religious poems, such as "Eleven Addresses to the Lord" and "Opus Dei," in which he put himself "under new management" by embracing a "God of rescue." One felt him standing, guilt-ridden and amazed, before the eternal. He also wrote needy, grief-stricken poems that one still returns to late at night. Such lyrics as "He Resigns," "Henry by Night," and "Henry's Understanding" have a terrifying clarity and simplicity. They have a dark vulnerability and honesty, a wounded splendor.

HENRY'S UNDERSTANDING

> He was reading late, at Richard's, down in Maine,
> aged 32? Richard & Helen long in bed,
> my good wife long in bed.
> All I had to do was strip & get into my bed,
> putting the marker in the book, & sleep,
> & wake to a hot breakfast.

> Off the coast was an island, P'tit Manaan,
> the bluff from Richard's lawn was almost sheer.
> A chill at four o'clock.
> It only takes a few minutes to make a man.

A concentration upon now & here.
Suddenly, unlike Bach,

& horribly, unlike Bach, it occurred to me
that *one* night, instead of warm pajamas,
I'd take off all my clothes
& cross the damp cold lawn & down the bluff
into the terrible water & walk forever
under it out toward the island.

87

ROBERT PENN WARREN

We must learn to live in the world.

ROBERT PENN WARREN's late poetry is his most enduring work. It has great spiritual earnestness, deep tragic grandeur and joy. Warren was at heart a seeker, and poetry was for him a form of exploration. He considered himself a "yearner," a modern man who longed for a beyond in which he could not believe. His biographer Joseph Blotner rightly called him a "man of religious temperament without religious faith."

Warren identified himself as a naturalist, yet his work continually pushes against mortal limits. It seeks sublime heights, "altitudes and extensions." His most emblematic figure is the evening hawk, which he identified with his own poetic vision. ("I saw / The hawk shudder in the high sky.") He was talking to himself as well as to others when he said that we have to figure out how to live in the world. As he eloquently formulated it in "Masts at Dawn": "We must try / To love so well the world that we may believe, in the end, in God."

Many of Warren's best poems take place in the middle of the night, at the hour of epiphany. He often presents himself as a man standing on the lawn at night, staring into the sky, asking eternal questions, seeking answers that never come. He asked, "Why have I wandered the asphalt of midnight and not known why?"

> Yes, why, all the years, and places, and nights, have I
> Wandered and not known the question I carried?
> And carry?

He was tormented by Pascal's infinite starry spaces and typically remembered: "So starward I stared / To the unnamed void where Space and God / Flinch to come."

Warren's late flowering lasted from 1966 to 1986. It began when he was sixty-one years old and did not let up until three years before his death. Harold Bloom compares Warren's poetic renascence to the final phases of Thomas Hardy, William Butler Yeats, and Wallace Stevens. Warren's outpouring began with the lyrics in *Incarnations* and reached sweeping heights with the narrative poem *Audubon: A Vision*. The splendors unfolded as *Or Else; Can I See Arcturus From Where I Stand?; Now and Then; Being Here; Rumor Verified; Chief Joseph of the Nez Perce;* and *Altitudes and Extensions.*

Here is Warren's most tender poem of old age:

AFTER THE DINNER PARTY

You two sit at the table late, each, now and then,
Twirling a near-empty wine glass to watch the last red
Liquid climb up the crystalline spin to the last moment when
Centrifugality fails: with nothing now said.

What is left to say when the last logs sag and wink?
The dark outside is streaked with the casual snowflake
Of winter's demise, all guests long gone home, and you think
Of others who never again can come to partake

Of food, wine, laughter, and philosophy—
Though tonight one guest has quoted a killing phrase we owe
To a lost one whose grin, in eternal atrophy,
Now in dark celebrates some last unworded jest none can know.

Now a chair scrapes, sudden, on tiles, and one of you
Moves soundless, as in hypnotic certainty,
The length of table. Stands there a moment or two,
Then sits, reaches out a hand, open and empty.

How long it seems till a hand finds that hand there laid,
While ash, still glowing, crumbles, and silence is such
That the crumbling of ash is audibile. Now naught's left unsaid
Of the old heart-concerns, the last, tonight, which

Had been of the absent children, whose bright gaze
Over-arches the future's horizon, in the mist of your prayers.
The last log is black, while ash beneath displays
No last glow. You snuff candles. Soon the old stairs

Will creak with your grave and synchronized tread as each mounts
To a briefness of light, then true weight of darkness, and then
That heart-dimness in which neither joy nor sorrow counts.
Even so, one hand gropes out for another, again.

88

HOWARD NEMEROV

I cried because life is hopeless and beautiful.
And like a child I cried myself to sleep
High in the head of the house . . .

THE SELECTED POEMS OF HOWARD NEMEROV (2003) introduces a new generation of readers to a poet whose subversive wit and urbane intelligence burnished American poetry for more than forty years. It is a spare, judicious survey that includes selections from thirteen books, beginning with *The Image and the Law* (1947) and concluding with *Trying Conclusions* (1991). Nemerov's poems have gone out of fashion in recent years, and I hope this edition of his work helps bring back his civilized voice and temperate tone, his crafty way of thinking in poetry, of undermining assumptions, and making unforeseen connections.

Nemerov was a secular Jew with a taste for theological questions. He had a wry sense of humor and a dark skeptical intelligence. He called poems "figures of thought" and often compared them to jokes and riddles. He had a taste for paradox and courted what the critic Willard Spiegelman calls his "didactic muse." His poems tend to be lessons and explorations. They contemplate the interplay between mind and world. They delight in learning and relish wisdom.

Nemerov thought that "[p]oetry is a way of getting something right in language." He was a master of the iambic line, who believed in clarity and tended to the plain style, though he once told me that he didn't think his work was quite as "plain" as all that. He could turn thinking itself into moments of high lyricism, of physical attainment, as in the last stanza of "The Blue Swallows":

> O swallows, swallows, poems are not
> The point. Finding again the world,

That is the point, where loveliness
Adorns intelligible things
Because the mind's eye lit the sun.

Nemerov's philosophical meditations are so adroit that it is possible for readers to miss the underlying heartbreak of his work. My favorite poem of his, "Einstein & Freud & Jack," associates an unknown figure, a sort of everyman, one of us, with two of the greatest instigators of our modernity, whom he links together in their failure to save us from ourselves, to rescue us from historical catastrophe. It was written for Allen Tate's seventy-fifth birthday.

EINSTEIN & FREUD & JACK

Death is a dead, at least that's what Freud said.
Long considering, he finally thought
Life but a detour longer or less long;
Maybe that's why the going gets so rough.

When Einstein wrote to ask him what he thought
Science might do for world peace, Freud wrote back:
Not much. And took the occasion to point out
That science too begins and ends in myth.

His myth was of the sons conspired together
To kill the father and share out his flesh,
Blood, power, women, and the primal guilt
Thereon entailed, which they must strive

Vainly to expiate by sacrifice,
Fixed on all generations since, of sons.
Exiled in London, a surviving Jew,
Freud died of cancer before the war began

That Einstein wrote to Roosevelt about
Advising the research be started that,

Come seven years of dying fathers, dying sons,
In general massacre would end the same.

Einstein. He said that if it were to do
Again, he'd sooner be a plumber. He
Died too. We live on sayings said in myths,
And die of them as well, or ill. That's that,

Of making many books there is no end,
And like it saith in the book before that one,
What God wants, don't you forget it, Jack,
Is your contrite spirit, Jack, your broken heart.

89.

KENNETH KOCH

Old age, here we are!

HOW DOES A POET write about testosterone, or psychoanalysis, or Jew-ishness? How does he think about his stammering and competitive-ness, or mention the unmentionable subject of orgasms, or summarize the decade of his fifties, which once seemed to mark the end of life, but now feels like a relatively young age to him?

The New York poet Kenneth Koch was always full of witty sur-prises, and in his book *New Addresses* (2000) he tried to solve the problem by taking on the classic poetic device of the apostrophe, or direct address. The word *apostrophe* derives from a Greek term mean-ing "to turn away," and here he turned away from the audience to speak directly to a wide range of things that figured crucially in his life.

Anything can be addressed in a poetic apostrophe: Bradstreet speaks to her book and Pound to his songs, Donne talks to Death, Schiller to Joy, Whitman to the Earth, and O'Hara to the Sun at Fire Island. I've always been moved by the unhinged grief with which Tennyson proclaims "Ring out, wild bells" in *In Memoriam*. The apos-trophe seems to take us back to the realm of magic ritual, to the ar-chaic idea that the dead can be contacted and propitiated, the absent recalled, the inanimate and nonhuman formally humanized and in-voked, called upon for help. Yet there is also something perennially fresh about celebrating the world by talking to it.

Many of Koch's direct addresses have an odd poignancy. They are clever, but with dark undertows. He asks Stammering, "Where did you come from, lamentable quality?" and declares, "Before I had a life

284

you were about to ruin my life." He tells Testosterone, "By the way you're making me anxious, which is another thing you do." He confesses to his Jewishness, "I decided to conceal / You, my you, anyway, for a while. / Forgive me for that." He expresses gratitude to Psychoanalysis, which, he says, gave him "an ideal / of conversation," an associative process that had invigorated and infiltrated all his feelings, a watch that he only reluctantly gave up after two years at five days a week:

I didn't want to leave you. I cried. I sat up.
I stood up. I lay back down. I sat. I said
But I still get sore throats and have hay fever
"And some day you are going to die. We can't cure everything."
Psychoanalysis! I stood up like someone covered with light
As with paint, and said Thank you. Thank you.

Most of Koch's new addresses speak to the past in one way or another. The nature of the apostrophe seems to have liberated him to write a strange, unforeseen, and angular kind of autobiography. The book comes to rest on a jaunty address "To Old Age":

You hurried through my twenties as if there were nowhere to look
For what you were searching for, perhaps my first trip to China.
You said, "I love that country because they love everything that's
    old
And they like things to look old—take the fortune cookie for
    example
Or the dumplings or the universe's shining face." I said,
"Chopsticks don't look old," but you were hurrying
Past me, past my love, my uncomprehended marriage, my
Nine or ten years nailed in the valley of the fools, and still you
    were not there,
Wouldn't stop there. You disappeared for a year
That I spent in Paris, came back to me in my father's face
And later in my mother's conversation. You seemed great in the
    palm trees

During a storm and lessened by the boats' preceding clops.
Looking at a gun or a tiger I never thought I was standing facing
    you.
You were elsewhere, rippling the sands or else making some boring
    conversation
Among people who scarcely knew each other. You were left by
    Shelley to languish
And by Byron and by Keats. Shakespeare never encountered you.
    What are you, old age,
That some do and some do not come to you?
Are you an old guru who won't quit talking to us in time
For us to hang up the phone? You scare me half to death
And I suppose you will take me there, too. You are a companion
Of green ivy and stumbling vines. If I could break away from you
I would, but there is no light down in that gulch there. Walk with
    me, then
Let's not be falling . . . this fiery morning. *Grand âge, nous voici!*
    Old age, here we are!

90

SWIMMING

Now I will you to be a bold swimmer . . .
—WALT WHITMAN, "SONG OF MYSELF"

WE PLUNGE into the icy river, or ride the high salty waves, or crawl across the light blue lanes. We cut the surface with our bodies and give ourselves up to the flow of the first element, water. What is swimming *like*?

Adam Zagajewski compares the breast stroke to praying. "Swimming is like prayer," he writes: "palms join and part, / join and part, / almost without end."

The next time you're hanging around a large pool, or sweating through thirty-two laps, you might think of Maxine Kumin's poem "To Swim, To Believe," in which she also finds a deeply religious element in the act of immersion, the work of swimming itself.

To Swim, To Believe

Centre College, Danville, Kentucky

The beautiful excess of Jesus on the waters
is with me now in the Boles Natatorium.
This bud of me exults, giving witness:

these flippers that rose up to be arms.
These strings drawn to be fingers.
Legs plumped to make my useful fork.

Each time I tear this seam to enter,
all that I carry is taken from me,
shucked in the dive.

Lovers, children, even words go under.
Matters of dogma spin off in the freestyle
earning that mid-pool spurt, like faith.

Where have I come from? Where am I going?
What do I translate, gliding back and forth
erasing my own stitch marks in this lane?

Christ on the lake was not thinking
where the next heel-toe went.
God did him a dangerous favor

whereas Peter, the thinker, sank.

The secret is in the relenting,
the partnership. I let my body work

accepting the dangerous favor
from this king-size pool of waters.
Together I am supplicant. I am bride.

My shortlist of fine contemporary poems about swimming includes James Merrill's "Swimming by Night" ("Without clothes, without caution // Plunging past gravity"); Michael Collier's "The
Swimmer" ("Nothing like him in Bosch or Breughel"); Gerald Stern's
"Thinking About Shelley" ("Arm over over arm I swam out into the
rain"); and William Stafford's sly parable about confronting a sudden
storm, "With Kit, Age Seven, at the Beach":

> We would climb the highest dune,
> from there to gaze and come down:
> the ocean was performing;
> we contributed our climb.
>
> Waves leapfrogged and came
> straight out of the storm.

What should our gaze mean?
Kit waited for me to decide.

Standing on such a hill,
what would you tell your child?
That was an absolute vista.
Those waves raced far, and cold.

"How far could you swim, Daddy,
in such a storm?"
"As far as was needed," I said,
and as I talked, I swam.

91

ROBERT BLY

*Some people love only money, and some people love
only eternity. I'm half-way in-between.*

THE SUFI POETS believed in a universe beyond the sensory world, a
place they called the *mundus imaginalis,* which is "a concrete spiritual
world of archetype-Figures, apparitional Forms, Angels of species and
of individuals," and it seems to me that it is there (or some place much
like it) that Robert Bly has often gone to create his best work. Bly's
poems keep opening up interior realms, like floors giving way, and
have great spiritual access. At times he is Thoreau in Minnesota,
scrupulously observing the natural world, preserving the wilderness
that is both within and without, unleashing his wrath against impe-
rial power. "The walls of my poetry are splashed with blood," he
writes in his poem "The Trap-Door," "I don't want to be inward." At
other times, he is like the fourteen-year-old Jabir the Brilliant arrang-
ing sounds so that they become holy. "Friends," he declares in the
same poem, "each day I crawl over and kiss some of the books I love."
Political outrage and spiritual reverence sit side by side in Bly's work.

These thoughts are occasioned by Bly's collection *The Night Abraham Called to the Stars* (2001), which received the Maurice English Poetry Award for a distinguished book of poems published during the
preceding calendar year by a poet over fifty. Maurice English, who was
a poet, a translator, and the director of the University of Pennsylvania
Press, had a keen intelligence and a lifelong devotion to poetry, and
Bly is a worthy recipient of an award in his honor.

Bly has often found models for his poems in other cultures, and in
this book he displays his reverence for Islamic poetry, especially the work
of Rūmī and Ḥāfeẓ, by adapting the ghazal form. He ignores some key

traditional elements of the ghazal, but he does capture its feeling of boundless surprise. What he especially loves about the form is how each stanza operates as an independent unit. The subject matter changes from stanza to stanza, which gives a sense of leaping around, of rapidly shifting landscapes. Meanings accrue through association, and there is a liberating feeling of freedom within the prescribed form.

A sacred sense of gratitude animates Bly's poems, which move fluently between the material and the ethereal. Like Abraham from the Koran, the figure he writes about so well in the title poem of his new collection, he is "a man in love with the setting stars."

THE NIGHT ABRAHAM CALLED TO THE STARS

Do you remember the night Abraham first called
To the stars? He cried to Saturn: "You are my Lord!"
How happy he was! When he saw the Dawn Star,

He cried, "You are my Lord!" How destroyed he was
When he watched them set. Friends, he is like us:
We take as our Lord the stars that go down.

We are faithful companions to the unfaithful stars.
We are diggers, like badgers; we love to feel
The dirt flying out from behind our hind claws.

And no one can convince us that mud is not
Beautiful. It is our badger soul that thinks so.
We are ready to spend the rest of our life

Walking with muddy shoes in the wet fields.
We resemble exiles in the kingdom of the serpent.
We stand in the onion fields looking up at the night.

My heart is a calm potato by day, and a weeping,
Abandoned woman by night. Friend, tell me what to do,
Since I am a man in love with the setting stars.

92

GARY SNYDER

How Poetry Comes to Me

*It comes blundering over the
Boulders at night, it stays
Frightened outside the
Range of my campfire
I go to meet it at the
Edge of the light*

For more than forty years Gary Snyder has been letting poetry bound toward him in just such a way, trusting that it waits outside in the dark landscape, getting up and going to meet it with great receptivity, entering a place where the light gives way to something strange and unknown. He is the most intimate and mindful of poets, a careful walker in the world whose most characteristic gesture has been a pellucid American speech. He is a maker of myths and texts, an observant explorer who delights in following and then leaving the ancient trail, taking the self into the wild, letting the wilderness into the open house of the self.

Here is an early poem of Snyder's that has stayed with me for thirty years. It comes from his first book, *Riprap and Cold Mountain Poems* (1959), a collection of transparent translations from the Chinese and of homemade American poems laid down carefully like rocks before the mind. It helps to know that "riprap" is a cobble of stone laid on steep slick rock to make a trail for horses in the mountains.

Riprap

Lay down these words
Before your mind like rocks.
       placed solid, by hands

In choice of place, set
Before the body of the mind
        in space and time:
Solidity of bark, leaf, or wall
        riprap of things:
Cobble of milky way,
        straying planets,
These poems, people,
        lost ponies with
Dragging saddles
        and rocky sure-foot trails.
The worlds like an endless
        four-dimensional
Game of *Go.*
        ants and pebbles
In the thin loam, each rock a word
        a creek-washed stone
Granite: ingrained
        with torment of fire and weight
Crystals and sediment linked hot
        all change, in thoughts,
As well as things.

The commitments and connections in Snyder's work are clear and precise. He is a singer of community. He speaks of three hundred million years ago and of the world right now. He writes from the American West, from the spiritual home called "Turtle Island," the name, based on creation myths, given to our continent by Native Americans. He has been instructed by the practice of Zen Buddhism; by the splendid simplicity of Japanese and Chinese poetry, especially of the T'ang Dynasty; by Ezra Pound's internationalism and William Carlos Williams's sense of the local; by Native American songs and stories; and, most of all, by rivers and mountains, by the variety and richness, the manifest transfigurations of the physical universe. "There is no single or set 'nature' either as 'the natural world' or 'the nature of things,'" he writes in the preface to *No Nature: New and Selected Poems*

(1992): "The greatest respect we can pay to nature is not to trap it, but to acknowledge that it eludes us and that our own nature is also fluid, open, and conditional."

Gary Snyder's poems are prayers that attend to our fluent natures. They honor the interwoven wholeness of the world, the ancient wisdom that can teach us how to live mindfully on our planet. "Taste all," he writes, "and hand the knowledge down."

93

DONALD JUSTICE

a love that masquerades as pure technique

DONALD JUSTICE (1925–2004) had an exacting imagination. He was a precisionist of loss, a meticulous craftsman forever thinking about the past, about vanishing American scenes and landscapes. He was born in Miami, Florida, and wrote beautifully about his native realm, summoning up luminous details from his childhood in the 1930s (one of his improvisatory poems is called "The Miami of Other Days"), evoking Depression-era America with scrupulous accuracy (another is termed "Cinema and Ballad of the Great Depression").

Justice had an elegiac imagination—the tone of his work is quiet, grave, and measured—and he approached his subjects with a deep feeling disguised as an exclusively formal interest. Influenced by Baudelaire and Stevens, he was in some ways a poet in the line of Thomas Hardy, an heir to the Southern Fugitives, a classically minded writer with a modern sensibility, a poet of forgotten worlds, which he seeks to rescue from oblivion.

A skilled and restless metricist, Justice liked to experiment with traditional forms, which he enlivened and roughened with variations. ("I like to leave a rough spot or two in handling any of the forms," he says, "a mark of authenticity.") He wrote one of the best modern pantoums ("Pantoum of the Great Depression") and two of the finest villanelles in English ("In Memory of the Unknown Poet, Robert Boardman Vaughan" and "Villanelle at Sundown"). His sestinas are models of ingenuity ("A Dream Sestina," "Sestina on Six Words by Weldon Kees," "Here in Katmandu"). In a moving elegy for his mother, "Psalm and Lament," he employs the structural strategies of the psalm—statement and reiteration—to encompass his sorrow. The first stanzas create the feeling:

> The clocks are sorry, the clocks are very sad.
> One stops, one goes on striking the wrong hours.
>
> And the grass burns terribly in the sun,
> The grass turns yellow secretly at the roots.
>
> Now suddenly the yard chairs look empty, the sky looks empty,
> The sky looks vast and empty.
>
> Out on Red Road the traffic continues; everything continues.
> Nor does memory sleep; it goes on.
>
> Out spring the butterflies of recollection,
> And I think that for the first time I understand
>
> The beautiful ordinary light of this patio
> And even perhaps the dark rich earth of a heart.

Justice showed a penchant for fragments. He treated free verse with the same rigor that he brought to traditional forms, and he experimented with chance methods, most notably in his book *Departures*. I have a special affection for his sonnets about taking piano lessons, one a portrait of his teacher, "Mrs. Snow," the other a clear-eyed and witty reminiscence—a reenactment—of being a hesitant student:

THE PUPIL

> Picture me, the shy pupil at the door,
> One small, tight fist clutching the dread Czerny.
> Back then time was still harmony, not money,
> And I could spend a whole week practicing for
> That moment on the threshold.
>   Then to take courage,

And enter, and pass among mysterious scents,
And sit quite straight, and with a frail confidence
Assault the keyboard with a childish flourish!

Only to lose my place, or forget the key,
And almost doubt the very metronome
(Outside, the traffic, the laborers going home),
And still to bear on across Chopin or Brahms,
Stupid and wild with love equally for the storms
Of C# and the calms of C.

94.

DANIEL HUGHES

He is survived by a welter of words.

THE POET Daniel Hughes, a radiant presence, left behind an enormous hole when he died in October 2003, at the age of seventy-four. He lived the majority of his adulthood in Detroit, where he had been a longstanding professor of English at Wayne State University. Hughes was deterred but not defeated by the debilitating illness of multiple sclerosis, which he suffered for forty years. All through his illness, which colonized his adulthood, he lived a pure life of the mind, and art—English Romantic poetry, Italian Renaissance painting, European classical music—was for him a kind of religion.

Dan and I taught together at Wayne in the late 1970s and the early 1980s. I have vivid memories of meeting him on the top floor of State Hall—first on his cane, then on his walker, finally in a wheelchair—and stopping to talk about poetry. He was a marvelous Shelley scholar, and the Romantics were always our touchstone. All his life he pursued the figures of Romanticism—what he called "the long chase of the Romantics"—with a kind of wild personal zeal. He took the deepest lessons of Romantic poetry to heart. He was an adept of Emily Dickinson's work. He also loved Robert Lowell's poetry, and had been good friends with John Berryman. Indeed, Berryman's dream song #35, "MLA," was dedicated to Dan and his wife, Mary, and I often used to call out the first stanza when I saw him:

> Hey, out there!—assistant professors, full,
> associates,—instructors—others—any—
> I have a sing to shay.

We are assembled here in the capital
city for Dull—and one professor's wife is Mary—
at Christmastide, hey!

The poem ends on a delicious note—"forget your footnotes on the old gentleman; / dance around Mary"—which I felt should be our theme song. Sometimes my conversations with Dan about poetry were so intense they had to be continued at his apartment in Palmer Park, which vibrated with the sound of opera blasting from the stereo. We also pored over art books and dwelt for a while together in the Italy of the mind.

Hughes published four individual collections during his lifetime: *Waking in a Tree* (1963), *Lost Title* (1974), *Falling* (1979), and *Spirit-Traps* (1984), which were then distilled and gathered into *You Are Not Stendhal,* a collection of new and selected poems (1992). His posthumous work, *Ashes & Stars,* may be his finest individual collection of all. His poems are filled with crafty ironies and witty refusals, with exact and exacting observations about the disappointments of life in a fallen time, yet they also present us with a singer who has slipped through the side door onto the main stage and sounded the flaming, reckless, operatic notes of a high splendor.

One of my favorite previous pieces, the poem "Too Noble," strikes a characteristic chord:

"Too noble," Rick said,
so we shut off the Beethoven
but still the sound
lingered about us, and lifted us
above the croissants and the jokes
we tried before we were awake.

No one's noble now—
we thought of the death of words, the slipping,
the history of disappointment,
but the sound stayed, as though the walls
claimed it.

We went for a walk in the bright morning.
The air was clarified, renewed, noble.

Hughes's poems often begin in disappointment but end on a note of noble attainment. It is as if the poet needed to overcome his own ironies to reach the state of rapture, which so called to him. He needed to be lifted up. In his poem "The Problem with Bliss," for example, he wondered if "bliss" was "one of those words gone forever":

But Campbell used it, the Upanishads use it,
and you ache toward it and speak it to yourself,
its sibilants rowing you out to the egoless sea.

Hughes's final work shimmers between the earth and the sky, between the grayness of ashes and the brightness of stars. One feels in reading him both the downward pressure of mortality and the upward swell of transcendence. Reading his last poems, I recognize that my old friend had a kind of epigrammatic mortal wisdom. He also had a spark of divinity in him. He believed that poetry itself could not be slain by time, and his own poems are filled with what Shelley called "our best and happiest moments . . . arising unforeseen and departing unbidden." He will be much missed, though his spirit lasts. It is inscribed in poetry.

95

DOROTHEA TANNING

Slept dreams, they say, take just a few seconds
no matter how long they are. Or how far

I walked on that bridge of spider silk
with the moon beside me like a friend.

Her light trapped us in a radiance of bliss so
pure, hours weren't hours, or minutes minutes

as we passed my old lecture hall, its professor
stopping in the middle of his question "Can

someone here tell me—?" to stare at us as we
floated along, my insouciance blurring a little

with a sense of guilt. Had I a right to this?
Could such joy be mine for free? . . .

AT NINETY-THREE, Dorothea Tanning, who has had a long and marvelous life as a visual artist, is our most surprising new poet. She is an audacious dreamer, and the spirit of creativity, the sheer joy of making things, is everywhere apparent in her restless, inventive, energetic, and triumphant first book of poems, *A Table of Content*.

Tanning takes her epigraph from Montaigne—"It's hard to be always the same person"—and turns it every which way. She is drawn in poetry, as in painting, to radical juxtapositions, collage-like effects, and longs for multiple lives, a multiplicity of selves. One of her characteristic signs is bliss ("Wild rapture spins over your personal landscape"), but the flip side is a sense of doomed singularity: "If it isn't too late / let me waste one day away / from my history," the speaker pleads in "Sequestrienne." "Let me see without / looking inside / at broken glass."

Tanning often draws metaphors from painting ("Oh, we were primed like canvas"), but embraces her role as wordsmith. She takes innocent pleasure in the sheer oddity of words, in the basic triggering power of the letters themselves. She probes the medium and plays with different line and stanza lengths to see what they will yield.

A Table of Content is organized around the alphabet and divided into four sections: A to G, H to O, P to S, T to W. It cleverly starts with a poem entitled "Are You?" ("Stay on the planet, if you can," the poet advises, "It isn't / all that chilly and what's more, / grows warmer by the / minute") and concludes with one called "Window Treatment" ("My windows are private-eyed," she observes. "They gape with authority: / what to let in, what to let out").

Tanning's poetry estranges reality. It has a way of being both whimsical and grave, charmingly lighthearted as well as deadly serious. It has a great deal to teach us about the nature of making art, about the life of a maker, and shines a light on our own lives. Here is a sonnet from the creative front:

REPORT FROM THE FIELD

Sublimation, a new version of piety,
Hovers the paint and gets her going.
Everything drifts, a barely heard sigh is the

Sound of wind in the next room blowing
Dust from anxiety. A favorite receptacle
Holds her breath and occasional sewing.

Only the artist will be held responsible
For something so far unsaid but true,
For having the crust to let the hysterical

Earnest of genuine feeling show through,
And watching herself in the glassy eyeing
Of *Art as seen through a hole in her shoe.*

Painter and poet, sometimes said to be lying,
Agonizingly know it is more like dying.

96

JANE MAYHALL

You think death is a nostalgic passivity;
wrong.

I'VE BEEN DEEPLY moved by the love poems—urgent, ravishing, grief-stricken—in Jane Mayhall's exceptional book *Sleeping Late on Judgment Day*. These thirty-eight poems, which constitute the second section of Mayhall's collection, celebrate her long bohemian marriage ("the bond of mystery") to Leslie George Katz. They seem poured out in a torrent, in a sudden rush of memories. At eighty-five, Mayhall has broken through a wall of silence and transformed the oceanic depths of feeling into the faithful nuances of art.

There is something wild and untamed in Mayhall's unsentimental memorial poems. She refuses easy comforts, false generalities. She is not seduced by sadness but overwhelmed by loss, ferociously recalling how her husband grappled with heavy medication and physical pain, with what in the poem "Paean" she calls "the crucifixion of dying":

> Not even
> doctors or poets were equipped to see the courage
> and congestion, as if the body were a whole
> city, in surges of wisdom and tragic scrutiny. Between
> bouts of morphine and enforced
>
> daze, he was steady. As well maintaining
> desire in the corrosion of hospitals.
> Thus counselors (protected by the rind of comic
> distance) said, "Nothing's that serious."
> No doctrine or bias can give

the glory to him. That from every portal,
the humble unreduced light outside, putting to flight
all generalities, siphoning the sun; the room,
his consciousness, I'll break
my mind to tell of.

There is something holy and crazed about an intensely personal grief. "My thoughts sway into violent, / black somnambulant, cold death / supplying the madness of your gone," Mayhall declares. But she also refuses to obliterate the agony of consciousness. The temptation is great ("Your absence is / a need to close my eyes"), but she doesn't want to numb or medicate her pain, to sleep it away. "Don't let me dream, doze and deny," she says, "like / a TV slob." Yet she feels no better off for waking. Elsewhere she defines love as "walking on broken rocks / where nobody goes."

Mayhall also refuses to let death be "the consummation of us." She is left alone, unguarded and inconsolable. "I am the slave of my ardor, nobody / knows your quality as I, who / sprang to your need," she recalls in one poem. "Our joy was Eden," she concludes in another. "But when you died, it was insane, // And nature didn't save us." The only anodyne is ardent creative work, the solace of making art, of defying time.

PAINKILLER

Ardent work is a painkiller,
like just your handwriting on a page,
and doing mathematics—that connects with central
neurological tracks, vast circulatory blood-

lights, into aphrodisiacal
forgetfulness. And the more aching a line
of poem, the more it lulls.
Intense dancers on broken toes

insist they never noticed. Like Tchaikovsky
using his tears on laboring music scores, the

melody narcotic. Or running the good
race eludes the hurt.

Mind over matter? It's the brandy gift
of life. Or from a crack in Nothingness—
creation of the world. And must have
been some backbreaking,

godless job. Enormous, long time
over-hours. Working like a dog, that
sweet analgesic postponement
of the End.

97

WILLIAM MATTHEWS

an oddball knows an oddball at forty or at 40,000
paces. Let's raise our dribbles glasses. Here's to us,
morose at dances and giggly in committee . . .

THE POET William Matthews (1942–1997), who had a lucky wit and
a startling intelligence, once offered, in characteristically ironic fashion, what he called "a short but comprehensive summary" of all the
subjects for lyric poetry:

1. I went out into the woods today and it made me feel, you
   know, sort of religious.
2. We're not getting any younger.
3. It sure is cold and lonely (a) without you, honey, or (b) with
   you, honey.
4. Sadness seems but the other side of the coin of happiness,
   and vice versa, and in any case the coin is too soon spent
   and on we know not what.

This condensed list, which comes from his essay "Dull Subjects" in his
prose book *Curiosities* (1989), is amusing not just because of its decid-
edly unromantic posture, but also because of its oddball accuracy. So,
too, it suggests that the real power of poetry lies not in subject matter, but in the capacity to transform that subject matter into language.

Matthews had a fluent capacity to think in poetry. His writing has
a conversational tone and a relaxed authority. Reading him is like
spending the evening with a deliciously intelligent friend. It may not
be the deepest experience, but it is wonderfully satisfying. He liked to
muse about jazz, food, and wine, about memory and childhood, time
and money, about language itself—three of his favorite oxymorons

were *friendly fire, famous poet,* and *common sense*—and, especially, about the daunting power of love. His editor, the poet Peter Davison, once described him as "a collector of experience, a gourmet of language, a notable expert in pleasure," who could, "without gulping, speak of 'death flickering in you like a pilot light.'" For all the ostensible variety of Matthews's different subjects, his list actually applies to his own poetry, since his work seems secretly powered by a secular but nonetheless genuine reverence for the world, by a poignant sense of aging, by the loneliness of (and within) love, and by the twin feelings of sadness and happiness, which are both so painfully fleeting, so deep and transitory.

Matthews's life's work is brought together in *Search Party: Collected Poems* (Houghton Mifflin, 2004). His writing demonstrates how ingenuity can serve emotion in poetry. One of my favorite of his poems is called simply "Grief." A public poem driven by private feeling, it moves forward by describing New York City on a recognizably snarled winter day that leaves everyone in an infernal mood. The lyric comes full circle by translating the line from Dante that serves as its epigraph. Thus the poem ends by explaining why the poet has been writing it all along. His real subject is the claim that suffering makes upon us.

GRIEF

E detto l'ho perché doler ti debbia!
—*INFERNO*, XXIV, 151

Snow coming in parallel to the street,
a cab spinning its tires (a rising whine
like a domestic argument, and then
the words get said that never get forgot),

slush and backed-up runoff waters at each
corner, clogged buses smelling of wet wool . . .
The acrid anger of the homeless swells
like wet rice. *This slop is where I live, bitch,*

a sogged panhandler shrieks to whom it may
concern. But none of us slows down for scorn;
there's someone's misery in all we earn.
But like a bur in a dog's coat his rage

has borrowed legs. We bring it home. It lives
like kin among the angers of the house,
and leaves the same sharp zinc taste in the mouth:
And I have told you this to make you grieve.

98

VIETNAM WAR POEMS

All the poet can do to-day is warn.
—Wilfred Owen

War poetry is very much on my mind these days, and recently I found myself pulling down an anthology I hadn't thought about for some time: Walter Lowenfels's *Where Is Vietnam?* I bought it in 1967 when I was seventeen years old, and it served as my introduction to many poets whose work later became important to me, such as Robert Bly, Galway Kinnell, and James Wright.

I remember how much I liked the title, which seemed apt, since most Americans didn't know where Vietnam was, just as today they probably don't know the location of Iraq. I was impressed that eighty-seven American poets, each represented by a single poem, had galvanized against the war. These antiwar poems still seem politically and historically necessary to me, though, like most protest poems, they tend to be overly didactic.

David Ignatow sets the tone with a satirical poem written during a bombing pause:

All Quiet

How come nobody is being bombed today?
I want to know, being a citizen
of this country, and a family man.
You can't take my fate in your hands,
without informing me.
I can blow up a bomb or crush a skull—
whoever started this peace

without advising me
through a news leak
at which I could have voiced a protest,
running my whole family off a cliff.

A body of stateside polemical poems (and there were key ones by
Allen Ginsberg, W. S. Merwin, Adrienne Rich, and others) eventually
joined with the poetry of returning veterans, who wrote not just in
protest against the war but also out of the trauma of combat experience. I am eager to recommend W. D. Ehrhart's *To Those Who Have
Come Home Tired* (1984) as well as his anthologies, *Carrying the Darkness* (1988) and *Unaccustomed Mercy* (1989). Bruce Weigl gives essential
testimony in *Song of Napalm* (1988), and so does Yusef Komunyakaa
in his fourth book, *Dien Cai Dau* (1988), which may be the best single
book of poems inspired—if that is the right word—by the war. Some
of the poems still leave me shaking, like this surreal one about a girl
burning:

"YOU AND I ARE DISAPPEARING"

—BJORN HAKANSSON

The cry I bring down from the hills
belongs to a girl still burning
inside my head. At daybreak
        she burns like a piece of paper.
She burns like foxfire
in a thigh-shaped valley.
A skirt of flames
dances around her
at dusk.
        We stand with our hands
hanging at our sides,
while she burns
        like a sack of dry ice.
She burns like oil on water.

She burns like a cattail torch
dipped in gasoline.
She glows like the fat tip
of a banker's cigar,
        silent as quicksilver.
A tiger under a rainbow
    at nightfall.
She burns like a shot glass of vodka.
She burns like a field of poppies
at the edge of a rainforest.
She rises like dragonsmoke
    to my nostrils.
She burns like a burning bush
driven by a godawful wind.

99.

NEW YORK CITY

In the deserts of the heart
Let the healing fountains start,
In the prison of his days,
Teach the free man how to praise.
—W. H. Auden, "In Memory of W. B. Yeats"

ONE LYRIC that often wells up in me when I come back to New York
City after a time away is Paul Goodman's poem of joyous and impatient homecoming, "The Lordly Hudson." It's not a public poem per
se, though I've thought it often in the past year, since it's infused with
such a deep American gratitude.

Goodman's poem is grounded in the spoken word ("Poetry starts
from good colloquial speech," he wrote in his splendid defense of poetry, *Speaking and Language*), but it rises almost to a chant through a
series of odd spoken repetitions. The repetitive dialogue, as well as the
imagery in this poem, makes it sound a little like an English ballad,
though the interpolations, the way the poet addresses himself, characterize the subjective personal lyric. The poem begins as a dialogue, but
it concludes as a monologue. "A monologue is not the same as talking to oneself," Goodman wrote. "It is more like daydream."

THE LORDLY HUDSON

"Driver, what stream is it?" I asked, well knowing
it was our lordly Hudson hardly flowing,
"It is our lordly Hudson hardly flowing,"
he said, "under the green-grown cliffs."

Be still, man! No one needs your passionate
suffrage to select this glory,

this is our lordly Hudson hardly flowing
under the green-grown cliffs.

"Driver! has this a peer in Europe or the East?"
"No no!" he said. Home! home!
be quiet, heart! this is our lordly Hudson
and has no peer in Europe or the East,

this is our lordly Hudson hardly flowing
under the green-grown cliffs
and has no peer in Europe or the East.
Be patient, Paul! home! home!

There have been many heartsick American poems in the last few years, and many of bewildered outrage, but only a few of these traumatized pieces have also been shocked into gratitude. One poem that shines in this regard is Deborah Garrison's "I Saw You Walking," which appears in a helpful anthology, *110 Stories: New York Writes after September 11:*

I saw you walking through Newark Penn Station
in your shoes of white ash. At the corner
of my nervous glance your dazed passage
first forced me away, tracing the crescent
berth you'd give a drunk, a lurcher, nuzzling
all corners with ill will and his stench, but
not this one, not today: one shirt arm's sheared
clean from the shoulder, the whole bare limb
wet with muscle and shining dimly pink,
the other full-sheathed in cotton, Brooks Bros.
type, the cuff yet buttoned at the wrist, a
parody of careful dress, preparedness—
so you had not rolled up your sleeves yet this
morning when your suit jacket (here are
the pants, dark gray, with subtle stripe, as worn
by men like you on ordinary days)

and briefcase (you've none, reverse commuter
come from the pit with nothing to carry
but your life) were torn from you, as your life
was not. Your face itself seemed to be walking,
leading your body north, though the age
of the face, blank and ashen, passing forth
and away from me, was unclear, the sandy
crown of hair powdered white like your feet, but
underneath not yet gray—forty-seven?
forty-eight? The age of someone's father—
and I trembled for your luck, for your broad
dusted back, half-shirted, walking away;
I should have dropped to my knees to thank God
you were alive, o my God, in whom I don't believe.

100

TOM SLEIGH

Art in the act of renovating itself always goes back to its archaic beginnings.
—GUY DAVENPORT

A SPELL IS an incantation or charm designed to produce magical effects. "It is exceedingly well / To give a common word the *spell*," the eighteenth-century poet Christopher Smart writes, punning on the word *spell*. Tribal peoples everywhere have believed that the act of putting words in a certain rhythmic order has magical potency, a power released when the words are chanted aloud. The very premise of a spell is that speech matters, that language can induce change.

Tom Sleigh's nine-part sequence "New York American Spell, 2001," which appears in his fine book *Far Side of the Earth,* is one of the most genuinely interesting, oblique, and forceful recent poems I've read. Two of the sections freely adapt spells from *The Greek Magical Papyri,* a repository of great religious literature that mainly dates from the second century B.C. to the fifth century A.D. These spells for knowledge and protection addressed to the sun god Helios take on odd relevance as Sleigh interweaves them with descriptions of looking out from the Brooklyn Bridge ("All you'd see if you were out there / Is air vanishing into clearer air") or standing in front of St. Vincent's Hospital ("A woman hugging another woman / Who was weeping blocked the sidewalk. / Nobody moved for a moment").

Here is Sleigh's "Spell Spoken by Suppliant to Helios for Protection," which has a kind of helpless poignancy in light of our dark American tragedy:

> This is the charm that will protect you, the charm
> That you must wear: Onto lime wood write

With vermilion the secret name, name of
The fifty magic letters. Then say the words:
"Guard me from every daimon of the air,
On the earth and under the earth, guard me
From every angel and phantom, every
Ghostly visitation and enchantment,
Me, your suppliant." Enclose it in a skin
Dyed purple, hang it round your neck and wear it.

The final poem in Sleigh's sequence is based on a Sumerian spell that dates to the second millennium B.C. The Sumerian text survives in cuneiform, an ancient wedge-shaped writing on clay tablets. Sleigh transcribed it from a French translation that he found in a Parisian museum, and then re-created it as a contemporary American lament, a prayer for compassion and hope:

LAMENTATION ON UR

from a Sumerian spell, 2000 B.C.

Like molten bronze and iron shed blood
    pools. Our country's dead
melt into the earth
    as grease melts in the sun, men whose
helmets now lie scattered, men annihilated

by the double-bladed axe. Heavy, beyond
    help, they lie still as a gazelle
exhausted in a trap,
    muzzle in the dust. In home
after home, empty doorways frame the absence

of mothers and fathers who vanished
    in the flames remorselessly
spreading claiming even
    frightened children who lay quiet
in their mother's arms, now borne into

oblivion, like swimmers swept out to sea
    by the surging current.
May the great barred gate
    of blackest night again swing shut
on silent hinges. Destroyed in its turn,

may this disaster too be torn out of mind.

THOMAS JAMES

The poet creates in trance as an angel, in moments of crisis as a man.
—MIGUEL HERNÁNDEZ

THOMAS JAMES (1946–1974) published one collection of poems in his lifetime. *Letters to a Stranger* (1973) is a book of dark intensities and deeply felt connections, both haunted and haunting, at once brooding, sensual, and lucid. Its poems are shapely and well fashioned, as if the poet had tested his demons by submitting them to the rigors of a formal control. These lyrics are strikingly pitched and modulated to the specifically human registers of a single speaking voice.

This is a poetry of crisis—of nervous and tensed fields, feverish hospital rooms, painful emergency wards. These intimate poems, which present themselves as "letters," are generally addressed to someone who is deeply removed and almost impossibly inaccessible: a remote reader, a blind cousin, a dying god. One of the book's most beautiful poems, "Letter to a Mute," gauges the distance exactly: "If I could reach you now, in any way / At all, I would say this to you." These communiqués attempt to cross the widest and slightest distances, the voids and gulfs between us.

Many of the poems in *Letters to a Stranger* have a slow, hallucinatory quality that one associates with a nearly complete isolation. In order to find a correlative for this overwhelming inner solitude, the poems often send their speakers alone into an open field. That field may be brimming with wildflowers, but it lacks any human resonance or contact. Sometimes it seems as desolate as the interior of the self. "Longing for Death," a poem strongly reminiscent of Anne Sexton's "Wanting to Die," begins: "I stepped out of my car door, into the black, / Searching for the rag ends of some dream." The speaker talks of wanting "to marry an absence" and to feel "the raw meat of a personal wound."

When two people do go out into a field together, it is ultimately to remove themselves from each other, to send them reeling back into themselves, alone. "Wild Cherries" concludes: "When you smile, / I see you dying in that single instant. / Walking back home, into ourselves, we enter / A far-off country neither of us wanted." James was deeply preoccupied with remembering and forgetting the Garden of Eden, some original innocent country outside of time, and keeps introducing a coiled snake ("Its eyes clouded with sun, its face a death mask") into his rich, earthly landscapes.

The other typical setting in *Letters* is the single bedroom where someone is seriously ill, either mentally or physically. This is usually a hospital room, and the book relies heavily on a language of contagion, laceration, and sickness. Always flowers are brought in, a striking contrast to the blank sterility of the surroundings, but also a contrast to the patient's inner and outer wounds. In these poems, many of which are reminiscent of Sylvia Plath's "Tulips," "the scent of carnations is too heady" ("Carnations"), the poinsettias disclose "brightness like an inflammation" ("The Poinsettias"), and the "peonies bloom like a cancer / Eating the heart out of this room" ("Peonies").

Letters also carefully constructs a strong family lineage for its preoccupation with the poet's inner turmoil. "Going Back," for example, situates the speaker between an insane uncle and an aunt who committed suicide by swallowing disinfectant before it announces forebodingly that "all this still gallops through my veins." In its steady preoccupation with madness and suicide, *Letters* shares the twin thematic concerns of two books that influenced it: Plath's *Ariel* (1965) and Sexton's *Live or Die* (1966).

One of the ways in which James circumvented the more restrictive limits of the so-called confessional voice was by displacing the "I" in many of these poems, imagining himself into other people's skins. This may partially have been a result of his strong interest in theater. Thus the "letters" retain their tone of intimacy and sense of emotional risk, but deflect any sense of self-display, projecting a diversity of other voices. These range from a bell-ringer haunted by the fact that "the saints have been turning to stone for a long, long time" to the mummy of a woman named Jemutesonekh whose body continues to hold its shape and who keeps on remembering how she died ("It was so simple!"). What these voices share is an intolerable isolation and a feverish obsession with sacrifice. Some of the strongest dramatic monologues engage the voices of emblematic Christians: "Sister Mariam Thérèse Takes the Veil," "Magdalene in the Garden," "Saint Francis Among the Hawks." All of these voices are haunted and steeled by the crucifixion, its terrible radiance and ever-receding distance. For them consciousness is pain, and they are obsessed by the pierced body and tormented by its remoteness. Their suffering is best summed up in the poet's own voice when he finally cries out in desperation: "Oh, Christ, you are so very far away. / Your hands are full of broken glass, / And I am too small to measure your imperfect gifts" ("Wine").

The voice in these poems—painfully lonely and filled with longing, estranged and religious—has stayed with me for more than twenty years. It deserves to be remembered.

REASONS

For our own private reasons
We live in each other for an hour.
Stranger, I take your body and its seasons,
Aware the moon has gone a little sour

For us. The moon hangs up there like a stone
Shaken out of its proper setting.
We lie down in each other. We lie down alone
And watch the moon's flawed marble getting

Out of hand. What are the dead doing tonight?
The padlocks of their tongues embrace the black,
Each syllable locked in place, tucked out of sight.
Even this moon could never pull them back,

Even if it held them in its arms
And weighed them down with stones,
Took them entirely on their own terms
And piled the orchard's blossom on their bones.

I am aware of your body and its dangers.
I spread my cloak for you in leafy weather
Where other fugitives and other strangers
Will put their mouths together.

102

STAN RICE

the egg of tenderness will break in our hearts

THE POET AND PAINTER Stan Rice died from brain cancer in December 2002 at the age of sixty. More than twenty years ago, the poet Gerald Stern read "Monkey Hill" to me on a park bench in the San Francisco Zoo. Rice was heading up the Creative Writing Program at San Francisco State at the time and Stern had just given a reading there, which is why he had the book in his pocket. The setting was memorable, with a chaos of monkeys splendidly squealing and rushing around in the background. The poem was first published in Rice's book *Body of Work* (Lost Roads, 1983), and it's reprinted in his new and selected poems, *Singing Yet,* which is the place to begin if you don't yet know his work.

MONKEY HILL

We will sit all day on a bench in the sun watching the spider
    monkeys.
It will at moments resemble an internal Eden.
But we will not know this.
We will think that we are just taking pictures with our minds.
The male will stand upright and scratch his silvery-gold chest.
It will sound rough and shameless.
Over and over the egg of tenderness will break in our hearts
at the sight of the baby spider monkeys.
For nothing could be more guileless or curious.
The mother will stand on all fours and stare into space

and we will see by her eyes that all of this is beyond her,
though she is intelligent she is unable to fathom
this sweet injustice nature has made cling to her back.
And we will wait for those moments
when out of the concrete slabs piled to resemble a hill
a splendidly squealing chaos of monkeys
rushes, some trespass or crime in monkeydom,
causing us to cry aloud, Look at that one!
And then also there will be those moments we are embarrassed
and only through a deliberate effort
will we not look away as the monkey
reaches backwards to pull at the indescribable
pink something that dangles from its bottom,
and we will feel our humanity is endangered
and that our intimate moments might lap over into the animal
     world
and our privacies be beheld with such ghastly frankness.
But no monkey does any one thing for very long.
So soon the candor will pass.
And gradually the shadows of the trees will touch our bench
and it will get cool, then uncomfortably cool, and there will be
     fewer
and fewer monkeys, and no one will be on the opposite bench
with detached and absorbed expression, and even the thief gulls
will have left the moat, and we will say these words as we stand;
     no;
think them: Oh God, whatever else be true, though nothing is
     permanent,
may the myth of our lives be like this memory of monkeys; that
     real.

I like the naked candor and directness of this poem. I like its
sweetness. It is set in the future ("We will sit all day on a bench in the
sun watching the spider monkeys"), which gives it a sense of anticipation and inevitability. The poem opens with a series of bald statements
("We will"; "It will") and develops the strategy throughout. It has a

simple incantatory rhythm and vivacious detail. The lines and the sentences coincide. The speaker admits that "the egg of tenderness will break in our hearts / at the sight of the baby spider monkeys." How keenly he observes the spider monkeys, how well he already knows them!

"Monkey Hill" is a poem of close observation that stretches beyond observation into a sexual and familial allegory ("It will at moments resemble an internal Eden. / But we will not know this"), a strategy Rice might have picked up from Ted Hughes or D. H. Lawrence, who perfected it in some of the great animal poems of the twentieth century. Like them, he doesn't shy away from what is embarrassing or unseemly in animal behavior, behavior that makes us nervous because it reminds us of ourselves. The poem becomes a love poem, a memorial wish for a couple spending a day—the day of their lives—watching the monkeys, who are both real and mythic.

103

ROLAND FLINT

Now I remember to you

My friend Roland Flint (1934–2001) was outraged by the Persian Gulf War. He wrote a poem about it set in late winter / early spring 1991, that still has shocking relevance today. The poem is simply called "Seasonal, 1991," and it appears in his outstanding final book, *Easy* (1999):

> The last freezing rain of winter
> or the first bona fide spring rain
> pittering its intermittent music
> on the roof and copper gutters
> is what you wake to a few days
> after the killing has almost
> stopped, in the Gulf. It is a sound
> filled with cleansing new shingles,
> wet and black, with crocuses,
> and, just behind them, forsythia,
> tulips, azaleas—spring. But it doesn't
> wash away last night's news, one
> hundred and fifty thousand Iraqis dead,
> mostly from our bombing: not
> the Elite Guards, but less loyal
> Muslims, Kurds, and Christian Assyrians,
> driven out to and trapped on
> the front lines of policies
> for which they did not vote or elect

to die, these weeks black rain fell
down, in light or dark, day in,
night out, a bloody, percussive
anthem to our great victory over
Saddam and the inhuman poor.
Now, while the lisping patter
genially wakens our house in
a birdsung Maryland suburb,
in Baghdad a season of heat and winds
of cholera and typhus begins.

"Seasonal, 1991" is exemplary in the way it exhibits a strong double consciousness; the poet scrupulously observes the natural world outside his suburban Maryland home even as he tries to wrap his mind around the human and political realities of what our country is doing halfway around the world.

Flint taught at Georgetown University for almost thirty years, but he never forgot that he had grown up on a small potato farm in North Dakota, which taught him something about caring for the land and something about hardship. Here is a poem that he wrote for his fifty-seventh birthday. The poem, a return to origins, is structured as a letter to his mother, but it now also takes on the retrospective shine of a self-elegy.

2-26-91

Well, mother, tomorrow night
I will be born, if this were 57
years ago, and you were 29.
Twenty-nine! How young you
would be to me now, mother!
A girl. Were you still
a girl at 29?—having your
fourth baby, your first after
the miscarriage, me?
If I'm thinking of you more,

am I getting ready to be born
again or do I miss you
from reading Juan Rulfo,
who lets the dead
son and mother talk
the way we did so long,
a month before you died,
seven years, 5 months
and 8 days ago, almost 50
years after that night
we beat the doctor
by 25 minutes or so.
Remember? I don't, but
you remembered it to me.
Now I remember to you,
everything, the 40 watt bulb,
the winter, your holding me
aside till the doctor
came to cut the cord.

104

M. WYREBEK

Be properly scared and go on doing what you have to do.
—Flannery O'Connor

The poet M. Wyrebek died in February 2003, at the age of forty-two. Wyrebek was a remarkably courageous person who had battled cancer most of her life. She was a deep intimate of illness and once told me that she could scarcely remember a time when she hadn't been sick. Doctors kept her alive and saved her time and again. I first met her at the Bread Loaf Writers Conference in the mid-1980s—a scrawny young woman with a working-class background and a Vassar education. She came from a large family in Waterbury, Connecticut, and lived most of her adult life in Sterling, Massachusetts, outside Boston. She had four brothers and four sisters and was completely devoted to her many nieces and nephews. She had fierce attachments. One could see immediately that she had a ferocious heart and a great love of poetry.

A few years later, I was delighted to be able to work with Wyrebek as my student in the outstanding low-residency M.F.A. program at Warren Wilson College. I'll never forget our first conference, in which she asked me to be as tough as possible on her poems. Her honesty was bracing. "You can't hurt my feelings," she said. "Nothing you can say can possibly be as shocking as what I've heard from doctors." She lived on the edge of calamity for many years, and she was determined to make art out of what had happened to her.

Wyrebek published one transfiguring book of poems, *Be Properly Scared* (1986), which was selected by Gregory Orr for the Four Way Books Intro Series in Poetry. The book characteristically took its title from a tough-minded statement by Flannery O'Connor, with whom she felt a great affinity. "Cowards can be just as vicious as those who declare themselves—more so," O'Connor asserted: "Don't take any romantic attitude . . . Be properly scared and go on doing what you have to do."

Wyrebek sought a poetry that was extreme and unflinching. She understood mortal panic and fear. She didn't like romantic posturing, and she wanted an art that took account of suffering. Her work could be playful, but its underlying depth of seriousness was never in question. One of my favorite poems of hers, "Night Owl," begins with her driving home from the hospital—it seems as if she was always getting terrible news—and gradually opens out into a great sense of mysterious encounter. It's as if a night owl becomes her Virgilian guide into the vast night.

Night Owl

You are nearing the land that is life.
You will recognize it by its seriousness.
                                        —Rilke

Driving my bad news the back way home
I know I'm in the land that is life
when I reach my favorite stretch of road—fields
flat and wide where corn appears soon after
planting the soil tilled, night-soaked
and crumbled into fists.
Ferguson's barn is somewhere
at the end of this long arm of tar
and as I near it, something grazes the back
passenger-side door, luffs parallel to my car—
a huge owl on headlight spray floating,
holding night over the hood to see
if this moving thing is real, alive,
something to kill—then gliding in
close as if to taste glass.
The road levitates, buffeted on a surf

of light, the fog-eaten farm disappearing
as I ride into starlessness, cells conspiring
so I am bright-flecked and uplifted—is this
what it feels like to be chosen—to be taken
under the wing of something vast
that knows its way blindly?

105

ROBERTA SPEAR, ERNESTO TREJO

the music of the earth
close to the earth.

ROBERTA SPEAR (1948–2003) was a California poet who kept close to the earth, the earthly. She had a wonderful way of looking attentively both at the plain valley spores and at the stars that guide us through hard nights. She had a gift for transfiguring the ordinary and pinpointing the mysteries at the heart of daily life. "We must still learn to share," she wrote, "what was never ours." Her most characteristic poetic strategy was to take a daily experience and ponder it until it yielded something spooky and mysterious, something extraordinary.

Spear published three books: *Silks* (1980, National Poetry Series), *Taking to Water* (1984), and *The Pilgrim Among Us* (1991). Her voice is clear, forthright, exacting, precise. Here is her poem "Meditation," which puns on her last name—she calls herself "a slow spear"—and has the watery undertow of a self-elegy, a disappearance:

> I could sit in this hot bath for hours
> both ends disappearing at once
> old skin sloughed and lacy
> as bits of lichen
> until only my navel
> a stone cast
> leaves rings on the surface
> and the water closes over it.
>
> I am the reed
> you peeled back and snapped

off your bare shoulder
a slow spear
that landed ever so lightly
on the glassy lake
and stayed afloat.

My arms
even my chin
are weightless . . .

and I could almost go under
without a breath—
the water like a mother
with her gloves and small parcel
saying *I brought you here*
and I can take you back.

I met Spear in Fresno many years ago through her mentor, Philip Levine, who also introduced me to Ernesto Trejo (1950–1991), another Fresno poet who passed before his time. Trejo wrote both in Spanish and in English. The poems in his one full-length collection, *Entering a Life* (1990), struggle to defy nothingness and death by re-creating other lives, by letting other stories enter into his own story, by seeking communion with the lost and marginal, the otherwise forgotten. His work was touched by death ("I learn one thing," he wrote, "death is no longer / remote") and filled with an odd foreboding of his own end, as in his moving poem "Some Sparrows":

Lately, I've been watching them, pecking
furiously at the ground,
then retreating into the eucalyptus,
where they stagger like compasses
before their tiny hearts quit and they drop,
stone-like.
     Sometimes my cat
will sniff them and jerk back

as if pierced on the nose by a needle.
In the dark they go on dying.
While burying them I have shoveled newspapers,
their bloody lips decayed, a child's
lucky penny, a rusted pipe
that goes nowhere, the roots of weeds
tangled like kite strings or hearts. . . .
Tonight, as if for the last time, I hold
my woman's face. Were I to die, my eyes' vaults
would crave light. When I go, place a dying sparrow
in my hands. My soul will find a tree to perch on.

106

PETER EVERWINE

How It Is

This is how it is—

> *One turns away*
> *and walks out into the evening.*
> *There is a white horse on the prairie, or a river*
> *that slips away among dark rocks.*
>
> *One speaks, or is about to speak,*
> *not that it matters.*
>
> *What matters is this—*

It is evening.
I have been away a long time.
Something is singing in the grass.

THERE IS SOMETHING shining and pure—a radiant clarity, a luminous stillness—at the heart of Peter Everwine's cleansing work, which is brought together in *From the Meadow*. His translations from Hebrew poets (T. Carmi, Natan Zach, David Vogel), as well as his adaptations of ancient Nahuatl texts, seem to come from the same voice—the same part of the self—as his own lyrics, which have a mysterious quietness, a grave simplicity. He is a pastoral poet, which suggests that he seeks to discover something essential in our natures by leaving the social realm behind and heading off into the natural world. It's as if he needs to hike into the fields in order to look back with equanimity at his own experience.

Everwine's poems create a zone of silence around them. They have an element of "pure poetry," which means that they are closer, say, to Mallarmé than to Neruda. They are shadowed by nightfall and typically leave the daylight world behind. The words themselves seem distilled and come from a great inner distance. They often have a nocturnal feeling, as if they were written by lamplight late at night. Everwine evokes "[t]he lamp / and the white paper / and the hour when words end / like many roads / before the same darkened house" ("Late Hour"). He declares: "Last night I lay awake / listening to the wind shake my house. / This morning I thought: if someone knocks / I will not answer" ("Night Letters").

For Everwine, as for some of the Hebrew poets he translates, singing comes before speaking ("First I'll sing. Later, perhaps, I'll speak") and carries greater weight, another kind of information. The titles of the poems themselves are often simple declarations: "It Was Autumn," "We Meet in the Lives of Animals," "How to Handle It," "I Dreamt," and so forth. In the end, the lyrics keep edging up to some essential silence, some vast darkness, which is when I find them most moving and beautiful. *From the Meadow* is a work of dark pastoral, and it deserves a place on the bookshelf next to like-minded works, such as Robert Bly's *Silence in the Snowy Fields,* W. S. Merwin's *The Lice,* and Mark Strand's *Darker.*

Distance

The light pulling away from trees,
the trees speaking in shadows
to whatever listens . . .

Something as common as water
turns away from our faces
and leaves.

The stars rise out of the hills
—old kings and animals
marching in their thin tunnels of light.

Once more I find myself
standing on a dark pier, holding
an enormous rope of silence.

107.

MICHAEL FRIED

PAPYRUS

Lubricated in fish blood, tears, semen.

WALTER BENJAMIN'S brilliant insight, his insistence that "[t]here is no document of civilization which is not at the same time a document of barbarism," has kept running through my mind as I've read and reread Michael Fried's third book of poems, *The Next Bend in the Road*. Best known for his stimulating and rigorous work in art history and criticism (I am eager to recommend *Art and Objecthood, Manet's Modernism,* and *Menzel's Realism*), Fried is highly conscious that great works of art, the most enduring human achievements, are inevitably entangled with the agon of history. Our joyous creations, our deep intimacies, are intertwined with the suffering of others.

The theme of interconnectedness runs like an electric current through this book, lighting it up. The first poem, a prefatory piece, introduces the motif in the most personal way. The poet sends off his collection ("Go, little book") and welcomes his child:

THE SEND-OFF

The hummingbird looks up from his flower punchbowl with an
    expression of pure dazzlement.
The May morning is that perfect,
our eleven-month-old daughter in her Grandma's-gift raspberry
    sundress is that astonishing.

She came here in stages
from Wuhan, China, where we adopted her
in the eye of a cyclone.

En route from the orphanage
all the while Anna slept in your arms
her birth mother's tears rose wavelike from the dusty earth
to speed us on our way.

The adoption of the poet's daughter is the touchstone of this work, which keeps accumulating figures and examples, noble precursors. All Fried's poems are "adoptions" of a sort, as Stanley Cavell suggests, lifting up "what had nearly been left behind." Fried apparently sees no gap—nor should we—between poems that deal with autobiographical subjects and poems that treat literary and artistic ones. Life and art are everywhere intertwined. All encounters are personal.

Many of Fried's lyrics and prose poems have an essayistic quality, the character of parable: "Kafka's Drawings," "Freud's Sacrifice," "Wittgenstein on Green," and so forth. The title poem, the first piece of a triptych, takes up the short-lived love affair in 1916 between Osip Mandelstam and Marina Tsvetayeva, who represent what is highest in Russian poetry. Both were cruelly broken on the wheel of Stalinism.

THE NEXT BEND IN THE ROAD

If there's a mention of eyelashes, then it's about Osip.
—NADEZHDA MANDELSTAM

The young man with long thick eyelashes is
unapologetically drunk with the world's beauty
despite or possibly because of the hollowness at its core
which he confirms in the slightly dead timbre
of the distant church bells sounding the hour.
Meanwhile the little horses jog onward without
the least appearance of strain, their breath issuing
visibly in twin dissolving plumes of cloud,
and the extraordinarily pretty woman (scarcely
more than a girl) whose head rests on the young man's
shoulder, although she has a husband to whom
she will return, is for the moment all his. Just beyond

the next bend in the road, or if not the next
the bend after that, still hidden by the towering
fir trees, their dark drooping vigorous branches
loaded with snow (I forgot to say that this
is a winter scene, that the youthful lovers are in
a sleigh, that they are both poets, that they will come
to similar ends), the Revolution waits.

108

MICHAEL RYAN

The writer has to judge himself with a stranger's eye and a stranger's scrutiny.
—FLANNERY O'CONNOR

MICHAEL RYAN brings a rigorous self-examination and scrutiny to his poems. He estranges reality and ruthlessly questions himself. His recently published *New and Selected Poems* represents three decades of work. It gathers together the equivalent of a new volume of poems with work from three previous collections: *Threats Instead of Trees* (1974), *In Winter* (1981), and *God Hunger* (1989), which lifted his poetry to another plane.

A ravenous spiritual appetite drives Ryan's best work, as in the poem "God Hunger":

> When the innumerable accidents of birth—
> parentage, hometown, all the rest—
> no longer anchor this fiction of the self
> and its incessant *I me mine,*
>
> then words won't be like nerves in a stump
> crackling with messages that end up nowhere,
> and I'll put on the wind like a gown of light linen
> and go be a king in a field of weeds.

Ryan has mastered at least two contemporary modes. One is a taut, Larkinesque lyric. Another is a free-verse narrative that takes an odd anecdote and interrogates it to uncover its significance. My favorites of this type—"A Burglary," "Passion," "Switchblade" ("Most of the past is lost, / and I'm glad mine has vanished / into blackness or space or whatever nowhere / what we feel and do goes"), "The Use of Poetry," and "An Old Book in Florence"—have a large sweep and un-remitting tension.

One of Ryan's best poems, "Not the End of the World," tells the story of a bird that flies down the chimney into the cold stove in his study. He scoops up the dull creature, carries it outside, and leaves it in the dirt. The helpless bird is swiftly surrounded by a group of iden-tical birds, mounting its back and pecking its body. The speaker can't tell if they are trying to rouse or to kill it, but he rationalizes that pick-ing it up would probably finish it off. He returns to his study but can't shake off a deeply ominous feeling:

> Do I need to say I was away
> for all of a minute
> before I went back to it?
> But the bird was gone.
> All the birds were gone,
> and the circle they had made
> now made a space so desolate
> that for one moment I saw
> the dead planet.

Ryan is a scrupulously observant poet with a gift for going for the jugular. Pain is one of the key subjects of his poems. How a hurtful past continues to haunt us is another. He thinks about human cruelty and puts individuals before us so that we can't look away or forget them. His work is finely honed, provocative, questing, and humane.

REMINDER

> Torment by appetite
> is itself an appetite
> dulled by inarticulate,
> dogged, daily

loving-others-to-death—
as Chekhov put it, "compassion
down to your fingertips"—
looking on them as into the sun

not in the least for their sake
but slowly for your own
because it causes
the blinded soul to bloom

like deliciousness in dirt,
like beauty from hurt,
their light, *their* light,
pulls so surely. Let it.

109.

LOUISE GLÜCK

The unsaid, for me, exerts great power.

THERE IS SOMETHING radically uncompromising about all of Louise Glück's work. Glück has published nine books of poems, each one an entity unto itself. She has redefined her project with each volume. Each one of her books is a significant station in her progress: *Firstborn* (1968), *The House on Marshland* (1975), *Descending Figure* (1980), *The Triumph of Achilles* (1985), *Ararat* (1990), *The Wild Iris* (1992), *Meadowlands* (1997), *Vita Nuova* (1999), and *The Seven Ages* (2001). She has also written one very forceful and clear-eyed work of prose, *Proofs & Theories: Essays on Poetry* (1994), which serves as a guide to her aesthetic and spiritual concerns.

Glück was mentored in poetry by Stanley Kunitz, her teacher at Columbia University. Her poems are austere and beautiful. She has an oracular voice, a fierce imagination, and an unsparing vision. Her short lyrics swell on the page. She has learned something about impersonality from T. S. Eliot, whose work she loves. She has a taste for asymmetry and writes a taut, irregular free verse. Like the Objectivist poet George Oppen, whom she calls "a master of white space," she typically employs a strategy of pauses and intervals, of "disruption, hesitation, silence." "I am attracted to ellipsis, to the unsaid, to suggestion, to eloquent, deliberate silence," she asserts.

Glück's subjects are painful ones and she embraces them with unflinching honesty. A massive isolation surrounds everything she writes. Loss is a given, like loneliness, like yearning. Often she seems disgusted with our flawed bodily desires, our sad needs, our human imperfections. Yet her work craves listeners and seeks connection.

THE SEVEN AGES

In my first dream the world appeared
the salt, the bitter, the forbidden, the sweet
In my second I descended

I was human, I couldn't just see a thing
beast that I am

I had to touch, to contain it

I hid in the groves,
I worked in the fields until the fields were bare—

time
that will never come again—
the dry wheat bound, caskets
of figs and olives

I even loved a few times in my disgusting human way

and like everyone I called that accomplishment
erotic freedom,
absurd as it seems

The wheat gathered and stored, the last
fruit dried: time

that is hoarded, that is never used,
does it also end?

In my first dream the world appeared
the sweet, the forbidden
but there was no garden, only
raw elements

I was human:
I had to beg to descend
the salt, the bitter, the demanding, the preemptive

And like everyone, I took, I was taken
I dreamed

I was betrayed:

Earth was given to me in a dream
In a dream I possessed it

110.

BILL KNOTT

GOODBYE

If you are still alive when you read this,
close your eyes. I am
under their lids, growing black.

BILL KNOTT has always taken the position of a nonjoiner, an outsider, a comedian and a crank, a deflator, a sufferer. "I wish to be misunderstood," he says wryly in his tiny poem "Wrong," "that is, / to be understood from your perspective." Knott is a sort of Bartleby the Scrivener of lyric poetry, a prolific writer who puns often on his name (*knot, not*) and has gone his own idiosyncratic way for thirty-five years and eleven volumes, which include *Laugh at the End of the World: Collected Comic Poems 1969–1999.* He is, to borrow the title of his most recent book, the quintessential "Unsubscriber."

THE UNSUBSCRIBER

Like all children, you were a de facto
Member of the Flat Earth Society,
Believing nothing but what you could see
Or touch or whatever sense led act to

Fruition: mudpies made summer beneath
A tree whose measured shade endowed decrees
Between light and dark: such hierarchies
Gave you implicit a sophistic faith—

(Fallacious fellowship!)—
                                        Youth's adherents

Ignore the fact that most factions reject
Their lyric league (which only fools have stayed

Striplings of) and none condone its nonsense:
No one loves that vain solipsistic sect
You'd never join, whose dues you've always paid.

Knott has cultivated a surreal wit and an offbeat vernacular style that has moments of high lyricism and deep despair. When I read his first book, *The Naomi Poems: Book One: Corpse and Beans* (Big Table, 1968), published under the pseudonym St. Geraud (1940–1966), the author's note stunned me ("Bill Knott [1940–1966] is a virgin and a suicide") and so did some of the radically short poems, such as this brief elegy:

DEATH

Going to sleep, I cross my hands on my chest.
They will place my hands like this.
It will look as though I am flying into myself.

Knott has always had a weird, self-deprecating sense of humor and a tortured sensibility. At times he seems like a lesser Robert Desnos, the French surrealist who combined a gift for associative thinking with a deep humanity. Like Desnos, Knott has a flair for strange images and a sneaky formal sense. He likes to play with the sonnet form (see his responses to Borges, Trakl, and Bashō in *Unsubscriber*) and thinks of a poem as "a room that contains / the house it's in." He likes to play with sound and count syllables (a typical title is "Romance [Hendecasyllabics]"), to coin words ("Neckcognition," "Transhendeculous") and compound them ("Forthfable," "Heilstyles").

Above all, Knott is willing to take in the subject of suffering, which he approaches from his own unconventional and genuine angle ("In the Orphanage, hell, even if they do tell / on you there's no one for them to tell it *to*"). Here is a four-line poem, for example, that seems to me to hover somewhere near Flannery O'Connor's zone:

CRUX

Do they let you still keep your crutches when
they crucify you, as if you could even manage
the goshdarn things with your hands out like that.
Heck, they'd have to nail them up to your armpits.

STUART DYBEK

Who are the great forgetters
Who will know just how to make us forget such and such a part of the world
Where is the Christopher Columbus to whom is owed the forgetting of a
    continent

            —Guillaume Apollinaire

Stuart Dybek is a splendid urban writer with a deep feeling for
music and an equally deep allegiance to dreams. His second book of
poems, *Streets in Their Own Ink*, is filled with moody nocturnes, with
long, rhythmic, solitary walks through city streets at night ("the rule
on city nights / is still: keep moving"). It has a gritty realism infused
with a sense of the marvelous, a religious aura:

> Alone, along a street that's suddenly
> like any other, you're blessed
> simply to continue
> another night's walk home.

Dybek is a cosmopolitan with strong roots in his native territory.
He begins with a ferocious loyalty to his neighborhood, to his Polish,
Catholic, working-class boyhood in Chicago, which he has evoked in
three extraordinary books of short fiction: *Childhood and Other Neigh-*
borhoods, The Coast of Chicago, and *I Sailed with Magellan.* In both poetry and prose, he sees the extraordinary in ordinary lives and blends
the quotidian with the fantastic. "There were autobiographies / at
every corner, / legends, litanies, manifestos, / memoirs in forgotten
tongues," he writes in his poem "Autobiography."

Dybek treats the past as both familiar and strange country. It can't
be simply recalled at will with any deep accuracy. "Suppose the past
could not be recalled / any more than we can foretell / the future, that

in order to remember / you'd have to visit an oracle," he posits in "Revelation":

> At such moments, the past
> would suddenly bloom into consciousness
> with a shock like clairvoyance.
> What *had* happened would seem to loom
> with the mystery of what *will* happen,
> and stunned by this unwanted gift, we'd pray
> for the revelation to be lifted.

Dybek's fierce nostalgia is balanced and even outweighed by a redemptive need to forget, hence his epigraph from Apollinaire's poem "Toujours." His greatest loyalty has always been to an inner city of dreams, the geography of the interior, our secret lives. For him, this inner life is inextricably intertwined with the outer one, which we cannot forget, which seems never to forget us.

WINDY CITY

> The garments worn in flying dreams
> were fashioned there—
> overcoats that swooped like kites,
> scarves streaming like vapor trails,
> gowns ballooning into spinnakers.
>
> In a city like that one might sail
> through life led by a runaway hat.
> The young scattered in whatever directions
> their wild hair pointed, and gusting
> into one another, they fell in love.
>
> At night, wind rippled saxophones
> that hung like wind chimes
> in pawnshop windows, hooting through

each horn so that the streets seemed haunted,
not by nighthawks, but by doves.

Pinwheels whirred from steeples
in place of crosses. At the pinnacles
of public buildings, snagged underclothes—
the only flag—flapped majestically.
And when it came time to disappear

one simply chose a thoroughfare
devoid of memories, raised a collar,
and turned one's back on the wind.
I remember closing my eyes
into a swirl of scuttling leaves.

112

MARK JARMAN

Lord of the returning leaves, of sleepers
Waking in their tunnels among roots,
Of heart and bush and fire-headed stag,
Of all things branching, stirring the blood like sap,
Pray for us in your small commemorations . . .

MARK JARMAN has a religious imagination. He treats poetry as a spiritual quest, and much of his eighth book of poems, *To the Green Man,* is a serious investigation of faith. He is the son and grandson of preachers and has taken the running quarrel between his father, a rationalist, and his grandfather, a would-be mystic, into the secular realm of his poems, where it becomes a dialogue about reason and the irrational. Poetry may have become his true church, as he seems to suggest in the anecdotal poem "In Church with Hart Crane," but he doesn't escape the hard questions of his upbringing.

Throughout *To the Green Man,* Jarman ponders the truth of a statement attributed to the Delphic Oracle—"Called or not called, God is present"—and repeatedly turns to the insoluble mystery of God's eternal absence or omnipresence. The poems often read like idiosyncratic prayers. "Let us think of God as a lover / Who never calls, / Whose pleasure in us is aroused / In unrepeatable ways," he writes in the first of "Five Psalms." "God Who Is Absent / God Who Is Present / God Who Finds Us / In Our Hiding Places," he declares in another: "God Whom We Name / God Whom We Cannot Name / When We Open Our Mouths / With the Name God Word God." Here is the fifth psalm:

Lord of dimensions and the dimensionless,
Waves and particle, all and none,

Who lets us measure the wounded atom,
Who lets us doubt all measurement,

When in this world we betray you
Let us be faithful in another.

Jarman's poetry is God-haunted. He writes as an unorthodox but essentially Christian poet who embraces paradox and treats contradiction, to use Simone Weil's phrase, as a lever for transcendence. The sense that faith is a necessary leap, an incredible gamble—and a gamble on the incredible—animates his work, which often turns to woods and fields to consider "the nature of the world." Suddenly coming across a fox, he wonders, *"What have I done to merit that regard?"* When he considers science, as in "Lord Chemistry" ("The kingdom is inside somewhere all right. / It's tucked in by a fold of time and space"), or confronts artworks—a twelfth-century Byzantine icon, Goya's *Saint Peter Repentant*—it is usually to consider "the elemental laws / Of God," which, "like gravity, seem whimsically selective."

The element of chance comes to the fore in his poem "Astragaloi"—the word for what the Greeks called "knucklebones," and we call dice. Knucklebones came from sheep or goats and were often used as a form of divination.

ASTRAGALOI

We know there must be consciousness in things,
       In bits of gravel pecked up by a hen
To grind inside her crop, and spider silk
       Just as it hardens stickily in air,
And even those things paralyzed in place,
       The wall brick, the hat peg, the steel beam
Inside the skyscraper, and lost, forgotten,
       And buried in ancient tombs, the toys and games.
Those starry jacks, those knucklebones of glass

Meant for the dead to play with, toss and catch
Back of the hand and read the patterns of,
Diversions to beguile the endless time,
Never to be picked up again. . . . They're thinking,
Surely, all of them. They are lost in thought.

113

NICHOLAS CHRISTOPHER

HAIKU

Etched on the moth's wings
the story of a man's life
powder to the touch

ONE OF OUR MOST inventive writers, Nicholas Christopher is a fabulist obsessed by transience and deeply troubled by mortality. His fiction often puts me in mind of Jorge Luis Borges and Italo Calvino, two time travelers who are his great precursors. His poetry tends to build on the work of Wallace Stevens, Elizabeth Bishop, and James Merrill. Like them, he has a taste for the exotic, the faraway, the displaced, the imaginary. He is a close observer with a romantic sensibility, an eager, even fervent, eye, and a long wistful gaze, the sense that the delicate lifelines—the story—of a person can be like "powder to the touch." To read his richly honed and sensuous work, which has so much tensile strength, is to visit other worlds and then return to our own, disturbed by time, but also refreshed and reawakened.

Christopher writes often as an American solitary, a restless traveler. He is an urban poet who loves islands and fantasizes about escaping from history, which he cannot do. His work keeps being pulled back to dark cityscapes (he has written an excellent critical book about film noir: *Somewhere in the Night: Film Noir and the American City*) and historical catastrophes. This is evident in his novels *Veronica; A Trip to the Stars;* and *Franklin Flyer.* Yet hot climes repeatedly call to him, hence the title of his selected poems, *Crossing the Equator.* Luminosities beckon. This is a poet who cherishes surfaces, which shimmer in the distance, and holds fast to what he sees, lest everything should disappear. Often his work seems literally overtaken by the past, the bright nostalgias, and a lost realm becomes an island he returns to, illuminates, and surveys. Above all, he loves the glamour of the physical world.

Crossing the Equator brings together a generous selection of new poems with work from seven previous volumes covering more than thirty years: *On Tour with Rita* (1982); *A Short History of the Island of Butterflies* (1986); *Desperate Characters* (1988); *In the Year of the Comet* (1992); *5° & Other Poems* (1995); *The Creation of the Night Sky* (1998); and *Atomic Field: Two Poems* (2000). It provides us with the opportunity to immerse ourselves in Christopher's drenched landscapes, what he sees, his highly tropical language.

Trópico

On the abandoned tennis court in the coconut grove
where the cows chew weeds along the baseline

and a halved ball like a temple's dome shadows
an anthill of powdered clay to which a column

of red ants marches out of the grass
lugging bread crumbs from a ditchdigger's

lunch scavenged by the roadside
and grape seeds spat out a truck window

by a girl with windblown hair returning barefoot
from a dance the previous night

and finally a fly's carcass minus the wing
that a straggler ant is struggling to carry

when a gecko slithers from the weeds to snap him up
before being snatched away himself hours later

asleep behind transparent eyelids on a fallen
palm by a trembler a nocturnal bird

whose plumage sparkles with stars as he flies
over the road where a truck is speeding

with no girl inside tonight to taste the wind
and drawing in his wings dives into the forest

a black curtain he pierces like a needle
allowing a pinpoint of light to escape

114

PHILIP SCHULTZ

You hear me speak. But do you hear me feel?
—GERTRUD KOLMAR

"I GET FAITH / and intuition and 5763 years of longing and despair, a passion / for hearsay, boogying and epistemology," Philip Schultz confesses in his exuberant, helpless, inquisitive, and exalted tragicomedy, *Living in the Past.* Schultz's book-length sequence is a Jewish coming-of-age story set in upstate New York ("This is Rochester, N.Y., in the fifties, when all the Displaced Persons / move in and suddenly even the elms look defeated") amidst an extraordinary mix of ethnic groups. "Grandma believes / they came here so we all could suffer," he declares at the outset, "that soon we'll all dress / like undertakers and march around whispering to the dead."

Schultz writes as one of the whisperers, a middle-aged man with a family of his own who finds himself compulsively returning to the landscape of his childhood, of his passage into manhood. He can't forget what determined him; he can't give up living in the past. He tracks the year leading up to his bar mitvah ("in another 248 days / I'll be bar mitzvahed and leave this valley of endless weeping"), and poignantly evokes his experience as an only child in an eccentric, anguished, and miserable family. "No one in this family ever suspects they're unhappy," he announces, "in fact, the less happy we are, the less we suspect it."

The family unit consists of his grandmother, who "climbs a chair to yell at God for killing / her only husband"; his uncle, who "walks around with a straightedge razor tied round / his neck on a red string, screaming and pounding on things"; his mother, who binges on Almond

Joys and hides bacon in the icebox; and his father, who "sleepwalks through / the wilderness of the living room, Odysseus disguised as a Zionist, / or a pickled beet." It is only partly a rhetorical question when the speaker wonders aloud, "Didn't everyone live in a house where everyone feels cheated, / ignored, and unredeemed?"

Living in the Past re-creates a quintessentially immigrant American world where everyone is hostile to everyone else and "no matter how far down you started from, you began again from the beginning." The entire neighborhood is marching forward while looking back. Schultz adeptly summons up a world where almost everyone is displaced by the war in Europe and "dickers with God." Mr. Schwartzman, who lost his wife and five children in Auschwitz, is the most haunting figure in the book, which is also shadowed by the ghost of Gertrud Kolmar—each section begins with an epigraph from her work—an immensely gifted Jewish poet who was born in 1894 in Berlin and disappeared in 1943 on the last transport to Auschwitz. "You hear me speak," Kolmar wrote. "But do you hear me feel?" Here is the poem in which Schultz brings together Mr. Schwartzman and Gertrud Kolmar, two doomed figures:

Mr. Schwartzman survived the Nazis but not Cuba Place, where
he takes long Saturday walks with his five dead children
who ride a carousel round the inside of his cracked eyeballs,
each a continent, a resume filed at Auschwitz, where Gertrud Kolmar,
his older sister's best friend, also was murdered, her poems
scratched in blood, flying over the Urals, singing, "Out of darkness
I come, a woman, I carry a child, and have forgotten whose it is."
He reads her at the back of his candlelit eyes, his kaddish voice
wears a tallis and skullcap, praising her soul's dark soliloquy: "I am
a continent that will sink without a sound into the sea."

There is a sparkling wit, a comic obsessiveness ("At night I go outside and reminisce, like an idiot"), a Whitmanian chutzpah, and an elegiac tenderness to Philip Schultz's deeply Jewish and radically American memorial work, which concludes with a lament:

I wish the dead would take their bodies with them when they die.
I wish they would not leave them behind. I wish they would take
their dreams and streets and cafes. That they would understand
    why
we cannot say or do with anyone else what we said and did with
    them.
Why we cannot forgive them for leaving us behind.

115

DEBORAH DIGGES

See how the first dark takes the city in its arms
and carries it into what yesterday we called the future.

O, the dying are such acrobats.
Here you must take a boat from one day to the next,

or clutch the girders of the bridge, hand over hand.
But they are sailing like a pendulum between eternity and evening,

diving, recovering, balancing the air.

DEBORAH DIGGES writes from the other side of fifty, from deep in midlife, in her luminous fourth book of poems, *Trapeze.* Like Elizabeth Bishop, an enabling model, Digges has been a keenly observant poet, a walker in the country, one of nature's intimates. So, too, as in Bishop, there is an underlying sense of peril—of mortal panic—driving her work, which is painfully sharpened by loss. "Call it a nearness like a room you make inside yourself for sorrow," she confesses in "Trillium." "Few are invited in." The twenty-five poems in *Trapeze* are written in what she calls "the aftermath of youth" and filled with stray moments of beauty held aloft and rescued from oblivion.

Digges has developed a rich, sensuous, and rhythmical free verse, a headlong vernacular style that at times reminds me of Galway Kinnell. The title of her previous collection, *Rough Music,* is apt. Her attack on a subject is often refracted, even oblique—she has an odd associative wildness—and yet her gaze is unwavering. I find something both tender and ruthless—a furious cherishing—in the way she looks hard at things. "The light / of earth says simply gone, yes," she declares in the strange and wonderful poem "Gown of Moleskins."

"As for your dead, they will be not be / returning. The leafless burial woods fill / with brilliant brutal light. How few / you've loved toward posterity."

There is great emotional courage in Digges's book of thresholds and crossings, of farewells and hard departures. She will not shy away from what she stumbles upon in her explorations, as when she comes across two young mothers watching their toddlers on a beach in late March. "Once they looked back to show me myself at fifty, / frightening to them, not yet recognizable, the self- / same, almost, in an old nightmare obsolete," she observes coolly at the end of "Boat." "O brilliant, trivial unmooring."

Some of Digges's most heartbreaking poems touch upon the illness and death of her husband. I'm especially taken by "Midsummer," "So Light You Were I Would Have Carried You" ("Light as you were / I would have carried you / from the room / of your death back / to our room, / climbed back, / crawled up the stairs / to our bed"), and "Seersucker Suit," an astonishing two-sentence elegy that rhythmically reminds me of Theodore Roethke's lyric "Child on Top of a Greenhouse." I love the way Digges takes maritime imagery, as Pablo Neruda does in his poem *"Solo la muerte,"* and applies it to a man's closet, all the while jerry-rigging a kind of music that builds to full sail:

SEERSUCKER SUIT

To the curator of the museum, to the exhibition of fathers,
to the next room from this closet of trousers
and trousers, full sail the walnut hangers of shirts,
O the great ghost ships of his shoes.
Through the racks and the riggings,
belt buckles ringing and coins in coat pockets
and moths that fly up from the black woolen remnants,
his smell like a kiss blown through hallways of cedar,
the shape of him locked in his burial clothes,
his voice tucked deep in his name,

his keys and the bells to his heart,
I am passing his light blue seersucker suit
with one grass-stained knee,
and a white shirt, clean boxers, clean socks, a handkerchief.

116

SUSAN STEWART

You understand these are questions you are asking of yourself.

IN HER WONDERFULLY imaginative fourth poetry book, *Columbarium*, Susan Stewart invents a type of poem she calls "shadow georgics." These poems respond to and reconfigure the traditional georgic, a didactic poem about rural life. The georgic goes back as far as Hesiod's *Works and Days* (eighth century B.C.), and reaches its high-water mark in Virgil's *Georgics* (37–30 B.C.), a sequence of four books that evokes the delights and dangers of country life. Stewart sometimes paraphrases and often calls to mind Virgil's discursive treatise, which is at once a practical guide and a celebration of the hard labor demanded by the earth. It serves as a weathervane for her highly constructed work.

I appreciate the instructive short lyric that inaugurates Stewart's intricately braided sequence. It has the deceptive simplicity of a Frostian parable, a made thing:

> I had a little dove
> made of paper and string.
> I pulled him along behind me—
> he could not sing.
>
> He was a made thing.
> I made him by heart.
> He did not sing at all
> and that was all of his art.

Stewart's "shadow georgics" are organized alphabetically by title: "Apple," "Bees," "Braid," "Cross/X," "Dark the star," and so forth on to "Weather," "Wings," "X/Cross," "To You and For You," and "Zero." The format suggests a parallel between language and nature, the alphabet and the elements. The carpentry is extensive; no two poems are alike, and each takes a radically different form. It's as if the endless mutability and metamorphic power of nature find an echo in a series of malleable poetic forms.

Stewart's difficult instruction manual is shadowed by doubts, haunted by childhood memories and night fears. The poet thinks hard about natural processes ("Born with the elm, you will die with it") and human history ("History starts / with the theft of a cow / and ends with the theft / of a temple"). Her poems are investigations and represent the dark unconscious of the georgic type, since they bring up what the didactic or all-knowing consciousness tends to repress: death itself. The speaker in this book is a brooder, mindful of absence, attentive to consciousness, and watchfully peering into the future, as in "Vigil": "Midnight much worry / in a little room— / strike a match and time / is burning toward you."

Stewart takes time in these poems to think about time. She thrills to nature and considers how we use it to make meaning. No subject is more fitting for the georgic than the cycle of the seasons, and here is Stewart's startling contribution. The death of the shepherd, like the poem itself, refers to James Thompson's *The Seasons* (1730).

THE SEASONS

Ice-jammed hard-clasped branches in the blocks a whole river of them
    yet at the same time, the time sensed
beneath the time walked, the time breathing in and out, the water
      almost
    eddying, still pushing there beneath
the milk-white surface, deep down and over the bed of rocks; you
      could call
    them frozen, though they never live

another state than less and less until they're gone, the water going on
    and on
   until it all accrues again. The seasons
always seemed to be a form of freedom, something good for making
    meaning,
   the kind of notion a founding father could
pull out now and then whenever
   the now and then would flag. Time
healing time, you know the saw.
   Lightning strikes and struck.
The shepherd fell down dead.
And then it all wound up again: a redbreast made a ruckus, the quick
    eternal sprung.

You wanted summer or you wanted death.
So death came again, and that was autumn.

117

STUART DISCHELL

My memory is an upright sweeping back.

THERE'S A DEEP sweetness in the way that Stuart Dischell, a romantic poet with a funny bone, returns to the past in his three books: *Good Hope Road* (1993); *Evenings & Avenues* (1996); and *Dig Safe* (2003). The title of his most recent collection, his best to date, derives from the brightly colored warning signs that construction workers spray-paint on sidewalks and roadways: "Steam rising from the coffee and exhalations / Of workers on break around a manhole cover, / The abbreviated utilities scribbled in Dig Safe" ("Crooked Wood"). Dischell cleverly employs the term "Dig Safe" as the reigning metaphor of the book, as both a wish and a command, for how to settle down and delve inward, approaching the treacheries of one's own past, the hard turning wheel of time lost and found and lost again. We're going to the erotic underground—the underworld—of a male psyche, and it's as if he's sending regards ("be well, dig safe") as we enter the danger zone where necessary but potentially hazardous psychological work always gets done.

Dischell's discursive lyrics have a light touch and a serious undertow. They have the jaunty quality of recollection, of trying to recall the past as honestly as possible, reporting back from the front. One thinks of them as invocations that come from the wide, middle regions of life, which is to say that they have a kind of equanimity about them. His particular way of approaching a subject, his strategy of attack, seems influenced by C. K. Williams and Robert Pinsky. It is close kin, say, to Carl Dennis and Tony Hoagland, both of whom also have

a neighborly way of piercing the inner mysteries and taking up—
taking on—the social world.

Dischell's poems typically operate by summoning the past, rather
than simply inhabiting it, as so many traditional lyrics seem to do.
Thus one poem characteristically begins: "Trying to remember what
it is was like to live / Here and how it was I used to feel and fit / Into
those days—like a convict in the movies / I have come back to put
on my old clothes" ("The Report"). "My memory is an upright sweeping back," he continues. "A man would be a scarecrow in a birdless
field." Another commences: "Hey it's been fourteen years since that
summer / We drove the little green Citroën out of Paris / Through
Lyon to the blue coast and went Mediterranean, / Wearing no or little
clothes, dozing in the bedchairs, / The naked democracy of the beach,
appreciating the sun / Who was now making famous European love"
("The Squanderers").

There's an antic strain humming through Dischell's writing
("When people say they miss me, / I think how much I miss me too, /
Me, the old me, the great me"), but his underlying subject is loss,
which is what gives his poems their poignancy. "A Tenant at Will" provides a strong example of how his sensibility works:

> I no longer live on Linnaean Street
> Where I watched the others going to work
> As I drank coffee and smoked a pipe,
> Inventing my current existence.
> I was not bothered by the phone much.
> No credit cards and little to bank.
> My typewriter had just gone electric.
> Nights I returned after drink and talk
> To the punctuation of the white spark
> On the trackless trolley wire.
> And the slow-moving populace of summer
> And the naked sub-lessee
> In the lamplight flossing her teeth
> Whether I looked or not were there.

Honks and voices and stereo speakers.
Those were the windows of that life.
Some faced a courtyard, the others a street.
I would like to visit who lives there now,
See how my face remains there framed.

118

OLENA KALYTIAK DAVIS

This may not be for the faint of heart.

OLENA KALYTIAK DAVIS's two collections of poetry, *And Her Soul Out of Nothing* (1997) and *shattered sonnets love cards and other off and back handed importunities* (2003), show her to be one of the most idiosyncratic, unpredictable, and compelling poets of her generation.

Davis is an extremely angular and elusive writer. Her voice is tormented, self-interfering, and at times desperate. She has an extremely sarcastic surface, but one detects under that surface a lyrical and effusive imagination. At times I feel as if I am reading the work of an alienated young Romantic poet through the lens of a shattered postmodern mirror. "You always knew you could not keep god's attention," she confesses in her poem "if you are asked":

> And it doesn't work, bulletproofing the heart.
> The phenomenology of the soul, you have turned
> And returned to it: the tending and the attending, the paying
>
> With only your attention.

There is a driving spiritual quest, a tremendous inner hunger, at the heart of Davis's radically fractured and ironic idiom. I responded deeply to her first book as a broken and chipped work of soul-making. "The situation is grave," she declares in her poem "All the Natural Movements of the Soul":

the way we lean over each other, the way years
later we emerge: hunchbacked, hooded,
with full grown tender things called souls.

I find Davis's second collection even more radically energetic and
visionary than her first. She has a strong attraction to archaic diction,
which she then feels the need to undermine and even humiliate, and
a sense that wordplay will lead her to stumble into hard truths. She
loves rhetoric, and loves even more to wring its neck. Typically, she
writes from the point of view, as she puts it in "notes toward the ab-
lation of the soul," of "The soul that faiths. Yet remains / faithless. The
soul that prefers / to decline." For all its defensiveness, this convulsive
book—at times funny, at times sick at heart—refracts and defends a
wondrous inner light.

Here is a characteristically odd, impeded, and spiritual poem,
which has antecedents in Gerard Manley Hopkins's so-called terrible
sonnets and John Berryman's "Eleven Addresses to the Lord," in lower-
case sonnets by ee cummings and experimental ones by Ted Berrigan.
It is as if, in this poet's point of view, an apology to God requires an
over-the-top capitalizing of every word.

SIX APOLOGIES, LORD

I Have Loved My Horrible Self, Lord.
I Rose, Lord, And I Rose, Lord, And I
Dropt. Your Requirements, Lord. 'Spite Your Requirements, Lord,
I Have Loved the Low Voltage Of The Moon, Lord,
Until There Was No Moon Intensity Left, Lord, No Moon
    Intensity Left
For You, Lord. I Have Loved The Frivolous, The Fleeting, The
    Frightful
Clouds, Lord. I Have Loved Clouds! Do Not Forgive Me, Do Not
Forgive Me LordandLover, HarborandMaster, GuardianandBread,
    Do Not.
Hold Me, Lord, O, Hold Me

Accountable, Lord. I Am
Accountable. Lord.

Lord It Over Me,
Lord It Over Me, Lord. Feed Me

Hope, Lord. Feed Me
Hope, Lord, Or Break My Teeth.

Break My Teeth, Sir,

In This My Mouth.

119

SARAH ARVIO

> ... *the experiences that are called "apparitions," the whole so-called*
> *"spirit world," death, all these Things that are so closely related to us,*
> *have through our daily defensiveness been so entirely pushed out of*
> *life that the senses with which we might have been able to grasp*
> *them have atrophied.*
> —Rainer Maria Rilke, *Letters to a Young Poet*

SARAH ARVIO has been channeling voices, splitting herself off and listening to her inner musings, carrying on dialogues with the dead. She has turned herself into a poet of two minds, a spiritual apprentice to those "abstracted / / from humanness on the physical plane." The result is a splendidly odd and compelling first book, *Visits from the Seventh,* which consists of conversations between a woman and a group of invisible presences.

Visits is nervy, fanciful, and unified. Each poem invokes airborne visitors from another realm who drop in and out of consciousness at will, like a ghostly chorus. The spirits occupy a transitional zone they call *the seventh sense,* "the one we sometimes share with you." It is possible to read the voices as actual presences, or if that seems too spooky or unlikely, as an extended metaphor for the interior life. "Was it an admission of arrogance / to say right out that I had visitors?" Arvio asks near the end of the book. "We were driving in the Jersey meadows, / / a gray purple sky, roving orange spots, / white clouds lit miasmic yellow. 'It might / be best,' one said, 'to call us a conceit.'"

There is a strong suggestion the poet has summoned the voices out of a deep need for them, out of loneliness and longing. "I longed for the river of what they were / to flow through the channel of what I was," she declares. And yet the spirits also need human beings to stand in for them. "By some means they implant their thoughts / into a person's mind. Mine for instance. / And then they go on growing and thriving."

Arvio treats the visitors with a blend of reverence and irreverence, skepticism and wonder. She trades quips ("They thought they were funny. Were they funny?"), banishes them from her presence, and inevitably welcomes them back. She learns desire is fundamental, nothing is certain, "*Now is ever.*" At times she uses the visitors to meditate upon the life she's led. She questions her sources and sources herself. In so doing, she has found an uncanny vehicle for addressing, undressing, and redressing experience.

LOVE

It was not to them I wanted to speak
but they were the only ones who listened.
Do you think I don't know the truth, I said.

Do you think I don't know the half, I said.
I've had a life to regret all those
regrettable acts of lovelessness. And

did I think he would follow me through them
whispering encouragement, or hissing
not that! not that! I might have hoped it, yes.

But no one could and no one did. I came
alone; I had myself; a bare self is
bare of persons, for they make us ourselves,

they dress us in ourselves. Hope of a self,
to dress in the person of another.
And some place, in some other, chosen life,

all rival Pamelas shall be unborn,
all plain, brown-haired girls fingering their pearls
with a factual air of what-makes-sense.

"What a waste of words!" But I saw his eyes,
I saw their wander and their wishfulness.
She thinks she got him but she never did.

She thinks she holds him but she never will.
I have him in his sleeping wish and kiss;
she has his truce and loss, his settlement.

120

DAN CHIASSON

Sometimes this song feels like a cure
sometimes it makes the hurt much worse.

I'M STRUCK BY how the dream world and the autobiographical impulse come together in Dan Chiasson's superb first book of poems, *The Afterlife of Objects.* The process of dreaming itself—or, perhaps more accurately, the process of writing and thereby crafting the dream—seems to give the poet access to essential aspects of his own being that he couldn't otherwise penetrate or know. He exploits the kinship between writing poetry and dreaming, and thus speaks back to experience with something more than conscious mind. He lets reverie enter the process and reimagines his own beginnings. Here, the imagination becomes "an organ of perception, a means of feeling," as Robert Pinsky formulates it.

There's a strong element of fantasy in how the speaker in these poems dreams his way into the life of objects from his own and even his family's past. These objects have an afterlife that somehow goes beyond memory and continues to reverberate in the imagination (hence the title). They have an almost talismanic power to summon back and reinvent a lost world. In the poem "Spade," for example, the speaker dreams of becoming the very instrument that his mother used to plant flowers:

> I dreamed I was the spade
> my mother used
>
> to dig her marigolds in spring,
> her *bloom* and *worry.*

Her digging, throwing, patting to bring
rows to life, each
bloom familiar

to worry, every row perfect, bloom,
rich dirt between, planned
absence and full, superfluous bloom—

I made the trench her hand proposed;

I was the pressure in her palm;

her *ache from planting*
was
my *presence in her life.*

This dream becomes a way for the poet to externalize and concretize in an object the feeling of a son's presence in his mother's life. The spade becomes the emblem—or so he fantasizes—of the worry, the joy, and the ache that she feels in tending and fostering his growth, his blossoming.

So, too, in the little Freudian poem "Purple Blouse" the speaker dreams of selecting the garment that his mother wore on the morning of his conception. In this way he catapults himself back to his own origin.

PURPLE BLOUSE

Then I dreamed I chose
the purple blouse my mother

wore the morning she conceived
me—dressed her, felt her

expectation as my own, her life
now distillate of her one wish

her saying *Yes* to the thing thrown
over her.

The *Afterlife of Objects* is a book of interventions and reckonings.
It is intensely personal, but in a way that widens the space for our own
reveries, our own reimaginings. It invites us to imagine ourselves back
into the selves—the worlds—we inherited.

121

CATHERINE BARNETT

C minus A and B equals—
Tree with no branch equals—

What grief looks like:
A knife rusted in the side of a goat.

No, no.
A coin falling in water

And the fist dart for it.

CATHERINE BARNETT's indelible first book, *Into Perfect Spheres Such Holes Are Pierced,* has a long fore-life and comes to us as a work of full maturity. It is a taut, heartsick, and grief-stricken sequence that keeps returning to the site of a life-changing catastrophe, to the inexplicable death of her two nieces in a plane crash. As she writes at the outset: "You can read one version in the newspaper / and another in the courts / and a third in my sister's face, / in my sister's sisters' faces, / in my mother's face— // in the candles burned down to their jars" ("Transcript"). This entire sequence, a book of female mourning, has the classic feeling and grandeur of a Greek tragedy.

Barnett's poems are scrupulously restrained and beautifully made, though the speaker in them is at times wild and even crazed with feeling, unappeased by sorrow. She is unremitting in her quest to investigate, embody, and understand a swamping sadness, which she sometimes holds at bay by writing about it. Indeed, she keeps seeking figures for grief (a knife rusted in the side of a goat, a coin falling in water) as the poems struggle to do what Freud called "the work of mourning." She writes of "the rations of illumination and grief" ("Theology") and "the grief archive [that] gave out its last ration" ("Book of Lies"). The title poem, the heart of the collection, is representative:

Into Perfect Spheres Such Holes Are Pierced

We unstrung necklaces into two glass bowls
and passed them round to the mourners.
The beads were onyx, agate, quartz, all manner

of stone. Everyone was to take two
and at the end of the service
put one back in my sister's hands.

What could she do but collect
the round weights all night?
She has not restrung them,

not wanting to be finished yet with death.

The stubborn refusal to let go, to give up grieving, is one of the key motifs of Barnett's collection. Images of domesticity keep turning into nightmares of mourning, as when her sister, the bereft mother, "strips the blankets // and strips the sheets / down to the mattress made of stone" ("The Disbelieving"). Barnett writes against erasure and disappearance ("The god of footprints accepts no prayers," she declares in "Refusal," "he's / a cheap and sweaty god who must have lost his mind") and keeps returning with her sisters to the ocean shore of the accident, though it seems to give no consolation. There are four poems called "Site" and two entitled "The Return" threaded through the book. I agree with Linda Gregerson that "[i]f death could be un-done by love—that deathless human wish—if death could be undone by formidable mindfulness and immaculate craft, these poems would revive the dead." They are an act of soul-making.

The Return, ii

My brother thinks it's best to distract my sister,
not ask her about longing and its dirty tricks,
its flirty tricks, her girls

oh, hiding under the sheet waiting to be found,
digging ditches in the dirt,
blowing out the candles—

He holds her up, his arm over her shoulders
so she won't see the eyelashes they leave there,
for luck, like she taught them,
for making wishes that can't be spoken aloud

but I know he hears them,
as she does,
asking the same thing again—

come with us—   *come with us—*

122.

A. VAN JORDAN

So many words hover around my head

A. VAN JORDAN combines the tragic poignancy of the blues with the cinematic sweep of a documentary in his deeply humane and highly imaginative second book, *M-A-C-N-O-L-I-A,* which focuses on the life of MacNolia Cox, a spunky thirteen-year-old girl who won the Akron District Spelling Bee in 1936. Cox was the first African American to advance to the final round of the national competition, but it is generally thought—and Jordan clearly believes—that the Southern judges kept her from winning by deviously tripping her up on the word *nemesis,* which was not on the official list. That stolen opportunity marked her for life, and she was never the same afterward. Hence this conclusive poem, which is spoken by a woman veiled in white:

N-E-M-E-S-I-S BLUES

I'd rather have no name, no name for my man to call
Say, I'd rather lose my name, no name to call
Than to use my name to make a poor girl crawl

They gon' and used my name, cruel as they can be
They up and broke my good name, cruel as they can be
Done set fire to my name and blown the smoke back at me

Smells like turpentine is in the drinks tonight
Yeah, *put* some turpentine in the drinks tonight
Might as well get crazy cause we gonna have to fight

My name must taste like a misspelled word
Poor girl, my name must taste like a misspelled word
But when it's all over, I'll show 'em how trouble gets stirred

Than to use my name to make a poor girl crawl
Man, I'd rather have no name, no name for my man to call
Hell, I'd rather *lose* my name, have no name at all

Jordan comes from Akron, and he stumbled upon Cox's haunting story, as he says, "while researching the lifestyles of African Americans in Ohio during the '20s and '30s." It is for him an emblematic tale—the word "macnolia," he tellingly suggests, means "a Negro who spells and reads as well as [if not better than] any white"—and it gives him a convincing way to concentrate on an individual life while also exploring social attitudes and racial prejudices of Depression-era America.

Jordan's primary strategy is to interweave voices to create a dramatic overall portrait of MacNolia's life. MacNolia speaks often, savoring words, and we hear often from her less-verbal husband, John Montiere, who exclaims on their wedding night: "let's strip off our words / to speak without our tongues. let's / try to tongue without / saying a word. let's turn speech / back into struggle tonight."

Jordan is a formally inventive poet who plays with the notion of the spelling bee, creates dictionary definitions to refer to MacNolia's experiences, and meditates on the nature of words. "Sometimes you learn words / By living them and sometimes / Words learn you / / By defining who you are," MacNolia declares in the poem "Infidelity."

This diverse sequence uses framing devices from the movies ("INTERIOR—NIGHT—Panning shot of MACNOLIA'S bedroom on her deathbed") and takes some of its highest notes from music. One feels more than a little grief-stricken and outraged for the gifted girl who never recovered from her lost or stolen chance, the A student who dropped out of school, married, and ended up working as a domestic in the home of a local physician. "They say she / Spelled like a demon as a child," Jordan has Dr. Wittenberg declare in 1948: "They say she was almost / The national spelling champ, would've / Been the second one we had / From Akron in as little as three years. . . . / I don't know, really, but I'm telling you— / She's the best damn maid in town."

123

NEBRASKA POETRY

A Winter Morning

A farmhouse window far back from the highway
speaks to the darkness in a small, sure voice.
Against this stillness, only a kettle's whisper,
and against the starry cold, one small blue ring of flame.

THE APPOINTMENT of Ted Kooser as poet laureate puts me in mind of other poets from Nebraska who have meant a good deal to me: Willa Cather (1873–1947), John Neihardt (1881–1973), Weldon Kees (1914–1955), and Loren Eiseley (1907–1977). Something about the Great Plains seems to foster a plain, homemade style, a sturdy forthrightness with hidden depths, a hard-won clarity chastened by experience. It is an unadorned, pragmatic, quintessentially American poetry of empty places, of farmlands and low-slung cities. The open spaces stimulate and challenge people. One's mettle is tested. Cather said that coming to Nebraska was like being "thrown onto a land as bare as a piece of sheet iron."

The poets from Nebraska tend to have a reticent manner and a determinedly accessible style, a sensitivity to the natural world. This is a modest, stubborn kind of poetry that owes a great debt to the Native American sensibility. Seasons rotate and weather matters. Natural disasters are real. The visible world informs the verbal one. Yet there are also spiritual presences. The seemingly ordinary world turns out to be extraordinary. If you can learn to read the signs, every landscape has a genuine story to tell. Here is Eiseley's poem "Prairie Spring," which shows something of his gift as a literary naturalist:

Killdeer screaming over the flowing acres
of bronze grass now the buffalo are gone
make a wide eerie silence. In the midst of crying
April has come but meadow flowers alone
spring up to greet her. No more the hooves will thunder
of bison moving northward in the spring.
No more the violet by wet black muzzles
will be cropped under—a long silence follows
after the flashing and exultant wing.

There is a sense of quiet amazement at the core of all Kooser's work, but it especially seems to animate his new collection of poems, a book of portraits and landscapes, *Delights & Shadows*. Every delight is shadowed by darkness in this book of small wonders and hard dualisms. The book begins with a poem called "Walking on Tiptoe" and ends with one entitled "A Happy Birthday." It takes an epigraph from Emily Dickinson— "The Sailor cannot see the North, but knows the Needle can"—but just as easily could have taken one from Wallace Stevens: "Death is the mother of beauty." Mortality is omnipresent and induces a deep attentiveness. Everyone here—a young woman in a wheelchair, a skater dressed in black, a group of mourners after a funeral, the poet himself—seems to be moving lightly over an invisible abyss. "There are days when the fear of death / is as ubiquitous as light. It illuminates / everything," Kooser writes in "Surviving." "Were it not for the way you taught me to look / at the world, to see the life at play in everything," he writes to his mother, who has been dead just one month, "I would have to be lonely forever."

A HAPPY BIRTHDAY

This evening, I sat by an open window
and read till the light was gone and the book
was no more than a part of the darkness.
I could easily have switched on a lamp,
but I wanted to ride this day down into night,
to sit alone and smooth the unreadable page
with the pale gray ghost of my hand.

124

BASKETBALL POEMS

play for mortal stakes . . .
—Robert Frost

The NCAA tournament has got me thinking again about the analogy between basketball and poetry. In one of my favorite books about basketball, *The City Game*, Pete Axthelm writes: "To the uninitiated, the patterns may seem fleeting, elusive, even confusing, but on a city playground, a classic play is frozen in the minds of those who see it—a moment of order and achievement in a turbulent, frustrating existence." At times Axthelm sounds oddly like an urban, streetwise version of Robert Frost, who called poetry "a momentary stay against confusion." A few years ago, watching a college basketball coach diagramming a play on the blackboard, it occurred to me that some men think about a basketball play the same way that I think about a lyric poem—as an imaginative event, an intimate way of focusing and extending a radiant moment, a breakthrough into epiphany, a momentary stay against confusion.

In his essay "Basketball and Poetry: The Two Riches," the poet Stephen Dunn, who once scored 45 points in the *Long Island Press* League, suggests that the most important thing that basketball and poetry have in common is the possibility of transcendence, which he characterizes as the opposite of labor: "In writing, every writer knows when he or she is laboring to achieve an effect. You want to get from here to there, but find yourself willing it, forcing it. The equivalent in basketball is aiming your shot, a kind of strained and usually ineffective purposefulness. What you want is some kind of flow, each next moment a discovery."

My shortlist of favorite basketball poems, lyrics that flow, includes

William Matthews's "In Memory of the Utah Stars" ("Each of them must have terrified / his parents by being so big, obsessive / and exact so young"); Quincy Troupe's "Poem for Magic"; Garrett Hongo's "The Cadence of Silk"; Yusef Komunyakaa's "Slam, Dunk, & Hook"; Marisa de los Santos's "Women Watching Basketball" ("to declare, *Divine is the flesh!* / and for once to believe it, believe it"); and B. H. Fairchild's "Old Men Playing Basketball," a poem, I must admit, that seems to have increasing relevance to me as the years keep coming on:

OLD MEN PLAYING BASKETBALL

The heavy bodies lunge, the broken language
of fake and drive, glamorous jump shot
slowed to a stutter. Their gestures, in love
again with the pure geometry of curves,

rise toward the ball, falter, and fall away.
On the boards their hands and fingertips
tremble in tense little prayers of reach
and balance. Then, the grind of bone

and socket, the caught breath, the sigh,
the grunt of the body laboring to give
birth to itself. In their tolling and grand
sweeps, I wonder, do they still make love

to their wives, kissing the undersides
of their wrists, dancing the old soft-shoe
of desire? And on the long walk home
from the VFW, do they still sing

to the drunken moon? Stands full, clock
moving, the one in army fatigues
and houseshoes says to himself, *pick and roll,*
and the phrase sounds musical as ever,

radio crooning songs of love after the game,
the girl leaning back in the Chevy's front seat
as her raven hair flames in the shuddering
light of the outdoor movie, and now he drives,

gliding toward the net. A glass wand
of autumn light breaks over the backboard.
Boys rise up in old men, wings begin to sprout
at their backs. The ball turns in the darkening air.

125

TONY HOAGLAND

I am asleep in America too,
And I don't know how to wake myself either.

TONY HOAGLAND has a smart and sassy way of thinking about America in his work. He is one of the few poets self-consciously trying to come to terms with—to find a way to think about—the apparent omnipotence and inescapability of mass culture that surrounds us like a sea. We are endlessly swimming through its waters. His third book, with its comic, self-mocking, and very American title, *What Narcissism Means to Me,* heads off into uncharted territory. It is his best collection yet.

Hoagland's poetry suggests that we're in the midst of an unprecedented cultural situation where everything feels like it is being spun all the time. It's hard to break through into genuine feeling. Thus a lovely summer night becomes the "Commercial for a Summer Night," the merchandise is wearing models again this year, and a friend says that of all the available systems ("There's Socialism and Communism and Capitalism, / . . . Feminism and Hedonism, / and there's Catholicism and Bipedalism and Consumerism"), "I think Narcissism is the system / that means the most to me."

When one of the teacher-poet's blue-haired, tongue-studded students declares that "America is for him a maximum-security prison / / Whose walls are made of RadioShacks and Burger Kings, and MTV episodes / Where you can't tell the show from the commercials," the speaker can't tell "if this is a legitimate category of pain, / or whether he is just spin doctoring a better grade." The concluding stanzas of "America" show the kind of zany insightfulness that Hoagland has into contemporary American culture:

And I look at the student with his acne and cell phone and phony
    ghetto clothes
And I think, "I am asleep in America too,

And I don't know how to wake myself either,"
And I remember what Marx said near the end of his life:

"I was listening to the cries of the past,
When I should have been listening to the cries of the future."

But how could he have imagined 100 channels of 24-hour cable
Or what kind of nightmare it might be

When each day you watch rivers of bright merchandise run past you
And you are floating in your pleasure boat upon this river

Even while others are drowning underneath you
And you see their faces twisting in the surface of the waters

And yet it seems to be your own hand
Which turns the volume higher?

Hoagland's vernacular has an odd lyricism. His discursiveness is image-laden. He feels that "deep inside the misery / of daily life, / love lies bleeding," and he's determined to go through the false bottoms of our reality to uncover it. Here he thinks about the allegorical situation of a friend shuttling between a hospital and an adoption agency:

MIGRATION

This year Marie drives back and forth
from the hospital room of her dying friend
to the office of the adoption agency.

I bet sometimes she doesn't know
what threshold she is waiting at—

the hand of her sick friend, hot with fever;
the theoretical baby just a lot of paperwork so far.

But next year she might be standing by a grave,
wearing black with a splash of
                                    banana vomit on it,

the little girl just starting to say *Sesame Street*
and *Cappuccino latte grande Mommy.*
The future ours for a while to hold, with its heaviness—

and hope moving from one location to another
like the holy ghost that it is.

126.

MARTÍN ESPADA

Vivas to those who have failed!
—WALT WHITMAN

MARTÍN ESPADA believes that the pursuit of social and political justice can and must be joined to the quest for art. These ideals are for him inseparable. He is a Latino poet who takes a cue from Whitman and dreams of an inclusive democracy. He stands up for what Whitman calls "the rights of them the others are down upon," and writes a fiery, impure, earth-tinged, human-centered poetry.

Alabanza, the title of Espada's new and selected poems, means "praise" in Spanish. It has a religious sense and derives from *alabar,* "to celebrate with words." Espada self-consciously uses poetry to celebrate those who don't usually find their way into literature—the unsung and marginalized, the overlooked and forgotten. He finds his title in some moving anaphoric lines from the poem "Oubao-Moin" by the Puerto Rican poet Juan Antonio Corretjer (1908–1985), which serve as an epigraph and set the tone for Espada's work over the past two decades:

> Gloria a las manos que la mina excavaran.
> Gloria a las manos que el ganado cuidaran.
> Gloria a las manos que el tabaco, que la caña y el café sembraran . . .
> Para ellas y para su patria, ¡alabanza! ¡alabanza!

> Glory to the hands that dug the mine.
> Glory to the hands that cared for the cattle.
> Glory to the hands that planted the tobacco, the sugarcane and the coffee . . .
> For them and for their country, praise! Praise!

Espada's poems are haunted by voices and memories. Refugees and immigrants call out to him. "I cannot evict them / from my insomniac nights," he writes, "tenants in the city of coughing / and dead radiators." He fantasizes that "this is the year that squatters evict landlords" and "those / who swim the border's undertow / and shiver in boxcars / are greeted with trumpets and drums / at the first railroad crossing / on the other side."

The title poem, "Alabanza: In Praise of Local 100," memorializes forty-three restaurant workers who lost their lives in the attack on the World Trade Center. "Praise Manhattan from a hundred and seven flights up, / like Atlantis glimpsed through the windows of an ancient aquarium," he declares in a poem that becomes a virtual roll call of poor countries. "Praise the great windows where immigrants from the kitchen / could squint and almost see their world, hear the chant of nations: / *Ecuador, México, Republica Dominicana, / Haiti, Yemen, Ghana, Bangladesh. / Alabanza.*"

Here is a villanelle that characteristically becomes a hymn to a group of Spanish-speaking prisoners who find themselves incarcerated in upstate New York:

THE PRISONERS OF SAINT LAWRENCE

Riverview Correctional Facility,
Ogdensburg, New York, 1993

Snow astonishing their hammered faces,
the prisoners of Saint Lawrence, island men,
remember in Spanish the island places.

The Saint Lawrence River churns white into Canada, races
past barbed walls. Immigrants from a dark sea find oceanic
snow astonishing. Their hammered faces

harden in city jails and courthouses, indigent cases
telling translators, public defenders what they
remember in Spanish. The island places,

banana leaf and nervous chickens, graces
gone in this amnesia of snow, stinging cocaine
snow, astonishing their hammered faces.

There is snow in the silence of the visiting room, spaces
like snow in the paper of their poems and letters, that
remember in Spanish the island places.

So the law speaks of cocaine, grams and traces,
as the prisoners of Saint Lawrence, island men,
snow astonishing their hammered faces,
remember in Spanish the island places.

127

YOUNG ASIAN AMERICAN WOMEN POETS

I won't only bloom where I'm planted.

THERE IS A rich and complicated way that many young Asian American poets, especially women, have been dealing with their ancestry and engaging the past. These poets create an art that looks forward by turning back. Their work confronts history and comes to terms with an array of cultural influences, a complex, divided inheritance.

I recommend, for example, Pimone Triplett's debut volume, *Ruining the Picture* (1998), which includes a marvelous group of longer poems that contain many scenes from her mother's Thailand. Triplett employs a golden style to confront a culture that is not entirely her own, but to which she is deeply connected.

Quan Barry's adventurous first book, *Asylum* (2001), is perilously poised between Vietnam, where she was born, and the United States, where she grew up. "Like all effective incendiaries," she writes in "Napalm," the last poem in her autobiographical sequence "Child of the Enemy," "I won't only bloom where I'm planted."

Barry is haunted by her origins, by the legacy of the Vietnam War, by American misconceptions about the land of her birth. She has developed an elliptical but determined way of approaching her subjects. I admire the five-part poem "Triage," which convincingly offers five viewpoints: "What Duc Said," "What Viet Said," "What They Said," "What Science Said" ("There were about 72 million litres of toxic chemicals / sprayed over Vietnamese land and Vietnamese people / during the war"), and "What I Said."

By conservative estimates the mangroves will not return
in this century. Neither will the eyes, the limbs twisted like roots.

Today Viet lies deep in the mosquito sickness—if he dies,
Duc dies too. There will be no time for separation, no time to airlift

the split being into surgery. Instead, the living half will wait passively
for what invariably will come rolling on, the roofs filling with people.

I didn't ask to survive.

Suji Kwock Kim's first book, *Notes from the Divided Country*
(2003), moves fluently between the living and the dead, the Korean
past and the Amerasian present. Her heartfelt and skillful work is
shadowed by the question of what is passed on through a long, blood-
soaked history. She tracks the generations through strong poems for
her great-grandparents, her grandmother, her father, and, especially,
her mother. She also traces the tormented, catastrophic history of count-
less others, many of them nameless, who figured in the making of more
than half a million new Americans.

FLIGHT

We ran from a home

                      we never saw again.

Saw nothing

                         remain ours.

My arm shot

                 from my body. My wife's broken

neck. Our son burned

                    into a wing of smoke.

A peeled face boiling with flies.

                      A man tearing

His gangrened leg off

            with his hands. A girl with her eyes

blown away. She was still

                                                screaming.

I know you

                                           cannot help us.

We will die before you

                                              are born.

Things flee

                                              their names—

Ash. Bone-salt. Charred embers

                                                of skull

The soot is

                                           mute.

128

BIRDSONG

Sir, we are a nest of singing birds.
—Samuel Johnson

Ruth Stone feels the connection between poetry and birdsong in "Poems," a lyric that indicates how inspiration comes to her. It's one of my favorite pieces from her book *In the Next Galaxy*.

Poems

When you come back to me
it will be crow time
and flycatcher time,
with rising spirals of gnats
between the apple trees.
Every weed will be quadrupled,
coarse, welcoming
and spine-tipped.
The crows, their black flapping
bodies, their long calling
toward the mountain;
relatives, like mine,
ambivalent, eye-hooded;
hooting and tearing.
And you will take me in
to your fractal meaningless
babble; the quick of my mouth,
the madness of my tongue.

Over the centuries, poets have often identified with cuckoos ("Sumer is icumen in— / Lhude sing, cuccu!") and mockingbirds, seagulls and herons, owls and nightingales ("Thou wast not born for death, immortal Bird!"). They have also noted their difference from us. They have watched them in their backyards (Anthony Hecht's "House Sparrows" nobly welcomes "these chipper stratoliners, / Unsullen, unresentful, full of the grace / Of cheerfulness"), followed them into the woods (Robert Burns, "Address to the Woodlark"; Amy Clampitt, "A Whippoorwill in the Woods"), and tracked them to the shore (May Swenson, "One of the Strangest"; Galway Kinnell, "The Grey Heron"). They have treated birds as messengers to and from the beyond, the very embodiment of a transcendent vocation.

For example, in his definitive compendium, *Shamanism,* Mircea Eliade points out that "[a]ll over the world learning the language of animals, especially of birds, is equivalent to knowing the secrets of nature and hence to being able to prophesy." He presents evidence that the Pomo and the Menomini shamans imitate birds' songs, just as birdcalls can be heard during séances among the Yakut, the Yukagir, the Chukchee, the Goldi, the Eskimo, and others. To mimic the natural call of a bird, or, more strongly, to become a bird oneself, "indicates the capacity," Eliade notes, "to undertake the ecstatic journey to the sky and the beyond."

It may be that a remnant of magical practice clings to a poet like Stone when she speaks of "crow time" and "flycatcher time," or when she mimics and even embodies "the fractal meaningless babble" of crow song. There is something irrational in poetry, which still trembles with a holy air. Shelley characterized the poet as "a nightingale, who sits in darkness and sings to cheer its own solitude with sweet sounds." I've always loved that moment at the end of "To a Skylark" when he calls upon the bird to teach him the ecstasy of its song. He seeks an energy that is both primitive and transcendental, the power of nature manifested through language. If he can learn birdsong, he declares, then he would sing with such "harmonious madness" that the awestruck world would pause and listen with the same rapt attention that he shows listening to the skylark's rapturous song:

Teach me half the gladness
   That thy brain must know,
Such harmonious madness
   From my lips would flow
The world should listen then—as I am listening now.

129

ROBERT PINSKY

Air an instrument of the tongue.
The tongue an instrument
Of the body. The body
An instrument of spirit,
The spirit a being of the air.

I'VE BEEN READING Robert Pinsky avidly for thirty years. I was lucky to start out with his first book, *Sadness and Happiness* (1975), which brought to contemporary poetry a rich discursiveness, a compelling new way of thinking, and a refreshing sense of other people. I've followed him through his book-length poem, *An Explanation of America* (1980), a remarkable meditation on being a citizen in our republic; *History of My Heart* (1984), which shows him to be an omnivorous thinker working at full power; *The Want Bone* (1990), which initiated a strange new lyricism into his work; *The Figured Wheel: New and Collected Poems: 1966–1996* (1996), an essential gathering that included twenty-one new poems; and, most recently, *Jersey Rain* (2000), a work of midlife reckonings. "Now near the end of the middle stretch of road / What have I learned?" he asks in the title poem. "Some earthly wiles. An art."

I recommend Pinsky's brilliant verse translation *The Inferno of Dante* (1990) and his highly engaging and unusually readable works of criticism: *The Situation of Poetry* (1977), *Poetry and the World* (1988), *The Sounds of Poetry* (1998), and *Democracy, Culture, and the Voice of Poetry* (2002), which thinks hard about the place of poetry in modern democracy. He has been especially alert to the way that poetry includes the social realm and argues that "[t]he solitude of lyric, almost by the nature of human solitude and the human voice, invokes a social presence."

In 1997, Pinsky founded the Favorite Poem Project during his tenure as the poet laureate of the United States (1997–2000). This project, a huge national resource, has culminated in three anthologies, which he edited with Maggie Dietz: *Americans' Favorite Poems; Poems to Read;* and, most recently, *An Invitation to Poetry: A New Favorite Poem Project Anthology,* which includes a DVD of people from all walks of life saying something about their favorite poems and then reading them aloud. The original meaning of the word *anthology,* which derives from the Greek, is "flower gathering," and these books compose a surprisingly diverse and colorful garden. These anthologies give us a strong sense of how single poems reach individual readers.

Here is one of my favorite poems by Pinsky. I once had the life-changing experience of teaching poetry to a group of deaf children in Westchester County, New York, and thus this poem has special relevance to me. It triggers memories and gives me back a sense of my students' secret creativity and power, their eerie silence and explosive imaginations.

If You Could Write One Great Poem, What Would You Want It To Be About?

(Asked of four student poets at the Illinois Schools for the Deaf and Visually Impaired)

Fire: because it is quick, and can destroy.
Music: place where anger has its place.
Romantic Love—the cold or stupid ask why.
Sign: that it is a language, full of grace,

That it is visible, invisible, dark and clear,
That it is loud and noiseless and is contained
Inside a body and explodes in air
Out of a body to conquer from the mind.

130

FAREWELL

Another year gone—
hat in my hand,
sandals on my feet.
—Bashō

GOOD-BYES ARE POIGNANT. They belong to the part of life that's hard to write about. I'd like to close with a special nod to the reader, whom I think of as a friend. I'd like to sign it with a wave and even a kiss good-bye, the lyric as farewell. As Wallace Stevens writes, "That would be waving and that would be crying, / Crying and shouting and meaning farewell" ("Waving Adieu, Adieu, Adieu").

My grandfather taught me that, when a friend or relative was leaving on the train, we should stand on the platform and continue waving until the train had disappeared. It was something he learned from a Japanese friend. I was delighted to find this notion confirmed in Robert Aitken's illuminating book *A Zen Wave,* in which he remarks that the Japanese say good-bye to the very end: "They wave and wave until their friends are out of sight." He points this out as part of a commentary on one of Bashō's poems, which Robert Hass renders:

Seeing people off,
being seen off—
autumn in Kiso.

Bashō seems to be saying that for him, fall in Kiso is the time of departures. It is almost the outcome—the upshot—of our leave-takings. Now we say good-bye to our friends; now our friends say good-bye to us.

The experience of seeing off a friend is also important in Chinese poetry. Here is Ezra Pound's version of a striking poem that the wanderer Li Po wrote in 754 about parting from a dear one in Hsuancheng. Pound's lyrical adaptation first appeared as one of "Four Poems of Departure" in *Cathay* (1915). (There is also a strong version of this poem in Red Pine's *Poems of the Masters*.)

Taking Leave of a Friend

> Blue mountains to the north of the walls,
> White river winding about them;
> Here we must make separation
> And go out through a thousand miles of dead grass.
> Mind like a floating wide cloud,
> Sunset like the parting of old acquaintances
> Who bow over their clasped hands at a distance.
> Our horses neigh to each other
>   as we are departing.

"Dear friend whoever you are take this kiss, / I give it especially to you, do not forget me," Whitman declared in one of his songs of parting, "So Long!" (He also boldly announced, "Camerado, this is no book, / Who touches this touches a man.") I'd like to close with lines of farewell from the twenty-fourth section of the 1860 edition of *Leaves of Grass*. Whitman was unabashed about addressing and embracing each stranger, each one of us, as a dear familiar, about imagining the exchange between poet and his unknown reader as a form of creative love. I leave these lines to each individual reader, to each one of you, as a fleeting final gesture of our shared participation in poetry:

> Lift me close to your face till I whisper,
> What you are holding is in reality no book, nor part of a book,
> It is a man, flushed and full-bodied—it is I—*So long!*
> We must separate—Here! take from my lips this kiss,
> Whoever you are, I give it especially to you;
> *So long*—and I hope we shall meet again.

NOTES AND ACKNOWLEDGMENTS

THE PIECES that comprise *Poet's Choice* were almost all first presented in the *Washington Post Book World*. Some of them have been emended and enlarged as my own view of the poetry horizon has expanded. I have added and changed things throughout to make a more complete book. There are still many poets I love whose work does not appear here.

I began writing the Poet's Choice column shortly after September 11, 2001, and the impress of that devastating event is heavy on my choices. It was clear from the powerful response of readers to the column that poetry sustains us in hard times. I have been fortunate to have had such cosmopolitan readers. I have reconceived the order of the pieces for the purposes of this collection and divided the book into two equal parts. The scope of the first is international, the second American. But my understanding throughout is that American poetry, too, participates in the larger world.

I owe a special debt of thanks to Marie Arana, the exceptional editor of the *Washington Post Book World*, for inviting me to write the Poet's Choice column and for her weekly encouragement throughout my three-year tenure. Her warm responsiveness and keen insightfulness have made all the difference. I am also grateful to Mary Morris, who secured the permissions for the *Post*, and to the various Book World editors, who generously worked on my pieces over the years.

My friend and agent Liz Darhansoff has given me wonderful support. I am also grateful to my many friends at Harcourt, especially David Hough, managing editor, and Jennifer Gilmore, head of publicity. This book is dedicated to my dear friend and editor, André Bernard, to whom I owe so much. He is like a brother to me.

PUBLICATION ACKNOWLEDGMENTS

"Patriotic Songs" from *Amen* by Yehuda Amichai. Copyright © 1977 by Yehuda Amichai. Reprinted by permission of HarperCollins Publishers. From *Poems of Nazim Hikmet*, translated by Randy Blasing and Mutlu Konuk. Translation copyright © 1994, 2002 by Randy Blasing and Mutlu Konuk. Reprinted by permission of Persea Books, Inc. (New York). César Vallejo's "Our Bread" (excerpt) from *The Black Heralds*, translated by Rebecca Seiferle. English translation copyright © 2003 by Rebecca Seiferle. Reprinted with the permission of Copper Canyon Press, P.O. Box 271, Port Townsend, WA 98368-0271. Whitman's lines from "Crossing Brooklyn Ferry" appeared in *Leaves of Grass*, 1856, revised 1881. "To the Nightingale," translated by Alistair Reid, from Jorge Luis Borges, *Selected Poems*, edited by Alexander Coleman. Viking. Copyright © 1999 by Maria Kodama. Translation copyright © 1999 by Alistair Reid. Reprinted with permission. Sappho fragment: "Sappho: A Garland: The Poems and Fragments of Sappho," translated by Jim Powell. Farrar Straus Giroux. Copyright © 1993 by Jim Powell. Reprinted with permission. "God's Grandeur" and "Pied Beauty" appear in *Poems and Prose*, by Gerard Manley Hopkins. Copyright © 1953, 1963, The Estate of W. H. Gardner. "Caedmon's Hymn" (Translated from Saxon Form). "Caedmon" by Denise Levertov, from *Breathing the Water*, copyright © 1987 by Denise Levertov. Reprinted by permission of New Directions Publishing Corp. "Ode VI" from *Epinician Odes and Dithyrambs of Bacchylides*, translated by David R. Slavitt. Copyright © 1998 by the University of Pennsylvania Press. Reprinted by permission of the University of Pennsylvania Press. Pindar excerpt from "Turn 1." Nisetich, Frank J., *Pindar's Victory Songs*, pp. 82. © 1980 by the Johns Hopkins University Press. Reprinted with permission of The Johns Hopkins University Press. From *Pure Pagan*, translated by Burton Raffel, copyright © 2004 by Burton Raffel. Introduction © by Guy Davenport. Used by permission of Modern Library, a division of Random House, Inc. Reprinted by permission of Farrar, Straus and Giroux, LLC: "Ode (iii.30)" from *The Odes of Horace* translated by David Ferry. Excerpt from "An Horation Notion," from *Split Horizon: Poems* by Thomas Lux. Copyright © 1994 by Thomas Lux. Reprinted by permission of Houghton Mifflin Company. All rights reserved. "Not a *Paris Review* Interview" by F. T. Prince appears in *Collected Poems: 1935–1992*, The Sheep Meadow Press. Copyright © 1993 by F. T. Prince. The lines from Frank Bidart's poem "Advice to the Players" appear in his chapbook *Music Like Dirt*. Copyright © 2002 by Frank Bidart. Reprinted with the permission of Sarabande Books. The lines from J. D. McClatchy's translation of Horace's "Ars Poetica" appear in his book *Twenty Questions*. Columbia University Press. Copyright © 1998 Columbia University Press. Reprinted with permission. Blaga Dimitrova's poem "Ars Poetica" appears in *Scars*, selected and translated from the Bulgarian by Ludmilla G. Popova-Wightman. Ivy Press.

Translation copyright © 2002 by Ludmilla G. Popova-Wightman. Reprinted with permission of Ivy Press. "My Country in Darkness," from *The Lost Land* by Eavan Boland. Copyright © 1998 by Eavan Boland. Used by permission of W. W. Norton & Company, Inc. Adaptations of poems by Nezahualcóyotl and Ayocuan Cuetzpaltzin. Reprinted with the permission of Scribner, an imprint of Simon & Schuster Adult Publishing Group, from *Collecting the Animals* by Peter Everwine. Copyright © 1969, 1970, 1971, 1972 by Peter Everwine. "Poem of Temilotzin" and the seven lines beginning "I comprehend the secret" in *Fifteen Poets of the Aztec World,* by Miguel Leon-Portilla. Copyright © 1992 by the University of Oklahoma Press, Norman. Reprinted by permission of the publisher. John Hollander's translation of an anonymous Anglo-Saxon riddle appears in his anthology *War Poems.* Alfred A. Knopf. Copyright © 1999 by John Hollander. Used by Permission. "A Riddle" is reprinted by permission of Louisiana State University Press from *Darkening Water: Poems* by Daniel Hoffman. Copyright © 2002 by Daniel Hoffman. Ella Bat-Tzion's poem "Peace," translated by Barbara Goldberg and Moshe Dor, and Eytan Eytan's "The Wind Grinds," translated by Merrill Leffler and Moshe Dor, appear in *After the First Rain: Israeli Poems on War and Peace,* edited by Moshe Dor and Barbara Goldberg. Syracuse University Press in association with Dryad Press. Copyright © 1998 by Syracuse University Press. Reprinted with permission. Kathy Fagan's "Little Bad Dream Charm" appears in her book *The Charm.* Zoo Press. Copyright © 2002 by Kathy Fagan. Reprinted with permission. Thomas Campion's poem can be found in *Campion's Works,* ed. by Percival Vivian. Oxford University Press, 1909. Excerpts from *I Am: The Selected Poetry of John Clare* edited by Jonathan Bate. "Epiphany" by Robert Fitzgerald, from *Spring Shade: Poems 1931–1970,* copyright © 1969 by Robert Fitzgerald. Reprinted by permission of New Directions Publishing Corp. "The Oxen" can be found in *The Complete Poems of Thomas Hardy.* Macmillan Publishing Company. Copyright © Macmillan London Ltd. 1976. All quotations come from Charlotte Mew, *Collected Poems and Selected Prose,* edited by Val Warner. Carcanet Press. Previously uncollected work copyright © The Estate of Charlotte Mew 1981, 1997. Introduction, editorial material and selection copyright © Val Warner 1997. Used with permission of Carcanet Press Limited. "Cuchulain Comforted," reprinted with permission of Scribner, an imprint of Simon & Schuster Adult Publishing Group, and with the permission of AP Watt Ltd on behalf of Michael B. Yeats, from *W. B. Yeats, The Poems: A New Edition,* edited by Richard J. Finneran. Poems copyright © 1983 by Anne Yeats. "Last Poems 10" and "Last Poems 13" from *Rabindranath Tagore: Final Poems* by Rabindranath Tagore, tr. by Wendy Baker and Saranindranath Tagore. English translation copyright © 2001 by Wendy Baker and Saranindranath Tagore. Reproduced by permission of George Braziller, Inc. All quotations from *Sonnets of Guiseppe Belli,* translated by Miller Williams, are reprinted by permission of Louisiana State University Press, translation copyright © 1981. Reprinted by permission of Farrar, Straus and Giroux, LLC: "In Memory Of" and excerpt from "Pilgrimage" from *Selected Poems* by Giuseppe Ungaretti, translated by Andrew Frisardi. Reprinted by permission of Farrar, Straus and Giroux, LLC: "Sit the noon out . . ." and "The Eel" from *Collected Poems 1920–1954* by Eugenio Montale, translated by Jonathan Galassi. "The Panther" and "The Gazelle" from *Slow Air,* copyright © 2002 by Robin Robertson, reprinted by permission of Harcourt, Inc. and Macmillan Publishers. Reprinted by permission of Farrar, Straus and Giroux, LLC: "Self-Portrait, 1969" from

In the Western Night: Collected Poems: 1965–1990 by Frank Bidart. Reprinted by perm—
sion of Farrar, Straus and Giroux, LLC: Excerpts from "Self-Portrait" by Rainer Mari.
Rilke, translated by Robert Lowell from *Collected Poems* by Robert Lowell. Ernst Stadler,
"The Saying," translated by Stephen Berg, from *The Steel Cricket: Version 1958–1997.*
Copyright © 1997 by Stephen Berg. Reprinted with the permission of Copper Canyon
Press, P. O. Box 271, Port Townsend, WA 98368-0271. Reprinted by permission of Far-
rar, Straus and Giroux, LLC: Excerpts from "O the Chimneys" translated by Michael
Roloff and from "Fleeing" and "Butterfly" translated by Ruth and Matthew Mead from
O the Chimneys by Nelly Sachs. Boland, Eavan; *After Every War.* Princeton University
Press. Reprinted by permission of Princeton University Press. "The Beggar Woman of
Naples" by Max Jacob, translated by John Ashbery. Copyright © 1979 by John Ashbery.
Reprinted by permission of Georges Borchardt, Inc., on behalf of the author. "The Yel-
low Star Agani" and "Artless Lines" appear in *The Selected Poems of Max Jacob,* edited
and translated by William Kulik, Oberlin College Press. Copyright © 1999 by Oberlin
College. Reprinted by permission of the publisher. Ikkyü, ["night after night . . ."] from
Crow With No Mouth, versions by Stephen Berg. Copyright © 1989, 2000 by Stephen
Berg. Reprinted with the permission of Copper Canyon Press, P. O. Box 271, Port
Townsend, WA 98368-0271. "Black as an Iris" from *In the Inmost Hour of the Soul: Se-
lected Poems of Marina Tsvetayeva,* translated by Nina Kossman. Copyright 1989 by The
Humana Press, Inc., used by permission. Reprinted with permission of Scribner, an im-
print of Simon & Schuster Adult Publishing Group, and with the permission of The
Wylie Agency, from *Osip Mandelstam Selected Poems,* translated by Clarence Brown and
W. S. Merwin. Copyright © 1973 by Clarence Brown and W. S. Merwin. Selections
from *Art in the Light of Conscience: Eight Essays on Poetry by Marina Tsvetaeva,* trans-
lated with Introduction and Notes by Angela Livingstone. © 1992 by Angela Living-
stone and reprinted by permission of Harvard University Press. "Incantation by
Laughter" and the untitled poem beginning "Russia, I give you my divine . . ." by
Velimir Khlebnikov. Reprinted by permission of the publisher from *The King of Time:
Poems, Fictions, Visions of the Future* by Velimir Khlebnikov, pp. 20, 53–54, Cambridge,
Mass.: Harvard University Press, Copyright 1985, by the Dia Art Foundation. Reprinted
by permission of Farrar, Straus and Giroux, LLC: "May 24, 1980" from *Collected Poems
in English* by Joseph Brodsky. "A Confession," "Gift" and selected lines from eight
poems, as submitted, from *The Collected Poems 1931–1987* by Czeslaw Milosz. Copyright
© 1988 by Czeslaw Milosz Royalties, Inc. Reprinted by permission of HarperCollins
Publishers. Reprinted by permission of Farrar, Straus and Giroux, LLC: "A Flame" and
"A Quick Poem" translated by Clare Cavanagh and "Fire" translated by Renata Gorczynski from *Without End: New and Selected Poems by Adam Zagajewski.* Kocbek, Edvard;
Nothing is Lost. Princeton University Press. Reprinted by permission of Princeton University Press. "Words" by Tomaž Šalamun, copyright © 1998 by Christopher Merrill and
Tomaž Šalamun from *Feast* by Tomaž Šalamun, copyright © 2000 by Harcourt, Inc.,
reprinted by permission of Harcourt, Inc. "Pleasures" and excerpt from "Twilight Metaphysics" by Radmila Lazic, translated from the Serbian by Charles Simic. English language translation copyright 2003 by Charles Simic. Reprinted from *A Wake for the Living*
with the permission of Graywolf Press, Saint Paul, Minnesota. Reprinted by permission
of the publishers, Farrar, Straus and Giroux, LLC and Faber and Faber Ltd: "Shema"

by Edward Connery Lathem. Copyright 1969 by Henry Holt and Company. Copyrig © 1936 by Robert Frost, copyright © 1964 by Lesley Frost Ballantine. Reprinted by pe. mission of Henry Holt and Company, LLC. "Ghazal-[The only language of loss left in the world is Arabic—]," from The Country Without a Post Office by Agha Shahid Ali. Copyright © 1997 by Agha Shahid Ali. Used by permission of W. W. Norton & Company, Inc. Reetika Vazirani, "It's Me, I'm Not Home," "Lullaby," and excerpts from "It's a Young Country" and "Beijing" from World Hotel. Copyright © 2002 by Reetika Vazirano. Reprinted with the permission of Copper Canyon Press, P. O. Box 271, Port Townsend, WA 98368-0271. Ibn Ammar's "Reading" from Poems of Arab Andalusia, City Lights Books. Translation copyright © 1989 by Cola Franzen. Reprinted by permission of City Lights Books. Reprinted by permission of Farrar, Straus and Giroux, LLC: "Reading: The Bus" from Flesh and Blood by C. K. Williams. "The House Was Quiet and the World Was Calm," copyright © 1947 by Wallace Stevens, from The Collected Poems of Wallace Stevens by Wallace Stevens, copyright © 1954 by Wallace Stevens and renewed 1982 by Holly Stevens. Used by permission of Alfred A. Knopf, a division of Random House, Inc. Reprinted by permission of Farrar, Straus and Giroux, LLC: Excerpts from "Homage to Mistress Bradstreet" from Collected Poems 1937–1971 by John Barryman. "Women's Labors" from Approximate Darling by Lee Upton. Copyright © 1996 by Lee Upton. Reprinted by permission of the University of Georgia Press. Three lines, as submitted, from "Metaphors" from Crossing the Water by Sylvia Plath. Copyright © 1960 by Ted Hughes. Reprinted by permission of the publishers, HarperCollins Publishers and Faber and Faber Ltd. "Genesis 1:28" and "Prayer for My Children" are reprinted by permission of Louisiana State University Press from Four Testimonies by Kate Daniels. Copyright © 1998 by Kate Daniels. "Nursling" appears in Kathleen Ossip, The Search Engine. The American Poetry Review. Copyright © 2002 by Kathleen Ossip. Reprinted with permission. "The Runner" by Allen Grossman, from The Ether Dome, copyright ©1979 by Allen Grossman. Reprinted by permission of New Directions Publishing Corp. "The Lesson," "The Guilty Man," "Father and Son," "Night Letter," "The Portrait," "Journal for My Daughter," from The Collected Poems by Stanley Kunitz. Copyright © 2000 by Stanley Kunitz. Used by permission of W. W. Norton & Company, Inc. "The Whipping." Copyright © 1966 by Robert Hayden, from Collected Poems of Robert Hayden by Robert Hayden, edited by Frederick Glaysher. Used by permission of Liveright Corporation. Adonis's poem "Beginning Speech," translated by Lena Jayyusi and John Heath-Stubbs, can also be found in Modern Arabic Poetry, edited by Salma Khadra Jayyusi. Columbia University Press. Copyright © 1991 by Columbia University Press. Reprinted with permission. The excerpt from Mohammed Shehadeh's "Letters to Childhood," translated by Aziz Shihab, copyright © 1998 by Mohammed Shehadeh, appears in The Flag of Childhood: Poems from the Middle East, selected by Naomi Shihab Nye. Simon & Schuster. Copyright © 1998 by Naomi Shihab Nye. Reprinted by permission of Naomi Shihab Nye, 2005. Nazim Hikmet's poem "The Optimist," translated by Randy Blasing and Mutlu Konuk, appears in Poems of Nazim Hikmet. Persea Books. Copyright © 1994, 2002 by Randy Blasing and Mutlu Konuk. Used by permission. Excerpt from "Staying at Grandma's" copyright © 2005 by the Estate of Jane Kenyon. Reprinted from Collected Poems with the permission of Graywolf Press, Saint Paul, Minnesota. Lucille Clifton, excerpt from "Daughters" from The Book of Light. Copyright

1993 by Lucille Clifton. Reprinted with the permission of Copper Canyon Press,
?. O. Box 271, Port Townsend, WA 98368-0271. Li-Young Lee, "I Ask My Grandmother
to Sing" from *Rose.* Copyright © 1986 by Li-Young Lee. Reprinted with permission of
BOA Editions, Ltd., www.BOAEditions.org. Lorine Niedecker's "Grandfather" appears
in *Lorine Niedecker: Collected Works,* edited by Jenny Penberthy. University of California
Press, May 2002. Reprinted with permission of the University of California Press.
"Ichabod!" appears in *John Greenleaf Whittier, Selected Poems,* edited by Brenda Wine-
apple. American Poets Project: The Library of America. Copyright © 2004 by Literary
Classics of the United States, Inc. Excerpts from "Old Timer's Day" from *Old and New
Poems* by Donald Hall. Copyright © 1990 by Donald Hall. Reprinted by permission of
Houghton Mifflin Company. All rights reserved. "The Freaks at Spurgin Field Road,"
from *Making Certain It Goes On: Collected Poems of Richard Hugo* by Richard Hugo.
Copyright © 1984 by The Estate of Richard Hugo. Used by permission of W. W. Norton & Company, Inc. "A Performance at Hog Theater" first appeared in Russell Edson's
book *The Childhood of an Equestrian.* Copyright © 1973 by Russell Edson. Used with
Permission of the author. By William Carlos Williams, from *Collected Poems 1939–1962,
Volume II.* "The Banner Bearer" copyright © 1944 by William Carlos Williams. "Aspho-
del, That Greeny Flower" copyright © 1948 by William Carlos Williams. Reprinted by
permission of New Directions Publishing Corp. From *Selected Poems of Amy Lowell,*
edited by Melissa Bradshaw and Adrienne Munich. Rutgers University Press. Copyright
© 2002 by Rutgers, The State University of New Jersey. "The Taxi" originally appeared
in *Sword Blades and Poppy Seed.* The MacMillan Company, 1914. "Parousia," "Route,"
and "Psalm" by George Oppen, from *Collected Poems,* copyright © 1965 by George
Oppen. Reprinted by permission of New Directions Publishing Corp. The lines from
J. D. McClatchy's translation of Horace's "Ars Poetica" appear in his book "Twenty
Questions." Columbia University Press. Copyright © 1998 Columbia University Press.
Reprinted with permission. From *The Poems of Charles Reznikoff, 1918–1975,* edited by
Seamus Cooney. Reprinted by permission of Black Sparrow Books, an imprint of David
R. Godine, Publisher, Inc. Copyright © 2005 by the Estate of Charles Reznikoff. "Yom
Kippur Sonnet, with a Line from Lamentations" appears in *Dead Men's Praise* by Jacque-
line Osherow. Copyright © 1999 by Jacqueline Osherow. Used by permission of
Grove/Atlantic, Inc. The stanza from "To a Friend on the Day of Atonement" from *Col-
lected Poems* by Robert Mezey. University of Arkansas Press, 2000. Reprinted by permis-
sion of the author. The lines from "Yom Kippur 1984," from *Your Native Land, Your Life:
Poems by Adrienne Rich.* Copyright © 1986 by Adrienne Rich. Used by permission of the
author and W. W. Norton & Company, Inc. "Gloss," "Missal," copyright © 2004 by
Brooks Haxton, from *Uproar: Antiphonies to Psalms* by Brooks Haxton, copyright ©
2004 by Brooks Haxton. Used by permssion of Alfred A. Knopf, a division of Random
House, Inc. Mark Strand's poem is from *The Dark Harbor* by Mark Strand, copyright ©
1993 by Mark Strand. Used by permission of Alfred A. Knopf, a division of Random
House, Inc. "A Postcard from the Volcano," copyright © 1947 by Wallace Stevens, from
The Collected Poems of Wallace Stevens by Wallace Stevens, copyright © 1954 by Wallace
Stevens and renewed 1982 by Holly Stevens. Used by permission of Alfred A. Knopf, a
division of Random House, Inc. "Delia Rexroth" by Kenneth Rexroth, from *Collected
Shorter Poems,* copyright © 1944 by Kenneth Rexroth. "The Love Poems of Marichiko:

VII" by Kenneth Rexroth, from *The Morning Star,* copyright © 1979 by Kenne[th] Rexroth. Both poems reprinted by permission of New Directions Publishing Cor[p.] Reprinted by permission of International Creative Management, Inc. Copyright © 1935–1978 by Muriel Rukeyser, from *The Collected Poems of Muriel Rukeyser,* University of Pittsburgh Press 2005. "What the Living Do," from *What the Living Do* by Marie Howe. Copyright © 1997 by Marie Howe. Used by permission of W. W. Norton & Company, Inc. Reprinted by permission of Farrar, Straus and Giroux, LLC: "Well Water" from *The Complete Poems* by Randall Jarrell. Reprinted by the permission of Farrar, Straus and Giroux, LLC: Excerpts from *The Dream Songs* by John Barryman. Reprinted by permission of Farrar, Straus and Giroux, LLC: "Henry's Understanding" and excerpt from "Defensio in Extremis" from *Delusions, Etc.* by John Barryman. Copyright © 1998 by the Estate of Robert Penn Warren. Reprinted by permission of William Morris Agency, LLC on behalf of the Author. The stanza from "The Blue Swallows" and the poem "Einstein & Freud & Jack" appear in *The Selected Poems of Howard Nemerov,* edited by Daniel Anderson and published by Swallow Press/Ohio University Press. Copyright © 2003 by Swallow Press/Ohio University Press. Reprinted with permission of Margaret Nemerov. "To Old Age" from "New Addresses" by Kenneth Koch. Copyright © 2000 Alfred A. Knopf. Reprinted with permission from the Kenneth Koch Literary Estate. "With Kit, Age 7, At the Beach" copyright © 1970, 1998 by the Estate of William Stafford. Reprinted from *The Way It Is: New & Selected Poems* with the permission of Graywolf Press, Saint Paul, Minnesota. "To Swim, To Believe," from *Selected Poems 1960–1990* by Maxine Kumin. Copyright © 1996 by Maxine Kumin. Used by permission of W. W. Norton & Company, Inc. "The Night Abraham Called to the Stars" and lines from "The Trap-Door" from *The Night Abraham Called to the Stars* by Robert Bly. Copyright © 2001 by Robert Bly. Reprinted by permission of HarperCollins Publishers. "How Poetry Comes to Me," from *No Nature* by Gary Snyder, copyright © 1992 by Gary Snyder. Used by permission of Pantheon Books, a division of Random House, Inc. Copyright © 1991 by Gary Snyder from *No Nature: New and Selected Poems.* Copyright © 2004 by Gary Snyder from *Riprap and Cold Mountain Poems.* Reprinted by permission of Shoemaker & Hoard. "The Pupil," "Psalm and Lament," from *New and Selected Poems* by Donald Justice, copyright © 1995 by Donald Justice. Used by permission of Alfred A. Knopf, a division of Random House, Inc. Reprinted by permission of Farrar, Straus and Giroux, LLC: "Dream Song #35" from *The Dream Songs* by John Barryman. The poem "Too Noble" and the lines from "The Problem with Bliss" copyright © 1992 by Wayne State University Press. Reprinted from *You Are Not Stendhal: New and Selected Poems* with the permission of Wayne State University Press. "Report from the Field" and excerpt from *Bridge, Moon, Professor, Shoes* copyright © 2004 by Dorothea Tanning. Reprinted from *A Table of Content* with the permission of Graywolf Press, Saint Paul, Minnesota. "Sleeping Late on Judgment Day," "Painkiller," from *Sleeping Late on Judgement Day* by Jane Mayhall, copyright © 2004 by Jane Mayhall. Used by permission of Alfred A. Knopf, a division of Random House, Inc. "Grief" from *Time & Money: New Poems* by William Matthews. Copyright © 1995 by William Matthews. Reprinted by permission of Houghton Mifflin Company. All rights reserved. David Ignatow, "All Quiet" from *Against the Evidence* copyright © 1993 by David Ignatow and reprinted by permission of Wesleyan University Press. Yusef Komunyakaa "You and I Are isappearing" from *Dien Cai Dau* © 1988 by Yusef Komunyakaa and reprinted by permission of Wesleyan University Press. "I Saw You Walking," copyright © 2006 by Deborah Garrison, from *The Second Child* by Deborah Garrison. Used by permission of Random House, Inc. Paul Goodman's "The Lordly Hudson" appears in *Collected Poems.* Random House. Copyright © 1972, 1973 by the Estate of Paul Goodman, permission by Sally Goodman. "Spell Spoken by Suppliant to Helios for Protection," "Lamentation on Ur," and excerpts from *Far Side of the Earth: Poems* by Tom Sleigh. Copyright © 2003 by Tom Sleigh. Reprinted by permission of Houghton Mifflin Company. All rights reserved. Excerpts and the poem "Reasons," from *Letters to a Stranger* by Thomas James. Copyright © 1973 by Thomas James. Reprinted by permission of Houghton Mifflin Company. All rights reserved. Stan Rice's poem "Monkey Hill" first appeared in *Body of Work*. Lost Roads. Publishers © 1983 by Stan Rice. "Seasonal, 1991" and "2–26–91" are reprinted by permission of Louisiana State University Press from *Easy* by Roland Flint. Copyright © 1991, 1992, 1994, 1996, 1997, 1998, 1999 by Roland Flint. "Night Owl" from *Be Properly Scared* by M. Wyrebek, © 1996. By permission of Four Way Books. All rights reserved. Excerpt from "Some Sparrows" is reprinted with permission from the publisher of *Entering a Life* by Ernesto Trejo. Houston: Arte Publico Press, University of Houston, © 1990. "Meditation" from *Silks: Poems by Roberta Spear* © 1980 by Roberta Spear. Reprinted by permission of Henry Holt and Company, LLC. Excerpts from Peter Everwine, "From the Meadow: Selected and New Poems." University of Pittsburgh Press. Copyright © 2004, Peter Everwine. Reprinted by permission of the University of Pittsburgh Press. From Michael Fried, *The Next Bend in the Road.* The University of Chicago Press. Copyright © 2004 by the University of Chicago. Reprinted with permission. "God Hunger," "Reminder," excerpt from "Switchblade," and the last stanza from "Not the End of the World" from *New and Selected Poems* by Michael Ryan. Copyright © 2004 by Michael Ryan. Reprinted by permission of Houghton Mifflin Company. All rights reserved. "The Seven Ages" from *The Seven Ages* by Louise Gluck. Copyright © 2001 by Louise Gluck. Reprinted by permission of HarperCollins Publishers. Reprinted by permission of Farrar, Straus and Giroux, LLC: Excerpt from *The Unsubscriber* by Bill Knott. Bill Knott, "Death" and "Goodbye" from *Laugh at the End of the World: Collected Comic Poems 1969–1999*. Copyright © 2000 by Bill Knott. Reprinted with permission of BOA Editions, Ltd., www.BOAEditions.org. Reprinted by permission of Farrar, Straus and Giroux, LLC: Excerpt from *Streets in Their Own Ink* by Stuart Dybek. All quotations from Mark Jarman, *To the Green Man.* Copyright © 2004 by Mark Jarman. Reprinted with the permission of Sarabande Books. "Haiku" and "Tropico" by Nicholas Christopher. Excerpts from *Crossing the Equator* by Nicholas Christopher, copyright © 2004 by Nicholas Christopher, reprinted by permission of Harcourt, Inc. Excerpt from *Living in the Past* by Philip Schultz, copyright © 2004 by Philip Schultz, reprinted by permission of Harcourt, Inc. All quotations are from *Trapeze: Poems* by Deborah Digges, copyright © 2004 by Deborah Digges. Used by permission of Alfred A. Knopf, a division of Random House, Inc. All excerpts are from Susan Stewart, *Columbarium,* copyright © 2003 by the University of Chicago Press. "A Tenant at Will," from *Dig Safe* by Stuart Dischell, copyright © 2003 by Stuart Dischell. Used by permission of Penguin, a division of Penguin Group (USA) Inc. From Olena Kalytiak Davis, "shattered sonnets love cards and other off and back handed importunities." A Bloomsbury/Tin House

INDEX

4/04

ml